Tax Reform in Russia

Tax Reform in Russia

Jorge Martinez-Vazquez
Mark Rider
Sally Wallace

*Andrew Young School of Policy Studies,
Georgia State University, Atlanta, USA*

Edward Elgar
Cheltenham, UK • Northampton, MA, USA

Published by
Edward Elgar Publishing Limited
Glensanda House
Montpellier Parade
Cheltenham
Glos GL50 1UA
UK

Edward Elgar Publishing, Inc.
William Pratt House
9 Dewey Court
Northampton
Massachusetts 01060
USA

A catalogue record for this book
is available from the British Library

ISBN 978 1 84064 644 3

Printed and bound in Great Britain by MPG Books Ltd, Bodmin, Cornwall

Contents

Preface

Tax reform is no easy task in any country, nor does it ever seem quite finished. The reform of the Russia Federation's tax system has been particularly challenging. This is hardly surprising given the dramatic changes that were occurring during this period in this newly formed country. Since the break-up of the Soviet Union, there have been wholesale changes to the political system and intergovernmental structures as well as privatizations of major industries and the housing stock, creation of a private banking sector and liberalization of prices. Meanwhile, this new country also had to deal with issues of corruption; hyper inflation; currency reforms and devaluations; wage, pension and tax arrears; and tax evasion. At times these challenges have been crippling to the country's fiscal system, and, consequently, there have been repeated calls for revenue mobilization and tax simplification. Through it all, the tension between levels of government and between government and its constituents have led to many proposals to reform the tax system. Many of the proposals that were implemented did not prove to be successful in the context of the political economy of the Russian Federation. Underlying problems with the economy, intergovernmental issues, weak tax administration and resistance to paying tax resulted in a situation in which the tax laws needed to be simplified on the one hand, while still keeping an eye toward development of a modern tax system and its effective enforcement on the other.

Despite the harsh environment, the Government of the Russian Federation viewed tax reform as a central policy issue in its move toward a market-based economy and its quest for economic development. Indeed, some of the early reforms, particularly the adoption of a value added tax and income tax, seem to have taken root. The experience of the Russian Federation over the last 15 years has shown more clearly than in most other countries the interconnectedness between the reforms in tax policy, tax administration and intergovernmental fiscal relations.

In this book, we describe the remarkable development of the Russian tax reform from 1992 through 2005 and provide an economic analysis of these reforms. The content of the book is based on economics, but it is put in the context of the political economy of Russia. By thoroughly examining the tax system in this way, we can better evaluate the path of reform.

We have benefited from conference presentations and discussions with colleagues, including Roy Bahl, Richard Bird, Galina Kourliandskia, Robert Ebel, Charles McLure, Luc Noiset, Sharon Hester, Bradley Moore, Natasha Kalinana, Olga Vorontsova, Olga Pavlova, Metin Ismailov, Mitch Mokhtari, Alan Firestone, John Mikesell and many others, and we thank them for their many insights. We also would like to thank a number of individuals who have helped track changes to the tax system and helped compile data to support this work: Paul Benson, Dmitry Shishkin, Alisa Axelrod, Andrey Timofeev, Vid Ardison, Attasit Pankaew, Riatu Qibthiyyah, Sandeep Battacharyia and others.

Jorge Martinez-Vazquez
Mark Rider
Sally Wallace
Atlanta, October 2007

1. Introduction

The dissolution of the Union of Soviet Socialist Republics (USSR) in December 1991 marked not only the end of the Soviet empire but also the collapse of the Soviet political and economic system. The leadership of the Russian Federation faced the enormous challenge of radically transforming the political, economic and social institutions with only very limited historical precedents. As opposed to the gradualist approach pursued by China, Russia attempted a 'big bang' approach to reform: a wholesale transformation of the political system from a totalitarian state to democracy, rule of law and civil society, and an economic transformation from a planned to a market economy. In addition, the role of the state in the economy and in particular the fiscal system had to be transformed to complement the new political and economic order.

In the grand sweep of history, the break-up of the USSR and the subsequent effort to reform both the political and economic systems of the Russian Federation surely ranks among the most momentous events of the twentieth century. An important element of the reform effort was the need to develop a modern tax system to complement the new political and economic order and stabilize the economy. This book is concerned with the effort to establish a modern tax system that provides an adequate, stable, fair and efficient source of revenue during the administrations of President Yeltsin and, subsequently, Putin. Accordingly, we focus on the effort by the central government to enact a tax code, adopt an appropriate system of intergovernmental fiscal relations and establish a modern tax administration. We contend that these three institutions are inextricably intertwined with one another. Consequently, successful reform of any one of these three institutions requires complementary reforms of the other two.

Before embarking on a detailed account of Russia's tax reform, it seems worthwhile to describe the political and economic context in which these reforms took place. Not only does this provide some perspective on the difficult challenges facing the government of Russia during this period, but it also provides context to some of the particular economic influences shaping policy.

In contrast to the Czech Republic, Hungary, Poland and several other East European countries, Russia has little or no recent experience with democracy, civil society, private property, the rule of law or a market economy. Until the abolishment of serfdom in 1861, two-thirds of the Russian population was deprived of civil rights. While abolishment of serfdom allowed peasants to have land, it was in the form of joint ownership or *obschina*: a group of peasants living in the same village. Until Stolypin's 1906 reform, exit from *obschina* was limited by law and private holding of land within *obschina* was regularly renegotiated. Moreover, in Tsarist Russia a number of legal acts necessary for a market economy, such as commercial law, were absent. In other words, not only did Russia have a longer experience under communism than other East European countries, but at the time of the communist revolution in 1918, Russia lagged behind these other countries in developing democracy, civil society, rule of law and private property. Perhaps most importantly, there was no tradition during either the Soviet or Tsarist periods of a system of checks and balances on the power of the executive.

McAuley (1997) describes Soviet planning as a system in which goods were distributed among the elite through membership in an exclusive group: the Communist Party. For the rest of the population access to goods was open but controlled by the state. Since all financial transactions were cleared through the state-owned banking system, it was a simple matter for the government to finance its activities by intercepting money from the accounts of enterprises as either taxes on payroll or turnover. As such, Soviet citizens had little or no experience with taxes and the role taxes play in financing the activities of the public sector in a modern market economy.

Another distinctive feature of the Soviet economic system is that government officials worked to assure that firms received the inputs necessary to fulfill their output plans and enterprises operated with a soft budget constraint. Since prices in planned socialist economies were arbitrarily set by the government's established economic plan and did not reflect scarcity, the cost of producing a particular good or service could exceed the sales revenues of the enterprise. In a command economy, the revenue from the sale of a loaf of bread, to take just one example, may not have been sufficient to cover the cost of the flour used to produce it. In such cases, the government covered enterprise deficits with credits from the banking system. As a result of such soft budget constraints, enterprises lacked any incentive to improve the quality of their products, innovate or conserve on the use of scarce inputs.

As discussed in greater detail below, the practice of using soft budget constraints proved difficult to abolish, despite a thorough privatization of major enterprises in the initial phase of the reform process. Consequently, private enterprises were able to postpone genuine restructuring because they were not compelled to do so by competition, hard budget constraints and bankruptcy in the case of default. As discussed in greater detail below, the legacy of enterprise soft budget constraints continued to bedevil the movement to a market economy and the establishment of a rational and sustainable fiscal system.

In November 1991, in response to the economic decline of the Soviet economy during the late Brezhnev years and the inability of the Gorbachev reforms to reverse this decline, the Russian leadership announced the appointment of a new Government and outlined its commitment to fundamental economic reform. The program included: (1) price and wage liberalization by the end of 1991; (2) a commitment to a tight monetary policy, fiscal reform and ruble stabilization; (3) privatization of up to 50 percent of all small- and medium-sized enterprises within three months; (4) halting the funding of defense, foreign economic aid and 73 all-Union ministries and committees; (5) supplementing the social safety net; and (6) a qualified commitment to an inter-republic Central Bank. Of these objectives, only the fourth one was implemented without delay, thus completing the process of extending Russian government control over Union government functions.

The transformation into a market economy was fraught with problems. As Aslund (1995) points out, the economy was set up for a bumpy ride characterized by high inflation and unemployment rates. Besides the lack of initial support by the International Monetary Fund and the international community, the financial crisis with high inflation rates was due to the expansion of the money supply by the Central Bank of Russia.

Russia's growth pattern during the transition years followed the usual U-shape of other transition countries (Figure 1.1). The fortunes of the federal budget mirrored quite closely the evolution of the real economy (Figure 1.2). The government sector did not experience a surplus until 1999, when GDP finally experienced positive real growth rates. Throughout much of the decade of the 1990s, at the very time when the country badly needed a stable, predictable and generous revenue structure to support and build a transitioning economy, tax reform seemed an elusive goal. The central and regional governments faced growing deficits and pressure from the IMF to put their fiscal houses in order. Massive government expenditures were being offloaded from the central government to subnational governments that had virtually no revenue-raising capacity.

The tax reform attempts of the 1990s were made under very difficult economic and political circumstances. The strength and stability of the economy was up and (mostly) down throughout the decade. Debt burdens and outside pressure for reform were great and the federal government had

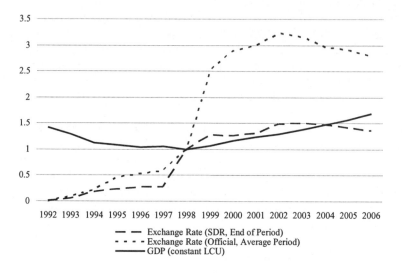

— — Exchange Rate (SDR, End of Period)
- - - - Exchange Rate (Official, Average Period)
——— GDP (constant LCU)

Source: World Development Indicators (Word Bank, 2006) and Government Finance Statistics (IMF, 2006)

Figure 1.1   *Indices of Real GDP and Dollar-Ruble Exchange Rate (1998=1)*

to deal with the regional governments in terms of intergovernmental fiscal relations. The economic crisis of 1998 further shook the confidence of the international community in Russia's long-term viability. The turnaround post-1998, fuelled in part by the growth of domestic production and the increasing world price of oil and natural gas, may have been a catalyst that allowed the government to move its tax reform efforts forward. The arrival of Vladimir Putin, his high approval ratings and the continued climb in the price of oil, may have breathed new life into the reform effort beginning in 1999. This book provides a close account of the important successes and failures of the tax reform effort in the Russian Federation from 1991 through 2006.

The remainder of the book is organized as follows. Chapter 2 provides a discussion of the different stages of tax reform during the Yeltsin years of the transition in the Russian Federation. The Russian Federation imposed several taxes inherited from the old Soviet regime, most significantly the profit, turnover and payroll taxes levied on and traditionally negotiated with state-owned enterprises. Tax reform efforts during this period were quite

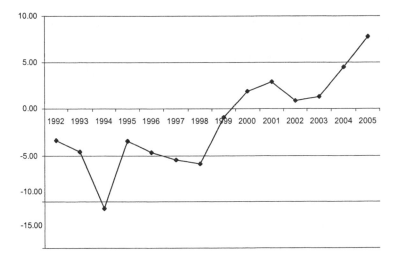

Source: Government Finance Statistics (IMF, 2006)

Figure 1.2   Government Balance as a Percent of GDP

incomplete and, in some cases, in the wrong direction. However, tax reform was quite obviously on the Government's agenda.

Chapter 3 provides an account of the implementation of a more or less complete tax code as well as major tax reforms aimed at reducing marginal tax rates. From the beginning of his appointment on January 1, 2000, President Putin stressed the critical importance of tax reform to Russia's recovery and acted quickly with the implementation of a tax reform agenda. Indeed, since his election to the presidency in March 2000, Putin has pursued an aggressive program of tax reforms and has had many important successes including the imposition of a flat rate income tax. The economics and political economy of Putin's reform efforts are detailed in this chapter.

In Chapter 4 we provide an analysis of the performance of the tax system including such things as revenue adequacy and tax incidence or the distribution of tax burdens across income groups. Tax effort by the Russian Federation was relatively low during the 1990s due to a variety of factors including noncompliance with the tax system, weak and corrupt tax administration and complexity of the system. However, in recent years, the level of tax effort has grown in the Russian Federation relative to that in other transition countries.

The structure of each of the major taxes is the focus of Chapter 5. There we present data and analysis that demonstrate the gains in the tax system, but also highlights the remaining problems. Chapter 6 discusses the evolution of tax administration in the Russian Federation. In the early years of the transition, the structure of the tax administration and the skills available to it were not adapted to the market economy. Chapter 6 also describes more recent attempts to modernize the tax administration apparatus. Finally, Chapter 6 covers the overall performance of tax administration in terms of tax arrears and noncomplaince and the evolution of tax morale among Russian citizens during the period under consideration in this book.

Chapter 7 discusses the reform of intergovernmental fiscal relations in the Russian Federation from the perspective of the tax system and tax policy reform. A major challenge for tax policy in Russia has been the issue of dual-subordination of tax administrators and the lack of revenue autonomy among subnational governments.

Chapter 8 concludes our review of the tax reform process in the Russian Federation. There we look at the next phase of tax reform – one   in which Russia is in a much stronger economic and political position than at the beginning of its tax reform journey in 1991. However, facing up to the challenges of designing and administering a revenue system may be increasingly difficult in Russia because of its growing dependence on the world economy, in particular the price of oil, and because subnational governments will continue to pressure the central government for 'their fair share' of budget resources.   More significantly, the country faces socioeconomic issues that will strain the revenue system, specifically, a negative population growth rate, increased demands for expenditures related to health and environmental clean-up and a growing elderly population. Thought needs to be given to future reforms of the tax system in Russia so that the tax system can be adjusted to provide the necessary level of revenue in a fair and efficient way.

2. Achievements and Failures during the Yeltsin Years

INTRODUCTION

For many years during the transition, the existence of a burdensome, unfair and uncertain tax system was generally perceived as one of the main causes for Russia's lack of investment, stagnant growth and the overall lackluster economic performance during the transition to a market economy. If not the most important factor, the inadequacies of the tax system have been ranked high among other factors, such as the lack of civil society institutions and the inability to enforce contracts, which are hindering the transformation of Russia into a full-fledged market economy. Given the importance of a sound fiscal policy to any economy, the paradox of fiscal policy in Russia during the transition has been, until very recently at least, the absence of comprehensive tax reform. Changes in the tax system, often for the better but sometimes for the worse, have occurred during the transition, but it was not until 1998 that significant breakthroughs occurred with the passage of the general portion of the tax code. This was followed in 2000 by a tax reform that was passed under the newly elected President Putin and further reforms through 2005. But even now, after all of these reforms, there are important deficiencies in the tax system.

Thus, despite the significant consensus of the importance of tax reform, an important question is why it took so long to occur. Tax reform is an arduous process in any country, but in Russia there were several important factors that contributed in peculiar ways to make the tax reform process so much more difficult. An important, perhaps the most important, factor impeding the progress of tax reform in Russia has been the absence of an historical tradition of the rule of law.[1] Of course, the lack of this tradition affected the reform of many other institutions in the country, as well. In addition, in Russia and most of the other former Soviet Republics, the exception being the Baltic countries of Estonia, Latvia and Lithuania, there was not a recognizable body of laws from the Tsarist period. In many cases, previously socialist planned economies of Central and Eastern Europe were able to jump-start their transition into market economies because they had

7

laws and institutions that could be dusted off to provide an institutional bridge to the development of a modern market economy. An additional reason, which is related to the two previous ones, is that unlike in other transition countries there was a lack of agreement and clear ideas as to where the country should go.

Given the acute needs of the early transition it should not be surprising that constitutional and legal reform in Russia were relegated to the backstage, and economic reforms took center stage. Only the passage of time made it clear that an approach that relied on their autocratic traditions could not sustain the transition to a market economy. Policy followed ad hoc and non-transparent procedures and the state bureaucracy was rampant with corruption. During the early part of the transition huge fortunes were made in the name of economic reform, through privatization of state enterprises, the assignment of export quotas for oil and the like. Under the loans-for-shares scheme, the new banker-plutocrats offered political and financial support for President Yeltsin's reelection in exchange for ownership and control of large stakes in Russia's most valuable companies at bargain or fraudulent prices.

It took four to five years for any serious attempts to create through legislation key institutions based on the rule of law, and this task remains in many ways incomplete. Hellman (1997) documents the development of some of these institutions including the Constitution and the need for more work in the area of institution building.

This chapter provides an account of the different stages tax reform has gone through during the Yeltsin years of the transition in the Russian Federation.[2] The next chapter reviews the process of tax reform after Vladimir Putin became President. Chapters 2 and 3 are meant to provide context to the more technical discussions in the remaining chapters of this book.

AN OVERVIEW OF TAX REFORM DURING THE YELTSIN YEARS

The Early Years of the Transition

At the time of the dissolution of the Soviet Union in 1991, Russia imposed several taxes inherited from the old regime, most significantly the profit, turnover, and payroll taxes levied on and traditionally negotiated with state-owned enterprises. Before the end of 1991, however, a new organizing law, 'The Basic Principles of Taxation' and new value added tax, enterprise profit tax and personal income tax laws had been approved. The law on the

Basic Principles served (and in some respects, still serves), with numerous amendments, until very recently as a substitute tax code on organizational, procedural and administrative issues.

This basic law also contains the formula for revenue assignment between the federal and subnational governments. It allocates 100 percent of value added tax and excise revenues, taxes on the revenues of banks, insurance companies, brokerages, transactions with securities and custom duties to the federal government and 100 percent of the revenues from the enterprise profit tax and personal income tax to subnational governments. These provisions of the law were never implemented because of opposition by regional governments. Actually, in the early stages some regions agreed to share taxes with the federal government but only on a mutually agreed upon or 'single channel basis'.[3]

The value added tax law, which for several years served as a model for other countries of the former Soviet Union, had some good features, such as a single rate, but the law also had many problems.[4] Other problematic pieces of tax legislation were introduced in succession following independence, including payroll taxes dedicated to extra-budgetary funds which were used to finance pensions, special excise taxes and taxes on natural resources. On the whole, from 1992 to 1997 a defective and complex tax system was put in place. Notorious offenders were the enterprise profit tax, which included a tax on excess wages which grossly exaggerated profits by disallowing many ordinary business expenses and a myriad of regional and local taxes. The most significant of these regional and local taxes fell on turnover and payroll, and were introduced during a period of several years when a presidential decree allowed subnational governments to introduce their own taxes. The resulting tax system gave Russia a reputation as one of the worst examples of tax reform among countries in transition, and was thoroughly criticized by Russian and international experts and organizations alike.[5]

The government made things more difficult for itself via its 'anti-taxpayer' approach to tax reform. In the early years of the Russian Federation, especially during the legislative rush of 1991 and 1992, many tax laws were put together practically overnight. One basic characteristic of this period was antagonistic to the rights of taxpayers and a punitive orientation toward tax enforcement, making taxpayers defenseless before an often corrupt, untrained and unwieldy tax administration. High taxes and even higher tax penalties, and capricious and often corrupt application of the tax law and penalties, drove many taxpayers into the underground economy and resulted in massive amounts of capital flight abroad. Estimates of capital flight during the early transition years vary widely, from $50–80 billion (US) per year in 1992–93 falling to $20 billion per

year, to higher estimates of $400–500 billion per year in the 1993–95 period
(Loungani and Mauro, 2001).

Despite many problems during the period up to the major reform
initiatives in 1997, the tax structure in Russia reflected a balance between
indirect taxes, principally the value added tax, an enterprise profit tax and
payroll taxes. The structure of the taxes followed western traditions in many
respects, but it differed in others. At least on the surface, the tax
restructuring that occurred shortly after the dissolution of the USSR led to a
tax system that was similar to that found in most Western countries.
However, the system that evolved in the early years reflected several
peculiarities of the Russian context. First, the Ministry of Finance initially
had difficulty asserting its views, and only over time was able to prevail
over the views of the Ministry of Economy and other more dominant
protagonists of economic policy of the Soviet Union. Second, tax reform in
Russia involved an increase in the perceived, if not the effective, tax effort.
Under the previous political structure, most taxes were invisible to
taxpayers. This structural change made it hard for the authorities to win
political and popular support for the new tax system. Third, the change in
political structure resulted in confrontation between the government and
state owned enterprises, which had previously enjoyed a cooperative
relationship. This confrontation hampered passage of new legislation and its
subsequent enforcement. Fourth, the change in the political structure
resulted in uncertainty regarding the ownership of assets and revenue
sources, as well as misunderstandings about the legal jurisdictions of
different governmental bodies.

During the period from 1991 to 1997, Russia established the three pillars
of a modern system of direct taxation – an enterprise profit tax, a personal
income tax and a payroll tax to fund a pay-as-you go pension system.
However, the enterprise profit tax differed in many important ways from the
corporate income tax used in many Western countries. For example, until
quite late in this initial period, the enterprise profit tax did not allow the full
deduction of wages, and furthermore wage income at the enterprise level
was subject to an 'excess wage tax'.[6] During the early years of the
transition, the enterprise profit tax was often used to promote or guide
certain types of investment activities through either tax incentives and
holidays or differential tax rates. On the other hand, Russia's enterprise
profit tax shared several features with the corporate income taxes used in
many Western countries: profits were taxed at 35 percent for most
companies (43 percent for banks, insurance companies and financial
intermediaries). Distributions of profits to individuals were taxed again
under the personal income tax, and dividends received by corporations were
taxed at source at a final rate of 15 percent. Other special treatments

included lower rates for agricultural producers, small businesses and joint ventures and higher rates on gambling and some financial intermediaries.

The calculation of the tax base of the enterprise profit tax underwent profound transformations during this period. Initially, Russia limited all deductions from enterprise revenues, including wages, depreciation allowances, interest, and expenses on research and development, environmental protection, and advertising. This is the main reason that the tax became known in Russia as the enterprise profit tax rather than a corporate income tax. The enterprise profit tax remained saddled for most of this period with special treatments and provisions. These measures contributed to lower collections directly and indirectly by facilitating evasion and avoidance behavior, increased the perception of unfairness of the tax system, and added to the distortions in the allocation of resources, particularly capital, in Russia.

The personal income tax was introduced in earnest in 1993. It was designed as a schedular tax on income, allowing for different bases and rates depending on the source of income. The tax base was a hybrid between consumption and income, since all types of labor and employment income were taxed (including fringe benefits, bonuses, allowances and other forms of non-cash income), but income from some capital sources were more lightly taxed or not taxed at all. The tax was levied on the worldwide income of residents and non-residents, allowing for personal allowances and certain hardship deductions computed in terms of the minimum wage. The rate structure was progressive, ranging from 12 percent to 35 percent of taxable income, with interest income above the refinancing rate subject to a rate of 15 percent until 1998 and 35 percent thereafter. Income tax was withheld at the source or paid directly by self-employed individuals. The top marginal rate for this tax of 35 percent was identical to the top rate of the enterprise profit tax from 1996 to 2001. In the case of social security contributions (payroll taxes), employers contributed 28 percent of payrolls to the pension fund, 9 percent to the social insurance and medical funds, and 1.5 percent to the unemployment fund. Smaller amounts were also contributed to various earmarked payroll tax surcharges.

The Russian Federation introduced a value added tax (VAT) in January 1992. This tax was largely patterned after the value added tax approved by the Supreme Soviet in December 1991, just before the dissolution of the USSR. On the positive side, the value added tax had a single rate (albeit a very high rate of 28 percent) and a fairly broad base covering most goods and services (food and children's goods face a lower rate and some services were and continue to be exempt). On the minus side, the Soviet model value added tax presented many peculiarities and problems. One of the most serious problems was the use of cash rather than accrual accounting in figuring out tax liabilities, compromising the effective application of the invoice-credit system, which is the cornerstone of most modern value added tax systems. This approach meant that manufacturers could claim value added tax credits even though the suppliers had not yet paid the tax because suppliers did not owe the tax until they received cash payment for the inputs. This arrangement resulted in deferral of payments, inflation and a loss of tax revenues. The credit-invoice method was used only at the manufacturing level. Liabilities at the wholesale and retail levels and most service sectors were calculated on the basis of taxpayers' gross margins, using a subtraction method value added tax. Using the subtraction value added tax at the wholesale and retail level undermined the self-enforcing properties of a credit-invoice method value added tax whereby unreported tax liability at one level of the production-distribution chain should be paid at the next level of the chain. A third problem with the Soviet era value added tax was that it denied credits for the value added tax paid on capital inputs which amounts to 28 percent tax on investment. This practice destroyed the consumption basis of the value added tax and introduced cascading elements in the tax, penalizing exports, among other things, even if they were zero-rated.

The value added tax also applied the origin method for trade among the Commonwealth of Independent States (CIS). Exports from Russia to other Commonwealth of Independent States countries were treated as domestic sales. As a result, they were subject to the value added tax, while imports to Russia from other Commonwealth of Independent States countries were exempt from the value added tax. In contrast, most countries with a value added tax use the destination method for international transactions with third countries. Under the destination method, exports are zero-rated and imports are subject to tax. The application of the origin method caused significant distortions and redistribution of revenues, especially favoring Russia. Also peculiar to the original value added tax was the fact that imports were not covered by tax. This was promptly changed so that imports from outside the Commonwealth of Independent States were subject to value added tax. The number of exemptions and special treatments significantly increased from the time of the original adoption of the value added tax to a considerable list of exemptions of both imported and domestically produced goods.

Early in the transition, Russia also introduced separate excise taxes on the traditional 'sin' commodities (tobacco products, alcoholic beverages and refined petroleum products) and on several 'luxury goods' (passenger cars and jewelry). Early on the list of excisable luxury goods was much longer, but the list was reduced to ease administrative burdens. In harmony with the origin method used for the value added tax for transactions within the

Commonwealth of Independent States, Russia exempted from Russian excise taxes excisable goods imported from other Commonwealth of Independent States countries. Imports of excise goods from non-Commonwealth of Independent States countries were subject to excise taxes. Because excise rates differed significantly within the Commonwealth of Independent States, a considerable trade developed within the Commonwealth of Independent States to arbitrage these differences. Contraband across the Commonwealth of Independent States borders also appeared to experience large increases. The excises were not inflation-indexed, which has led to significant erosion in real revenue over time.

This period was characterized by a widening budget deficit. Meanwhile, high tax rates discouraged voluntary compliance, investment and work effort, at least in the formal sector, and drove businesses into the underground economy. Tax rates remained high because the tax bases de facto were narrow. The tax administration did not collect an adequate share of this narrow base, causing a vicious cycle of increasing tax rates, further narrowing of the tax bases, revenue short falls, another round of tax rate increases and so on during this period of the transition. Tax arrears, negotiated tax settlements and tax amnesties became normal operating procedures.

One main problem was that revenues were inadequate and did not grow rapidly enough to cover the growth in government expenditures. The government deficit during this period ranged from 4 percent of GDP and upwards, while spending on infrastructure and social services remained low. The periodic changes in tax rates in an attempt to increase revenues heightened the feelings of uncertainty held by taxpayers and potential investors. That government revenue claimed a smaller share of GDP in Russia than in previous times was not the problem. One of the fundamental expectations from the start of the transition was that government should reduce its role in the economy, meaning also a decrease in the share of total output taken in taxation. One of the main reasons for the persistently high fiscal deficits throughout most of the 1990s resulted from maintaining high levels of government expenditures while tax revenues declined largely due to weak tax enforcement. The government's revenue share of total output had to increase to a level that would keep the deficit in an acceptable range or the government expenditure share of total output had to come down.

The sluggish and erratic behavior of revenues in response to changes in the economy was also an issue. Year after year, the tax system failed to yield the revenues forecasted in the budget. Periodically, the shortfall in collections was quite dramatic. These events almost routinely led to the introduction of emergency measures, often under pressure from the International Monetary Fund. The emergency measures on the policy side further complicated the tax structure. From the administrative side, the emergency measures often appeared to have been artificial because of their lack of durability. Many state tax inspectorates in the regions, and the territorial tax inspectorates within these regions, met their planned collections by asking for advance tax payments from taxpayers. Inevitably, this type of remedy led both to sharp increases in revenues followed after a few months by renewed precipitous declines in revenues.

Bad tax policy often originates with a chronic revenue crisis. Raising the tax rate on a poorly defined tax base may only compound problems; the enactment of a special value added tax rate has a similar effect, and 'new' taxes on foreign investors heighten uncertainty and dampen investment. The reasons for the revenue adequacy problem were numerous.

First, the growth of the Russian economy was sluggish. Actually, real GDP continued to decline almost consistently from 1992 to 1997. Revenue bases shrank or grew slowly. However, this did not explain why the ratio of taxes to GDP fell. The decline in the tax ratio occurred because some of the faster growing sectors of the Russian economy remained outside the tax base either because they were legally exempt, taxed in a preferential way or successfully evaded taxes, with significant earnings filtered to off-shore banks. The latter explanation quite likely held for the 'hard-to-tax' private entrepreneurs and the underground economy.

Second, taxpayers resisted paying taxes and enforcement remained weak, with the result that only a fraction of true liabilities were collected. The lack of tradition with voluntary compliance hurt tax collections from the start.

Third, many sectors of the economy were afforded preferential treatment under the tax laws, eroding the base and slowing revenue growth. It took a long time to tone down this interventionist tradition.

Fourth, the most powerful reason for the poor performance of the tax system was the inadequacy of the tax administration apparatus. The problem of weak administration had not been created, but was inherited.

The tax system had substantial structural defects. Some of these defects were mentioned above and are summarized here.

- First, the list of exemptions under the value added tax and preferential treatments under the income tax were inconsistent with international best practice and, more importantly, directly and indirectly eroded revenue potential. The cash versus accrual basis for determining value added tax liability was a major detriment to an efficiently operating value added tax, causing a revenue lag and dampening the incentive for enterprises to fully collect receivables. It also encouraged an increase in inter-enterprise arrears. The value added tax method used by manufacturers differed from that used for other firms, which created a horizontal inequity in the value added tax. This also added complexity to the system and raised compliance and administrative costs. Also, because the appropriate method was not clearly set forth in the law, it invited tax avoidance. The application of the origin method for the Commonwealth of Independent States trade also introduced the potential for tax evasion (Summers and Sunley, 1995).

- Second, excise tax rates on certain sumptuary and luxury items were low compared to those in other countries, particularly on motor fuels, alcohol, cigarettes and certain luxury items.
- Third, the enterprise profit tax base overstated profits because it did not allow for full deduction of the costs of doing business (for example, advertising, interest on some loans, business travel and entertainment expenses and training expenses were not allowed as deductions). Also, capital allowances may have significantly understated the full cost of capital depreciation. A host of other problems with the enterprise profit tax related to loss carry forwards, excessive exemptions and accounting rules also were present. Dividends were also subject to double taxation – at the corporate and the individual level.

The Struggles of the Tax Code during 1997–2000

In 1997, the Ministry of Finance submitted a comprehensive Draft Tax Code to the Duma. This Draft Tax Code had been put together over a period of more than two years under the leadership of the then Deputy Minister of Finance, Sergei Shatalov, and in consultation with foreign experts and international organizations. The Shatalov Draft Tax Code passed on the first of the three required readings of the State Duma on June 19, 1997.[7] The State Duma passed the code in the first reading under significant pressure from the government. President Yeltsin had threatened to dissolve the Duma if they did not vote on the code before the summer recess. The Draft Tax Code had little real support in the State Duma, was adamantly opposed by many regional governors, and was criticized and lobbied against by the private sector, especially the banking and natural resource oligarchs who had consolidated their economic power after their support for Yeltsin's reelection in 1996 in the 'loans for shares' scheme. After passage on the first reading, the Duma got a revenge of sorts by presenting over 4,000 amendments to the code to be discussed in the fall of 1997, before a second reading of the draft tax code.

The government withdrew its cohesive support of the tax code during this period as Yeltsin himself suggested that the government withdraw the tax code. The events culminated in November 1997, when the State Duma voted in an unusual second reading to reject the draft tax code and sent it back to the government. At this time the State Duma also opened up the field through the solicitation of alternative draft codes from interested parties. By that time, President Yeltsin had appointed a new finance minister, Mikhail Zadornov, who until then had been chairman of the Budget, Taxation, Banking and Finance Committee of the State Duma. A new deputy finance minister in charge of tax policy was also appointed, Mikhail Motorin, who until then had been chief of staff of Zadornov's Duma committee.

Though far from perfect, the Shatalov Draft Tax Code would have improved the tax structure in many significant ways. It clearly defined the scope of powers for each level of government, relative to the imposition of various taxes; it introduced taxes based on a closed list defined in the appropriate articles; it moved the value added tax to an accrual basis by 1999 and a consumption base by allowing credits for tax paid on capital inputs; it significantly expanded deductible expenses under the enterprise profit tax; it introduced an asset tax on banks (which were paying hardly any taxes); it moved to a broader use of schedular taxes and withholding at source for the personal income tax and avoided double taxation of dividends; and it would have also improved revenue assignments by allocating 100 percent of the value added tax to the federal government, allocating 100 percent of the enterprise profit tax and personal income tax to subnational governments, and eliminating many distortionary and nuisance taxes at the local levels. The Shatalov Draft Tax Code provided the tax administration with adequate tools for enforcement, such as the ability to issue regulations, bringing penalties to more realistic levels and introducing formal and fairer appeals procedures.

Many reasons were given at the time for the failure of the Shatalov Draft Tax Code. The most frequently mentioned was that the draft ignored and very often contradicted the previously approved Civil Code. As we discuss further below, the document lacked broad support. It invited opposition from the regions because of the reformed revenue assignments and opposition from business because of the asset tax on banks, among others. There was also general opposition politics played by the Communist-dominated Duma, which made it difficult for the different Yeltsin governments to pass any major legislation. There was also a lack of understanding of market economy tax concepts by deputies, and accusations that the draft was a reflection of the United States Internal Revenue Code rather than a Russian product adapted to the needs and special features of the Russian economy and institutions. A press release from the Ministry of Finance under the Zadornov-Motorin team in January 1998 announcing the new draft from the Ministry of Finance paid particular attention to its differences from the Shatalov Draft Tax Code. According to the press release, the new draft eliminated the following 'problems':

- language not consistent with the Russian Civil Code, such as 'charity or religious organizations' or 'passive and active economic activities';
- the ability of the tax administration to issue regulations, other than tax forms;
- the use of consolidated returns, which the regions opposed because of fears of losing revenue;
- the use of the accrual method or any other accounting method different from the financial accounts; and
- the asset tax on banks.

Following the government's withdrawal of the Shatalov draft from the State Duma in late 1997, the legislature requested the submission of alternative draft tax codes, either from deputies or from outside the State Duma. In the winter of 1998 many tax codes were submitted, including a new draft tax code from the Ministry of Finance. The State Duma considered all these drafts throughout the first part of 1998. At the time of submission, some of these drafts were considered serious contenders against the Ministry of Finance draft. The diversity and often extreme nature of the different drafts, most of them originating with State Duma deputies, were indications of the tax policy objectives the State Duma pursued, and in some cases the lack of a good understanding of the principles of tax policy design (see Box 2.1).

The discussion of the alternative draft tax codes by the Budget Committee of the State Duma during the months of February and March of 1998 led to the unsurprising, with hindsight, selection of the government's new Draft Tax Code in early April, 1998. This draft was far superior in structure and content to any of the alternatives that had been presented. However, as discussed below, the content of some of the other draft codes had a lasting impact. The State Duma passed the government's new draft in the first reading on 16 April, 1998. The Tax Code received 312 votes, 17 votes against and 1 abstained. To win votes, the Government promised to take into account all comprehensive ideas from alternative drafts.

In substance, the government's new draft tax code was a deep revision of the 1997 Shatalov Draft Tax Code. The Tax Code of Russia is comprised of two parts. Part I contains the provisions for tax administration and basic

---

Box 2.1   The Contending Draft Tax Codes of 1998

During the months of January and February over ten draft tax codes were submitted to the Duma's Budget Committee competing for a first position for recommendation by the Budget Committee to the full Duma for approval in a first reading. The draft tax codes differed in completeness and length and also in overall quality. The Budget Committee reviewed some of them in one single afternoon session but took others more seriously. The following is a description of some of the features of the draft codes.

Several common themes appear in most of these draft tax codes: the elimination of the value added tax and sometimes of the enterprise profit tax, the considerable strengthening of taxpayer rights (sometimes to the point that taxpayers can only be asked to pay taxes through court proceedings), and the protection and enhancement of revenue sharing going to the regions.

Black Earth: This draft code was presented by a regional association, and proposed the elimination of the value added tax and enterprise profit tax, allegedly in a quest for fairness in the system. Some of the revenue shortfall was made up by increases in the personal income tax and taxes on assets.

While property and asset taxes would be assigned to the federal government, the progressive personal income tax would be assigned to regional governments. The combined changes in these major taxes would have resulted in a reduction of total revenue of approximately 20 percent. In terms of tax administration, this code would allow taxpayers to refuse to pay a tax bill and take relatively simple matters to court for resolution.

Bratischev Draft Tax Code: This draft code was sponsored by Duma Deputy Bratischev and was technically titled 'On the Universal Taxation Systems in the Russian Federation'. This draft was even more radical than the Black Earth draft in that it contained no tax administration provisions. Most peculiarly, this draft did not contain tax rates per se, but rather a set of formulas, at times advanced mathematical algorithms, for the computation of tax liabilities. The draft had no provisions for the adjustment of tax bases such as exemptions or deductions and put a heavy emphasis on the taxation of monetary outlays of legal entities. Revenue assignments at different levels of government would have been calculated according to a complex formula based on a benchmark figure of basic needs, tax revenues available and a wage fund.

Sverdlosk Oblast Draft Tax Code: This draft code would have reduced the effectiveness of the tax administration by requiring routine intervention by the courts and in many cases the payment of taxes in kind. This draft code would also have reduced revenues through lower rates for enterprise profit tax and excises, and by cutting social security or payroll taxes by one-third.

Golov Draft Tax Code: This draft code, developed by Duma Deputy A.G. Golov, was the most concise draft tax code. It also made itself noticeable by offering the most extreme protection of taxpayers' rights. This draft required a court order for the enforcement of any aspect of the tax system. The draft also abolished the enterprise profit tax. The Golov draft would have relied heavily on taxes on exports and discriminatory taxes on foreign enterprises.

Gratchev Draft Tax Code: The draft code authored by Duma Deputy I.D. Gratchev eliminated the value added tax and excluded the possibility of any

> *Box 2.1 The Contending Draft Tax Codes of 1998 (continued)*
>
> type of sales tax. On the other hand, it introduced a minimum tax on income of enterprises based on gross income. Regarding tax enforcement it allowed taxpayers to refuse to pay taxes and required the tax administration to take them to court.
>
> Taxes of Russia: This draft tax code was developed by a political group which had as the foremost objective the simplification of the tax system. Its hallmark was the elimination of the enterprise profit tax, while at the same time it advocated the introduction of a 70 percent tax on the use of inputs.
>
> Mashinsky Draft: Duma Deputy Mashinsky's draft tax code would have eliminated the value added tax and made up for the shortfall in revenue by imposing additional taxes on energy carriers and by introducing a new luxury tax. The draft was quite vague about any other aspects of the tax system and its enforcement.
>
> Zhirinovsky Draft: This draft tax code, submitted by Duma Deputies Parshakov and Zhirinovsky, was in many respects similar to the Shatalov draft tax code. The most important difference was that the Zhirinovsky draft would have assigned most of the existing taxes to the regional and local levels of government. The federal government would have kept state duties, customs duties and fees, federal license fees and the tax on the use of symbols of the Russian Federation. To compensate for the loss in revenues to the federal budget, two flat-rate taxes would be introduced as federal taxes. First, a territorial tax (equal to a tax of 10,000 rubles per square meter of territory). Second, a capitation or poll tax levied at 1,150 rubles per person. The resulting federal tax burdens meant that Moscow residents would pay 1,163 rubles per year, whereas a resident of Yakutia in Siberia would pay 30,044 rubles per year.

tax assignment, while Part II contains the specific tax laws. Both parts of this government's version differed from the 1997 version in a number of ways. Some of the major themes and changes included the following:

- the Tax Code was a self-enforceable law and prohibited the use of decrees and regulations to complement it by any executive authority, including the Ministry of Finance or the State Tax Service;
- taxpayers' rights were fully supported. In particular, penalties would be levied only based on a court judgment, and the burden of proof would rest with the tax authorities;
- consolidated returns were not required or allowed;
- the definition of fair market value was clarified as 'the transaction price to be treated as the market price of a good or service. The tax administration would only be allowed to adjust prices in the event of transactions between related parties, barter transactions, and significant deviations from normally accepted prices';

- the basic features of the existing value added tax were retained, repudiating accrual accounting, maintaining the origination principle for trade with the Commonwealth of Independent States countries, maintaining a large list of exemptions, and no clear definition of zero-rated goods. The proposed general rate of the value added tax was reduced from 20 percent to 18 percent;
- some additional business expenses were made deductible under the enterprise profit tax, and the top rate was reduced from 35 percent to 30 percent; the additional or excess profits tax for oil and gas exploitation was applied only to new fields, and excise taxes on oil and gas were retained;
- a new final sales tax with a maximum rate of 5 percent was introduced as a regional government revenue source, which, if the regions chose to introduce it, would substitute for some of the existing turnover and payroll taxes at the subnational level;
- the introduction of the real estate property tax, assigned to the subnational level, and which would substitute for the existing property taxes on land, buildings and business assets, would be postponed until the pilot experiments in the city of Novgorod and Tver were completed (more information will be provided on this experiment at the end of the chapter);
- gains on property sales (real estate, securities, intellectual property rights and copyrights) were exempted from the personal income tax and subjected to a specific capital gains tax, with rates from 7.5 percent for long-term gains (more than one year) and 10 percent for short-term gains (less than one year) and amendment of personal income tax rates;
- provisions were made to reduce payroll tax contributions to the social funds and the road fund over a two year period; and
- the introduction of a chapter on special tax regimes to cover the following: small businesses that use the simplified tax system, agricultural enterprises that use the flat agricultural tax, retail sellers with no clearly delineated selling space and casinos and other gambling businesses. These taxes were mostly assigned to the subnational level.

While the government Draft Tax Code prevailed in the final vote of the State Duma Budget Committee and passed in the first reading of the full Duma in April, 1998, it did not survive much longer. First, it became clear that the Duma would not discuss and submit the new draft tax code in its entirety to a second reading. Instead, the discussion and vote would proceed in stages with the general part, or Part I, of the draft being discussed first.

The general part contained closed lists of federal, regional and local taxes, and the sections on tax administration, taxpayer rights and obligations, and other general issues and procedures pertaining to all specific taxes. The second part of the Draft Tax Code contained all the articles pertaining to the different taxes, including the major ones – the value added tax, enterprise profit tax, personal income tax, and special excises – as well as minor ones, including those at the regional and local level, which would be discussed and voted upon separately.

As the discussion of the general part of the new Draft Tax Code proceeded in the Budget Committee, a respected jurist and Duma deputy, Andrei Makarov, led a revision of this general part. This redraft became known as the Makarov draft, and it radically transformed many provisions, swinging the pendulum to the extreme protection of taxpayer rights and practically tying the hands of the tax administration to enforce taxes. Makarov's draft reflected to a large extent the sentiments expressed on these issues in the alternative draft tax codes that had been presented to the Duma in the winter of 1998. The second reading of the general part, the Makarov draft, took place on July 3, 1998, with a third reading and final approval on July 16.

The general part of the draft tax code was signed into law by the President on July 31, 1998 and became effective in January 1999. Under pressure from the government and international financial institutions, amendments to the general part were discussed for the better part of a year and were finally approved by the Duma on June 23, 1999. The majority of the amendments were technical in nature, clarifying certain poorly drafted sections of the original version as well as conforming various code terms with those contained in other legislation such as the Civil Code. It should also be noted that many conceptual amendments, if adopted, would have resulted in greater improvement of this piece of legislation. However, most of these amendments were rejected by the Duma. Examples of these amendments include an expansion of the definition of related parties for transfer pricing regulations, regulations allowing the tax authority to receive bank statements (on interest) of natural persons, addition of cases of excise tax evasion to the criminal code, and allowing the tax administration to maintain an office within certain large companies, among other important amendments.

The second part of the Draft Tax Code, which contained provisions regarding specific taxes, suffered a worse fate.[8] The Budget Committee of the Duma set the priorities for discussing first the draft code chapters on the enterprise profit tax and the personal income tax. Several working groups were created for that purpose, with members drawn from Duma deputies and representatives of the Ministry of Finance and State Tax Service, which later became the Ministry of Taxation. Other new taxes including the value added tax and special excises were tabled for discussion at a later date.

Progress was slow in the working groups, and it became clear that if any component of the second part of the draft tax code were to be passed it would have to be in 1999. As discussed below, the sharp devaluation of the ruble and debt default crisis of August 1998 took the wind out of the sails of further comprehensive tax reform. The Duma, prodded by the government, started to think of a dual track for reform in which the draft tax code would continue to be reviewed; meanwhile, other bills would be introduced with the objective of changing concrete features of existing laws.

As of March 2000, under a new administration, not a single specific tax in the draft tax code had been submitted to the Duma for a second reading. Most progress seems to have been achieved with the chapter on the draft enterprise profit tax, discussed in the Duma working group chaired by Svetlana Orlova. As a result of this work, the draft was significantly amended, and it was significantly different from the version passed in the first reading in June 1997. At this time, the Ministry of Finance was still hopeful of a second and third reading in 2000.

As of early 2000, Russia's tax system had many of the characteristics of tax systems in other countries, but it still presented serious problems. In addition, the culture of tax payment and voluntary compliance had not permeated the psyche of the country. As a case in point, the deputy head of the tax administration's personal income tax department was hopeful that 4 million tax returns would be filed in tax year 1999 based on projections of those with multiple jobs or significant capital income. In fact, this would have been a stretch as the number of returns filed in previous years did not top 1 million. Officials kept hoping, without much success at least through 2000, that stronger enforcement and the actual levy of fines for non-compliance eventually would increase voluntary compliance.

WHAT WENT WRONG WITH TAX REFORM DURING THE YELTSIN YEARS?

Several factors may account for the failure to accomplish comprehensive tax reform in the Russian Federation through early 2000. Specifically, as will be discussed in greater detail below, the push for comprehensive tax reform could not overcome the lack of a political strategy to pass the implementing legislation; the need for quick passage of emergency fiscal measures during the economic crisis of August 1998; and weaknesses in tax administration and other legacies of the Soviet period.

Before proceeding with the discussion of the Yeltsin attempt to pass comprehensive tax reform, two general observations should be noted, even if they may seem contradictory. First, the three obstacles noted above, when added together, would have been powerful enough to defeat comprehensive tax reform not only in Russia but in practically any other country. Second, despite these obstacles, the Putin government was able to gain passage of more or less comprehensive tax reform in the summer of 2000, mostly on account of the political prowess and high popularity of President Putin. In the following section, we examine the obstacles to successful tax reform. In the next chapter, we examine the more successful Putin tax reforms of 2000.

Failures in Reform Strategy

Beyond the general principles of more equitable and efficient taxes and a simple tax structure (which in itself can mean different things to different people), tax reform, and especially comprehensive tax reform, has been a difficult and controversial process in many countries. On the other hand, there are countries, including transitional countries, where comprehensive tax reform, even with some problems, has been achieved (for example the Baltic countries, Kazakhstan and Georgia).[9]

The failure of the Shatalov Draft Tax Code to pass the Duma in 1997 was said to have been caused by its differences with the Russian Civil Code, its Western influences, and even technical and conceptual errors. Purportedly, the new draft tax code submitted by the Ministry of Finance in early 1998 had been adapted to Russian institutions. In particular, it had been made compatible with the Civil Code, and it had been cleansed of certain other problems and influences and of what appeared to be divisive or controversial measures. In the end, however, the new Draft Tax Code did only slightly better than the Shatalov Draft Tax Code, despite the fact that the requirement that it be discussed and approved as a single piece of legislation had been relaxed.

One problem with both the Shatalov Draft Tax Code and the government's Draft Tax Code of 1998 was the failure to adopt explicit and well thought-out strategies that would focus not only on the substance and quality of the draft but also on successful passage into law. Successful comprehensive tax reform in democracies has often required full support and commitment from the top of the political structure and the empowerment of a tax reform commission with broad representation from the Ministry of Finance, tax administration, parliament and representatives of business and labor interests in the private sector.[10] Clearly, this was not the approach followed in Russia. The first comprehensive draft tax code was put together in isolation in the Ministry of Finance by Vice

Box 2.2   Successful Tax Reforms

Tax reform is difficult in any country; however there are some significant success stories over the past several decades. In most cases, the integrated work of a knowledgeable support staff (often a group of domestic and expatriate tax policy experts) and an influential commission of politicians, business leaders and academics have increased the chances of success in the tax reform arena. The following are some examples (Gillis, 1989 and Thirsk, 1997):

Jamaica: A successful tax reform was enacted based on work of the Jamaica Tax Structure Examination Project from 1983 to 1987. Reforms of the individual income, company income, property and value added taxes were enacted from 1986 to 1991. The Jamaica tax reform survived a change in administration, and its success is in part attributed to the fact that the entire administration was engaged (up to and including the Prime Minister), the underlying analysis for the reform was done based on extensive field work and a close working relationship with Jamaican officials and experts, resources supported quality expertise, and the expat team could assist with implementation and early analysis of the impacts of the reform. The reform was carried out during difficult economic times, which may have increased the sense of urgency in achieving a successful reform. Analysis of the reform suggests that it was successful in its goals of increasing the competitive position of the country by bringing down tax rates and broadening the tax base, while considering the overall equity of the tax system.

Colombia: Tax reform has been a long, ongoing process in Columbia. Tax reforms in 1974, 1986, and 1988 were marked by significant changes in policies over the years. Despite the length of time required the tax reforms seem to have moved tax policy in a positive direction. McLure and Zodrow (1997) report that over the years, improvements have been made in reducing tax incentives, unifying taxation of corporations and partnerships, simplifying the tax treatment of families, eliminating the deductions for personal expenditures and reducing the negative impacts of inflation and bracket creep.

Indonesia: The country's dependence on oil revenues was one reason for developing a tax reform agenda in the 1980s. Low levels of tax effort leading to differential effective tax rates among individuals and sectors in the economy were another. In 1983, a package of tax reform measures was introduced in order to diversify the revenue structure, reduce tax-induced distortions, simplify the tax law and increase administrative efficiency, while remaining cognizant of the tax burden on low-income individuals. Analysis of the reform suggests that it was successful at increasing the role of non-tax revenues in the overall revenue structure of the country. Furthermore, the tax bases were broadened, fewer individuals were statutorily subject to the income tax, and the tax administration was reorganized to increase administrative efficiency (however, this is difficult to measure empirically), but economic efficiency may have been compromised by differential enforcement by type of income, sector and activity.

Minister Shatalov and a small staff. Except for consultations with international experts, there were very few consultations with the tax administration, other parts of the executive branch of government or Parliament. Other significant stakeholders, including the private sector, in particular large enterprises, and the regions were neither consulted nor included in any kind of dialogue. The absence of a political strategy to gain support among some of the stakeholders may have been compounded by the adoption of measures that in theory were correct, but would also have ensured the open opposition of the regions, such as the changes in revenue assignments, and measures securing opposition by at least parts of the business sector, such as the assets tax on banks and other financial institutions.[11]

The difficulties of tax reform in Russia were not different from those in many other countries. Tax reform inevitably creates winners and losers. The winners tend to be numerous and realize only small benefits from the reform; whereas the losers, although often fewer in number, may suffer significant losses. In Russia, the losers were also politically and economically powerful – the large businesses dominated by the oligarchs as well as the powerful regional governors.

The strategy adopted by the new team in the Ministry of Finance in late 1997 was to 'clean up' the previous Draft Tax Code and rush it to the State Duma again without opening a dialogue or trying to build some degree of consensus among stakeholders. Considerable blame should also go to the Duma for rushing the review schedule and opening an invitation to any individual or group to submit draft tax codes. In the rush to meet extremely short deadlines, the Ministry of Finance practically did not consult with the State Tax Service on crucial provisions that would have hampered the tax administrations ability to enforce the tax laws. But even with a well-organized political strategy for tax reform, the government likely would have faced very significant difficulties with an opposition-dominated Duma. In hindsight, it may have been easier and more effective to try to gain political support for the draft tax code before submitting it to the Duma.[12]

With the exception of the extraordinary push by President Yeltsin to have the Duma pass the Shatalov Draft Tax Code in the first reading, the tax reform process lacked a unified and strong voice for passage from the government during this period. In many ways, the draft tax codes were only an affair of the Ministry of Finance and international advisers. The rapid political changes during this period, with four prime ministers from March 1998 to August 1999, of course, did not help to bring focus to any policy initiative, including passage of the Draft Tax Code.

The August 1998 Economic Crisis and Emergency Legislation

The financial crisis and the tumultuous economic environment that immediately preceded and then followed the devaluation and default of August 17, 1998, may have been enough to bring fundamental tax reform to a halt. In addition, the State Duma was occupied just before and after the August crisis with a series of emergency revenue and other economic measures submitted by the government. Often these measures were in response to concerns raised by the International Monetary Fund and the World Bank and increasingly became an attempt to convince the international community of the resolve of the Russian government to straighten out its fiscal house and put the economy back on the reform path. This confusing array of 'plans' and draft bills took the emphasis off fundamental tax reform. What ensued was tax reform on a piecemeal basis dominated by a desire, at times desperate desire, to raise revenue. De-emphasizing fundamental tax reform was welcomed by some observers who felt practical and effective tax reform had been long held hostage to the Draft Tax Code.[13]

Although there were all kinds of proposals, on the whole much of the tax legislation passed on a piecemeal basis represented improvements over the current law by broadening tax bases, lowering rates and reducing discriminatory treatment among different groups of taxpayers. The most important of these measures are described in Table 2.1. Passing some of these emergency laws was a struggle, and many of these measures were tabled or later repealed. In addition, not listed in Table 2.1, there were numerous other tax-related measures drafted during this period, many of which fizzled out as governments came and went during this tumultuous period.

The most important 'tax packages' during this period included the following: the Kirienko Stabilization Package of July 1998; the 19 bills associated with the 1999 federal budget proposal of December 1998, which came to fruition in April 1999; the spring 1999 stabilization package; and the tax bills associated with the 2000 federal budget proposal. Many of these bills represented substantial departures from current law and sometimes also major departures from the tax policy principles contained in the draft tax code.

The internal government debate over the future of the value added tax in late 1998 and early 1999 is a good example of the changing views and lack of a unified strategy. The introduction of a regional sales tax in July 1998 was expected to compensate for the revenue foregone as a result of lowering value added tax and was at least in theory consistent with the intent of the draft tax code. But this measure also marked the beginning of a change in the government's position regarding the value added tax. This issue was brought to a head as a major internal government dispute arose regarding the appropriate balance between revenue from the value added tax and a retail sales tax. In late December, 1998, the government debated the positions of the Ministry of Finance and the State Tax Service, which by then had become the Ministry of Taxation, with responsibility for tax policy and tax administration. The Ministry of Taxation (MinTax), headed by Gregory Boos, a former Duma deputy, wanted a reduction of the general value added tax rate to 10 percent, with the institution of a 10 percent regional sales tax. The Ministry of Finance was pushing for a package which would reduce the existing turnover taxes and slightly reduce the value added tax rate, with no increase in the sales tax rate, which was 5 percent at that time. A compromise was achieved and a belated budget proposal under the name of the '19 laws' went forward, with a value added tax rate of 15 percent and a regional sales tax of up to 10 percent. These proposals were ultimately rejected by the President and/or the State Duma.

Other Significant Impediments to Effective Tax Reform

The adoption of an incomplete and perhaps naive strategy for comprehensive tax reform and the tumultuous economic and political circumstances associated with the August 1998 crisis would seem to be sufficient reasons for the derailment of comprehensive tax reform. But even if those obstacles had not been present, there were several features of the Russian economy that should have been expected to hamper, if not derail altogether, the tax reform process. The pervasiveness of some of these problems may even have compromised the effectiveness and 'curative powers' of an approved tax code.

First, the multifaceted legacy of the Soviet Union had not been shed. In the economy, a substantial number of enterprises, even after privatization, continued to operate with negative value added to the economy but survived because they bartered with each other, much as they did during the Soviet period, in what became known as the 'virtual economy'.[14] Survival of these enterprises in the non-cash economy was favored by the fact that they were allowed to pay liabilities for taxes, energy consumption, and transportation costs through mutual offsets and other non-monetary transactions at grossly overvalued prices.

Negotiated taxes were the main feature of the tax system in the Soviet Union. After all these years of transition and tax reform, Russia's tax system still retains an important element of negotiation. This was most apparent in the way in which settlements were reached on the payment of tax arrears. The practice of tax offsets, or mutual cancellation of tax arrears

Table 2.1 Important Tax-Related Measures: July 1998 – September 1999

Measures	Explanations
Kirienko Stabilization Package: June–July, 1998	This package of 20 bills was submitted to the Duma in July 1998. Among the more important bills were the following: *Passed July 1998:* - Imposition of a regional sales tax of up to 5 percent. - Imposition of a regional imputed income tax for certain types of activities of up to 20 percent. - Reduction of enterprise profit tax rate from 35 to 30 percent (vetoed by the President). - Introduced a tax on gambling activities. - Curtailment of tax exemptions on closed administrative territories. - Reduction of excise taxes on crude oil (vetoed by the President) - State reporting requirement for large taxpayer expenses (cars, furs, jewelry; postponed until January 2000). *Rejected by Duma, enacted by presidential decree or government resolution:* - Indexing land tax rates (subsequently repealed). - Accrual method for value added tax enacted by resolution and then ruled out unconstitutional by the Supreme Court. - Reduction of social insurance taxes. - Increase of customs tariff for imported goods (subsequently repealed). Limitation of goods subject to the 10 percent value added tax (subsequently repealed). *Rejected:* - Uniform 20 percent value added tax rate. Change in personal income tax brackets and equivalent treatment of capital gains and interest income
19 Laws (1999 Federal Budget Package)	The first and second readings of these bills were held from December 1998 through April 1999. Among the more important bills were the following: *Passed April, 1999:* - Suspension of item 1, article 5, part 1 of the tax code of the Russian Federation so that the federation and regions could impose new taxes before 1 January, 2000. - Indexing of tax brackets and rate increase in personal income tax (45 percent rate effective 1 January, 2000 although never enacted); introduction of a 3 percent rate accrual to the federal budget.

Table 2.1   Important Tax-Related Measures: July 1998 – September 1999 (continued)

Measures	Explanations
19 Laws (1999 Federal Budget Package) (continued)	- Reduction of the enterprise profit tax rate to 30 percent (from 35 percent). - Indexation of excise tax rates - Expansion of the imputed income tax to additional activities. - Reduction and tightening of federal tax exemptions for closed administrative entities by limiting exemptions for enterprises with less than 70 percent of assets and 90 percent of activities in the closed zones. *Rejected by the President in April, 1999:* - A value added tax bill which would have reduced the value added tax rate to 15 percent, and also provided for caterers and retailers to become part of the value added tax credit-invoice system, and allow crediting on construction inputs. - A bill on hard currency controls which would have had the State Tax Inspectorates act as foreign currency control agents. Rate increases for the property tax on natural persons.
19 Laws (1999 Federal Budget Package)	*Rejected or tabled:* - Excise tax rate increases. - Amendments to the law on the State Tax Service which would have expanded the role of the STS in foreign currency and import/export operations. - Amendments to Part One of the tax code which would make mandatory the registration of alcohol-producing entities at the place of production. - A bill which would allow the Tax Service to receive banking statements of individuals. - A change in the calculation and payment of the tax on highway funds which would reduce the tax base. - A 10 percent sales tax for the goods subject to excise taxation. - Inclusion of outstanding debts into the tax base of the enterprise assets tax.

by taxpayers and budgetary arrears by the government (see below), also continued to allow federal and regional authorities to settle and protect particular groups of taxpayers. In fact, tax burdens were tailored made for each taxpayer because these arrangements included negotiations over the value to attach to the goods and services that the taxpayer provided to the government to settle tax arrears. These issues are further discussed in Chapter 4.

Other features of the Soviet tax system have persisted. Under the previous regime, taxes completely lacked transparency. Often, enterprises did not know what other taxpayers facing similar circumstances paid in taxes and the population at large were neither aware of taxes nor had any perceptions of tax burdens. Very few individuals actually filed tax returns, paid taxes during transactions or were aware of the existence of turnover taxes or profit taxes. That tax system created a taxpayer culture of mistrust of government and of noncompliance that endures to this day. Taxpayers continue to believe that tax burdens are distributed arbitrarily and that the government is wasteful if not corrupt. Tax evasion has continued to be a problem, including non-filing, underreporting of income, misclassification of income, exaggerating deductions and exemptions and delinquent payment of tax liabilities.

The broad perception among taxpayers of corruption of government officials continued to be a contributing factor to an unwillingness to pay taxes. The research institute, Information for Democracy, has conducted surveys of individuals and businesses to quantify the level of corruption and graft in the country. In 2002, the institute estimated that individuals paid about $3 billion in bribes, and businesses paid $33 billion in various payments to officials. Worse, the corruption of officials has undermined the basic fabric of society. Although high-profile cases of possible corruption captured the attention of the international media during the last years of the Yeltsin era, at least as damaging to the tax system has been the belief by Russian taxpayers that tax administration officials are corrupt. However, there are no formal studies of the size or significance of this type of corruption. The problem seems to be primarily at the middle- and lower-rank level of the tax administration, among those who have direct contact with taxpayers. It comes as no surprise that middle ranking officials who benefit from corrupt practices are interested in maintaining the status quo. However, the corrupt practices of this group has done less harm through its effect on the tax reform effort and much greater harm by demoralizing ordinary taxpayers and the restrictions legislators have felt compelled to impose on tax enforcement as a result of such behavior.

Another legacy of the Soviet Union is a weak tax administration system. Although in Soviet times tax administration lacked capacity, it was able to enforce taxes because taxpayers were large in size and small in number; the state bank monopoly operated the payment system; and, in fact, tax administrators could retroactively adjust rates and procedures to meet revenue quotas. The transformation of the old administrative system into a modern tax administration capable of enforcing taxes in a market-based economy has been painfully slow. The State Tax Service (STS) of the Russian Federation was introduced right after independence as a federal agency through the 'nationalization' of previously semi-autonomous regional and local offices. The STS continued to struggle for most of the transition period with the most basic reforms, including restructuring along functional lines rather than by type of tax or by type of taxpayer. An extremely weak central tax apparatus continued to struggle during the transition with the necessity of controlling the operations of a system in which the majority of functions are exercised at the lowest level of administration, the local tax inspectorates.

The control exercised by the headquarters of the Federal Tax Service over collections, returns, processing, audit or appeals in the local and regional offices continues to be weaker than in most other tax administration systems around the world. To the extent that regional and local governments have continued to pay for housing, bonuses and other aspects of the compensation of local administrators, there continues to be a significant de facto allegiance of tax administrators to the interests of subnational governments which in many cases differ from the interests of the federal government. This de facto dual subordination of local tax administrators has been a constant source of problems with the tax system during the transition.[15] Another major issue is that the tax administration continues to be collections-oriented, not taxpayer-oriented, which has contributed to the creation of a climate of distrust and suspicion among taxpayers. High compliance costs are imposed on taxpayers, who often must purchase tax forms and instructions and are required to file taxes in person, in many cases on a monthly basis. The lack of reform of the tax administration to some degree trivializes the lack of comprehensive tax policy reform. The efforts to modernize Russia's tax administration system are discussed in Chapter 6.

Tax evasion continued to be widespread and remained high during the entire transition period. Estimates of the amounts of taxable income moved offshore every year are in the magnitude of US$10 billion to US$20 billion or equal to between one- and two-thirds of projected total government revenues for 2000. As we discuss further in Chapter 4, the existing estimates of tax evasion show significant leakages in Russia's tax system, with personal income tax compliance estimates at approximately 50 percent, enterprise profit tax compliance around 60 percent, value added tax in the

range of 38 to 55 percent and special excises on alcoholic beverages close
to 50 percent throughout the 1990s. These estimates add up to a huge loss in
revenue due to noncompliance.

Another aspect of tax noncompliance that has played a particular role in
Russia is tax arrears. These late or non-payments of acknowledged tax
liabilities have been a pervasive phenomenon permeating all facets of the
Russian economy and with nefarious effects on the performance of the tax
system. Accumulated tax arrears, composed of delinquent payment of taxes
and deferred payments as agreed between the tax authorities and taxpayers,
at the end of 1998 were nearly equal to total tax collections. Between 1995
and 1998, tax collections at the federal and subnational level increased by
149.3 percent while tax arrears increased by 584.8 percent. The growth in
tax arrears between 1996 and 1999 was dramatically enhanced by the
federal and subnational governments' practice of tax offsets. Both
enterprises that can pay and those that cannot pay their tax liabilities on
time could benefit from tax offsets and the development of arrears. Granting
tax offsets became standard behavior in federal and subnational budgetary
practices. Despite the many problems created by tax offsets, they offered
the fiction of higher levels of expenditures and more balanced budget
execution. The use of periodic tax amnesties to combat arrears by the tax
authorities appears to have been yet another factor in their growth.[16]

However, the situation improved considerably in 1999 and, as we see
below, the positive trend continued through 2001. As will be discussed in
more detail in Chapter 4, one of the main causes of tax arrears during this
period was the availability of tax offsets. At the beginning of the transition,
offsets were simply mutual cancellations or settlements of accrued debts by
taxpayers to government and by government to supplies in the private
sector. Over time, offsets grew in many different ways, including the
government writing off tax arrears in lieu of cash payment for the purchase
of goods and services from the private sector. The progress made since
early 1999 in controlling tax arrears was the control of government
expenditure arrears via much more realistic budgeting which began in 1999,
and also the policy of discontinuing tax offsets at the federal level after the
months immediately following the August 1998 financial crisis. The use of
tax offsets, and therefore tax arrears, has been harder to control at the
subnational level. Although it does not appear that tax arrears expanded in
1999 at the subnational level, offsets of different forms and kinds continued
unabated that year.

Several important reforms were introduced in 2000 that have made the
use of tax offsets much less attractive, and therefore the incentives to
accumulate arrears at the subnational level diminished as well. For one, the
Budget Code, which became effective January 1 of that year made illegal all

non-cash transactions at any level of government (including offsets). Also important was the fact that beginning in 2000, the federal government changed the rules of the game for sharing tax revenues. Beginning in 2000, the federal government shared in total tax collections (cash and non-cash). Previously, revenues collected in a non-cash form had not been shared with the federal government.

Reforming a tax code is a difficult and complex procedure and it requires support and compatibility with other laws and institutions in the system. Actually, as pointed out above, the demise of the Shatalov Draft Tax Code was predicated, at least in part, on its inconsistency with other laws, in particular the Civil Code. This problem was supposedly addressed in the new draft tax code sent to the State Duma in 1998. However, there are still other laws and government institutions that represent powerful barriers to the implementation of the tax code.

A case in point, which highlights the difficulties of developing significant changes in tax legislation, is the experiment with the introduction of the real estate property tax.[17] This tax was proposed in the draft tax code as a substitute for three Soviet era property taxes still in force: the land rent tax, the tax on buildings and the tax on enterprise assets. Its introduction was postponed initially until a pilot tax project was completed in the cities of Novgorod and Tver. The arduous history of this experiment provides a good example of the difficulties faced in the modernization of the tax system in Russia. One of the main problems with the introduction of the real estate property tax has been the lack of coordination among government officials at various levels of government and among different laws of the Russian Federation that do not provide appropriate institutions or clear lines of authority. Title registration alone has been under the purview of four federal agencies; meanwhile, privatization of land and some structures (examples) is still crippled by politics.[18]

The lack of success of the property tax experiment in Novgorod and Tver remains a good example of how diverse interests in government and the private sector have worked hand in hand to slow down or, as in the case of the property tax, actually blocked reform (see Box 2.3). The draft on extending the experiment was signed by the President on July 28, 2004. Initially, it had been rejected by the Federation Council and considered within the Conciliatory Committee. The draft extended the experiment to 2005; revenue sharing stays unchanged; that is accruable to the budgets of the given cities. As of this writing, the tax has still not taken hold.

Box 2.3   Real Property Tax Experiment

The development of a real property tax has been conducted via an 'experiment' in the cities of Novgorod and Tver. The process has been a long one, beginning in late 1995 and continuing today. The following description of part of the process may help to give an indication of the complicated interplay among agencies, governments, and individuals that has been part of this one reform.

Introducing a fiscal cadastre: Development of a fiscal cadastre requires the review of title registration for properties. In many instances, the property committees of the cities had incomplete records, or misleading records (falsification of title ownership via shadow business, for example). Because the title registration process has not been fully developed, the cities had to do much investigative field work on their own. This held up the creation of the cadastre and additional resources had to be allocated for its creation. Federal legislation regarding title registration and property rights clarification has not been forthcoming. Such legislation is under the purview of the State Land Committee, Ministry for State Property and the State Committee for Construction. Because it relates to taxation, the Ministry of Finance would also have a role in the legislation.

Valuation of properties: There is no legal framework for valuation methodology at the federal level. Development of a legal framework needs to be a coordinated effort of federal, regional and local officials. There was also the obvious public reaction to market-based valuations of properties. Many individuals and business owners were very skeptical at first and believed it meant higher taxes. In fact, discussions of a property tax in some well-off municipalities around Moscow were promptly dropped due to citizen reaction.

Intergovernmental fiscal relations: The original intent of the real property tax was that it be a local government (city) revenue source and replace certain other local taxes. Both the federal and regional governments lobbied at various times to list the tax as a federal or regional tax, to be shared with the local governments. Debates arose regarding which level of government should pay for the creation of a fiscal cadastre, title registration, valuation and so on. The current pending federal legislation on the property tax states that the tax is to be shared between the regional and local government.

Compliance: Because the real property tax is a new tax, the regional tax administration had no experience administering such a tax. In addition, due to political and technical difficulties, the tax administration will have difficulty obtaining the fiscal cadastre data.

There was a need, too, for coordination regarding billing. The property tax committee in each city (newly established) could not technically issue bills, but the tax administration could not do so, either due to administrative constraints (the property tax was not listed as one of their collectible taxes, and they did not have access to the valuation and cadastre information). In the end, a compromise was reached whereby the property tax committee would issue 'bills' without a statement of liability, but would include all necessary information for the taxpayer to determine their liability (assessments and tax rates).

Box 2.3   *Real Property Tax Experiment (continued)*

Below are the results of the experiment upon the year 2003 submitted to the Federation Council:

During the first phase – 1997–99 – a new concept for introducing real estate tax was developed, envisaging gradual transfer to paying the given tax – taxpayers are defined as organizations, which hold property titles for buildings, structures, facilities and land plots the above are situated on. Production assets are exempt. The costs for carrying out the experiment including the costs for creating a tax register of real estate objects, and valuation of property at market prices rest with the city administrations.

During the second phase – 2000–03 – the concept was put into practice. The tax was introduced in Veliky Novgorod from January 1, 2000 for enterprises with full property titles. In 2000, 10 enterprises used the system, in 2001, 14, in 2002, 22, on November 1, 2003, 40 enterprises. In 2000, revenues were 388.9 thousand rubles, in 2001, 923.9 thousand rubles, in 2002, 1,740 thousand rubles and the forecast for 2003 was 4,653.8 thousand rubles. On the results of 2000 expected budget losses from transfer to the real property tax were offset in full by increasing the profits tax liabilities of the same taxpayers. No losses were reported in 2001. In 2002, no losses had been envisaged, but losses were reported in 2001. In 2002 though no losses had been envisaged, but with land tax rates having been doubled, real estate tax became lower than the land tax. Envisaged losses from the participants to the experiment were offset by the growth of collections from the enterprise profit tax and the personal income tax, as well as by the increase of land plots which were bought by enterprises of the cities. It is expected that the number of taxpayers will increase as a result of newly built enterprises with foreign investment. Demand for land plots is on the rise. In 2001, 29 were bought out, totaling 52 hectares. On November 11, 2003, there were 136, totaling 867.7 hectares.

Despite the fact that no real estate tax has been introduced in Tver, the city administration from 1998 to 2003 has made active use of the developments for the real estate register to enhance the efficiency of using real estate, namely, city zoning has been carried out, and coefficients for market valuation have been established varying from 0.03769 to 3.13853. The methodology for rent computation has also been developed and is being improved for non-residential estates (except for industrial objects), which belong to municipalities; the real estate register has served as a base for developing the register of municipal property; the market approach to rent computation for non-residential municipal property has allowed city revenues to increase by 30.5 million rubles, and rental payments to all budget levels by 60.8 million rubles.

CONCLUSIONS

Several lessons can be learned from the Yeltsin period. The first is that fundamental reform requires the full support of the government. In 1998–99, the attention of the government had been diverted to many other issues, and it lost its zeal and unified support, if it ever existed, for the draft tax code. A significant factor in the overall confusion was the fact that during this period, the Tax Policy Department of the Ministry of Finance lost its leading role in the tax reform effort of the government. The position of the Tax Policy Department was challenged by the Presidential Decree of December 25, 1998, which created the Ministry of Taxation (MinTax) from the State Tax Service. Under this decree, tax policy was brought under the purview of MinTax. However, since the middle of 1999, the role has gone de facto back to the Ministry of Finance.

A second lesson is that effective tax reform does not have to be done in an all-or-nothing fashion. Piecemeal reform can be positive. In fact many of the tax changes introduced during 1998–99 were in the direction of lower rates, reducing differential taxation among forms of income and reducing the complexity of the current system. These changes represented improvements, albeit small, in Russia's tax structure. Whether the continuation of the piecemeal approach would have been effective in tackling the major reform issues was at the time, and remains, an open question.[19] Of course, piecemeal reform also had its downside. For example, the desperate search for revenue led to the passage of administrative measures that unreasonably increased the compliance costs for taxpayers. At other times, contradictory legislation was passed but was unable to be administered.

NOTES

1. The lack of an historical tradition with the rule of law and its impact in modern Russia has been discussed quite extensively. See, for example, the collection of papers in Sachs and Pistor (1997), and in particular Owen (1997). In the mid-to-late 1990s, the issue of 'who lost Russia' nearly developed into a cottage industry. The phrase can be linked to many authors but was a central theme in a September 1998 report by the U.S. Congress on Russia's devaluation in August 1998.
2. Both Cohen (2001) and Freeland (2000) point out underlying structural problems with the politics and political economy of Russia as reasons for Russia's lack of economic stability. Stiglitz (2000) points to the influence of private interests in developing policies (such as privatization) that provided private benefits but public chaos. Klebnikov (2000) discusses the impact of the oligarchs on the process of privatization and other 'reforms' of the Russian economic and political systems.
3. Parts of this chapter draw on Martinez-Vazquez and Wallace (1999).
4. These regional governments retained all tax collections and made a single payment to the federal government. See Wallich (1994), Bahl (1994), and Martinez-Vazquez and Boex (2001).
5. See Martinez-Vazquez and McNab (1998).
6. The excess wage tax supposedly was introduced for two reasons: to discourage de-capitalization of the firm by workers who granted themselves unlimited pay increases; and to raise revenues. The excess wage tax was an unsatisfactory solution to the more pressing problems of eliminating labor management and imposing stricter budget constraints on enterprises. The excess wage tax in fact discouraged innovation and hampered productivity

       growth by preventing firms from raising wages to attract and retain highly skilled and motivated workers.

7.   The history and circumstances of the Shatalov Draft Tax Code are discussed in detail in McDonald (2001).

8.   We can only speculate why the general part of the Code has enjoyed better fortune than the specific part. Perhaps there was more groundswell demand for addressing what have been perceived as abuses by the tax administration and the general part was generally viewed as providing a significant increase in taxpayer rights; Duma deputies would have been hard put not to support this. See for example Zolt (1999) for the cases of the United States and Japan cases.

9.   See Ebrill and Havrylyshyn (1999).

10.   The work of this type of commission has been typically supported by a technical staff from the government, sometimes assisted by domestic and international experts. The work of the supporting staff is to provide information on best practices, advantages and disadvantages of particular approaches and complete information on the revenue and distributional consequences – gainers and losers of particular measures.

11.   See Shleifer and Treisman (2000).

12.   As a legislative body, the Duma was particularly ineffective, not only with the draft tax code but also in all fiscal matters. The overall ineffectiveness of the State Duma has been explained as due to the dual-channel or parallel design of the Duma in the Constitution, with both partisan factions and issue-oriented committees which require basically representation from all factions (Ostrow, 2000). There has also been a limited group of Deputies who understand tax related issues.

13.   See for example Antel (2002).

14.   See Karpov (1997) and Gaddy and Ickes (1998).

15.   Some other large former Soviet republics, such as Kazakhstan and Ukraine, have experienced similar problems in the transition arising from the de facto dual subordination of local tax officials but to a much lesser extent than in Russia.

16.   These issues are discussed further in Chapter 4. See also Alexeev (1998), Ivanova and Wyplosz (1999), Kurlyandskaya (2001), USGTA (1999a), and Alm, Martinez-Vazquez and Wallace (2006).

17.   The real estate property tax is discussed in Chapter 5.

18.   Land ownership reform is in the agenda for reform during 2001-2002.

19.   See Lapina (1995) and McDonald (2001) for discussions of the pros and cons of codification in the Russian case. McDonald (2001) also discusses the piecemeal approach to tax reform in Russia prior to the Shatalov Draft Tax Code of 1997 (Shatalov, 1996).

3. Tax Reform under Putin

INTRODUCTION

Vladimir Putin became acting President on December 31, 1999 and was sworn in as President on May 7, 2000. President Putin used an unprecedented level of direct influence and involvement to achieve consensus within the executive branch regarding the details of the government's tax reform package. He also exerted a great deal of influence to guide the tax reform through the parliamentary process. A described in greater detail below, the highlights of the Putin tax reform include a bold reform of the personal income tax with a flat rate of 13 percent; the consolidation and reduction of the social fund taxes; the substantial reduction and eventual elimination of the subnational turnover taxes; substantial increases in excise taxes; and an optional local piggyback enterprise profit tax up to a maximum of 5 percent.

THE SETTING

Two major political events helped to turn around the prospects for fundamental tax reform in the Russian Federation. First, the legislative elections to the State Duma in December 1999 crippled the stranglehold the Communist Party had exercised for practically the entire transition period by reducing the number of communist deputies from roughly one-half to one-third.[1] Second, Vladimir Putin was elected President with an overwhelming popular mandate in March 2000. These changes broke the legislative logjam that had stopped tax reform during the Yeltsin years. The turnaround in the economy in 2000 and 2001, also helped create the right economic and political climate for fundamental tax reform. The continued strength of the Russian economy could also have supported long-term fundamental change.

Post-Yeltsin, the Russia Federation saw significant changes in the pace of tax reform. From the beginning of his appointment as acting President, Putin stressed the critical importance of tax reform to Russia's recovery and acted early with the implementation of a tax reform agenda. Indeed, since his election to the presidency in March 2000, Putin has pursued an aggressive program of tax reforms that continued to move forward at least through 2006 (see Box 3.1).

Several other changes created more favorable circumstances for tax reform beginning in 2000. President Putin brought Sergei Shatalov back as deputy minister in charge of tax policy. Although not particularly loved by Duma deputies, Shatalov was the author of the first comprehensive draft tax code in 1997 and he was widely respected among tax specialists as the right person to spearhead the passage of the second part of the tax code. The Duma also made some immediate moves, which indicated a renewed interest in moving the tax code forward. In December 1999, Alexander Zhukov was renamed chair of the influential Budget and Tax Committee. Zhukov reiterated a need to develop tax reforms aimed at reducing the level of taxation in the country for business and individuals. Other reformers also participated as active members of the tax policy debate, including Mikhail Zadornov, former Minister of Finance and Georgy Boos, former Minister of Taxes and Fees.

As early as January 2000, the government put together an agenda in support of the passage of the second part of the Tax Code and other measures (see Box 3.2). This time, as before, some Duma deputies advanced their own program for reform but without the force or the chaos surrounding this process in early 1998.[2]

Perhaps the best news that accompanied the progress with tax reform in the early 2000s was the host of other reforms that were actively pushed by Putin's administration that complemented overall tax reform. These included a new land code, deep reform in the legal and judicial system, business de-regulation and in the longer term, pension reform, new labor and customs codes and regulations on corporate governance. Even with the central government tightening up on the regions and some major enterprises, significant gains have been made under Putin in the area of tax reform.

It may be helpful to recapitulate here at what point Putin took over the process of tax reform. Partially in response to the economic crisis of August 1998, the first part of the new Tax Code, containing the general principles of taxation and tax administration procedures, was passed by the Duma in 1998. However, after that significant first step, the government's tax reform efforts stalled, and the second part of the Tax Code, with measures for the specific taxes, became bogged down at the Duma. This impasse reflected to a large extent the lack of political consensus within the executive branch itself on substantive issues for the various taxes.

But in the months following his election to the presidency, Putin used an unprecedented level of direct influence and involvement to achieve

---

Box 3.1   The Economic Situation and Fiscal Performance

The economic recovery beginning in 2000 and 2001 has been widely attributed
to the improved relative price advantages introduced by the devaluation of
August 1998 and the high oil prices over this period, which boosted export
earnings, foreign reserves and government revenues. In particular, the enterprise
profit tax and the personal income tax have performed very well, especially the
latter, and this despite (or possibly because of) the significant cuts in marginal
tax rates. The Ministry of Finance in April 2001 reported that revenues from the
enterprise profit tax were up in the consolidated budgets of Russia's regions to
2.1 percent of GDP in the January-February 2001 period, as opposed to 1.7
percent of GDP for the same period in 2000. In the case of the personal income
tax, collections increased to 2.5 percent of GDP in 2001 in comparison to 1.7
percent in 2000. Information from the Ministry of Finance also shows that
personal income tax collections increased by 70 percent during the first quarter
of 2001 relative to the previous year. Personal income tax revenues grew to 3.4
of GDP by 2003 and then settled back to 3.3 percent in 2005. Payroll tax receipts
as a share of GDP increased from 2001 to 2002 and then fell slightly as a share
of GDP. Since the early 2000s through 2006, the general state of public sector
finances has improved, with gains coming from most revenue sources. The
overall budget position since 2000 has been in surplus (general government as
well as federal government). This has been supported by strong GDP growth,
with levels of growth reaching over 7 percent in 2003 and 2004.

Inflation has been considerably tamed from the high levels of the earlier years
of the transition and runs now at 1 percent per month. The rebound in GDP
growth has also led to falling unemployment rates, recently standing at just
above 10 percent. The share of the economy subject to arrears and barter has
decreased significantly after its peak of 50 percent in the aftermath of the August
1998 crisis to less than 25 percent in the early 2000 era.[3] By the middle of 2001,
there was increasing fear that domestic inflation had eroded the comparative
price advantage gained from the devaluation in 1998, but that later seemed to be
an unfounded worry in the following years.

Despite the recovery in aggregate production and the increase in GDP during
2000-01, household income and employment levels continued to be depressed
through 2003. More significantly, the general indicators of demographic and
health conditions have continued to falter during the transition and there are no
clear signs of a turnaround on this front.

Capital flight has been a difficult complication in Russia during the transition
years. As of 2002, estimates of capital flight remained close to $20 billion
annually (2004 estimates were $12 billion). There remains little access to credit,
especially long-term credit for the productive sector.

---

consensus within the executive branch regarding the details of the
government's tax reform package. Putin also exerted a great deal of
influence to guide the tax reform through the parliamentary process.[4]

A major element in the ultimately successful strategy was the explicit
formulation of a clear and unified vision of the needed reforms within the

---

Box 3.2   Yeltsin-Putin Hand-off: Year 2000 Government Initiatives

Early in 2000, the Ministry of Finance and the Ministry of Taxes and Fees (which reverted back to the non-ministerial tax service) became quite vocal about a number of tax code related issues, and the following tax policy measures were supported by Putin:

Part II of the Tax Code (for the second official reading, the Duma voted that this legislation be included in the priority consideration list for 2000);

- Reduced turnover taxes;
- Increase in deductions for businesses;
- Widening of personal income tax brackets;
- Indexation of the standard deduction for the personal income tax;
- Measures aimed at reducing capital flight (restrictions on foreign currency conversion and elimination of bank secrecy laws);

Further amendments to Part I of the tax code including more precise definitions of 'related parties' and 'place of business' to increase the likelihood of taxation of foreign subsidiaries.

---

executive branch of government. This vision was articulated in Sergei Shatalov's contribution to the Commission on Policy Goals which was established by Putin in early 2000 and headed by German Gref. The basic goals behind the new government's vision were to simplify and rationalize the tax structure and lower the overall burden of taxation.[5] Attainment of these immediate goals, it was hoped, would improve the business climate, lead to new investment, promote capital repatriation and foster sustained economic growth.[6] The strategy also involved a significant re-centralization of revenue sources (see Box 3.3).

REFORM CONTENT

It is worthwhile to review in some detail the contents of the Putin administration's plans for tax reform when he took over the process, among other things because the legislation actually passed by the Duma in the summer of 2000 differs, at least in some respects, quite considerably from the main tenets of that strategy. More importantly, the strategy reveals the kinds of analysis and evaluation that were behind the proposed tax reform, and the reforms from 1999 and 2001 reflect some of the boldest reforms in the post-Soviet period. The reforms that followed through 2006 are in large part based on that strategy, and we turn to a summary of those later in this chapter.

As pointed out above, one of the main thrusts of the Putin tax reform was to lower the overall tax burden on the economy. This goal was formulated more on the basis of nominal tax burdens as opposed to actual burdens. If there was 100 percent compliance with all of taxes in force in 2000, it was estimated that the overall tax burden would have been in the neighborhood of 41 percent of GDP, while the actual taxes collected were half that amount (IMF, 2004). The goal was to drastically reduce this nominal burden over a period of three years to approximately half of what it was in 2000 and then to clean up the system over a period of several years. This would be accomplished by the elimination of some taxes but mainly through the reduction in the rates of some taxes, accompanied by tax base broadening and improved tax administration.[7] The plan was to eliminate the most distortionary taxes, such as the turnover taxes and small nuisance taxes at the subnational and local levels.

Box 3.3   The Re-Centralization of Revenue Sources

There has been a clear trend toward the re-centralization of revenues at the federal level since 2000. While revenue sharing arrangements were relatively stable from 1994 to 1997, several substantial changes were made in revenue sharing arrangements leading up to, and in the wake of, the economic crisis of August 1998. Changes in the assignment of revenues, especially the assignment of personal income tax collections, reflect a tug-of-war over resources between the federal government and regional governments. Although regional governments had received 100 percent of personal income tax collections since the beginning of the transition (with the exception of a 3 percent federal surcharge during 1995–96), in 1998 the federal government increased the federal share of personal income tax collections to 40 percent.

In 1999, personal income tax collections were once again fully reassigned to the regions while the 3 percent federal surcharge was reintroduced, resulting in an effective regional sharing rate of 90 percent. In another policy reversal, the budget law for 2000 eliminated the surcharge and imposed a new sharing regime altogether, assigning 84 percent of personal income tax collections to the regional governments while allocating the remaining 16 percent of personal income tax revenues to the federal government. In 2001, 1 percent of the tax went to the federal government and 99 percent to the regional government and a new flat rate income tax structure was introduced. Beginning in 2002, the personal income tax reverted back to 100 percent to the regions. The gradual reassignment of value added tax collections to the federal government contributed to an important increase in the centralization of public sector resources. From 1994 until the first quarter of 1999, the value added tax was shared between the federal and regional governments on a 75/25 percent basis. Over this period, the regional share of the value added tax contributed between 15 and 20 percent of subnational own-source and shared revenue collections.

Box 3.3 The Re-Centralization of Revenue Sources (continued)

Starting with the second quarter of 1999, however, the regional government's share of value added tax collections was reduced to 15 percent and since 2001, 100 percent of the value added tax collections are assigned to the federal level. While this move eliminates the problems with the apportionment of value added tax collections between regions, the centralization of value added tax revenues reduces regional revenue autonomy. While the land tax has became an exclusive regional assignment in 2003, the share of taxes on lucrative oil and gas extraction has been centralized, with only 5 percent of the tax on oil extraction left for regional governments. The cumulative impact of the tax reforms and the reassignment of revenue sources since 1998 on the vertical fiscal balance is reflected by the changing distribution of resources across the different levels of government over time. During the early years of the transition there was a steady decline in the federal share of overall tax revenues. Specifically, in 1992 about 60 percent of overall tax collections were assigned to the federal level, by 1997 the federal share had declined to 42.5 percent. A sharp reversal in this trend can be observed starting in 1998 and continuing through the 2000s. Since the low point in 1997, the federal share of consolidated tax revenues has steadily increased over time. The federal government's share of overall tax collections is once again in the range of 60 percent or more. Thus, after a period of decentralization of fiscal resources early o in the transition, the vertical fiscal balance in Russia has shifted in favor of the federal government in recent years.

The elimination of these taxes was consistent with the pursuit of a second important objective, namely tax simplification. Also moving in this direction, the plan was to consolidate levies for the pension fund, social insurance fund and mandatory medical insurance fund into a single 'social' tax fund. Similarly, there were plans to consolidate the many different taxes falling on transportation into just one or a few taxes.

At the same time, the elimination of preferential treatments was intended to increase the horizontal equity of the system, although there was awareness of the need to keep some preferential treatments for deserving groups that could not be easily targeted by the expenditure side of the budget, such as the disabled or the victims of Chernobyl.

The 'Long-Term Development Strategy for the Russia Federation for 2001-2010' developed under the direction of German Gref (Russian Federation Government, 2001) also paid close attention to the modernization and computerization of the tax administration apparatus in the Russian Federation, paying special attention to fighting illegal capital flight and different forms of tax evasion.

For each tax, the plans differed quite considerably. In the case of the value added tax, the structural changes planned were quite minimal. There was a clear intention to leave intact this reliable source of revenue. In particular, around 2000, there were no plans to lower the general rate from 20 percent, which was considered to be competitive and lower than in some neighboring countries, such as Finland, Hungary, Poland and Sweden. However, future plans did include an additional reduction to 18 percent (in 2004). In 2000, there was an intention to switch to accrual accounting with a transition period, perhaps using installment payments, and a move to a destination-based value added tax with the Commonwealth of Independent States countries, using bilateral agreements when necessary. Importantly in light of subsequent events, the plan was to retain the then current law, a multiple-rate structure of the value added tax. A single rate value added tax was not seriously considered and remains a potential issue for future reforms.

For excise taxes only minor reforms were foreseen. The most significant changes would include the introduction of an excise tax on diesel fuel and motor oils as a substitute for the existing sales tax on fuel and lubricants, raising the excise rates on gasoline, and transferring the responsibility to pay part of the excise tax on alcoholic products from manufacturers to accredited wholesalers. The idea was to reduce the incentives for the illegal production of beverage alcohol. Because Part I of the Tax Code requires an explicit rate in the Code for natural gas, the proposal was to set an excise rate of 15 percent on natural gas at the point of shipment for domestic sales and those to Belarus, and 30 percent for all other exports. Although indexing the excise rates for inflation was discussed, it did not form part of the government's plans at the first stage of the Putin transition.

There were much more comprehensive plans for the reform of the enterprise profit tax, some of which have only recently been implemented. One main problem to be addressed in the government's plans was the disallowance of deductions for some regular business expenses. The principle would be to allow all expenses incurred for production and marketing as a deduction from income in the current period. This would mean that the existing restrictions on expenses for advertising, insurance, interest payments, and personnel training would be repealed. Another major area of reform would be the system of capital depreciation allowances. The existing system (1998-99) of differentiated depreciation rates would be simplified by using seven consolidated depreciation groups, much as is practiced in, for example, Canada.[8] The plans were also to introduce more accelerated rates of depreciation, on average 35 percent faster than existing ones, and also allow other depreciation schemes besides the straight-line method. This would allow enterprises to expense a sizable fraction of their capital investment during the first years of their use. In exchange for more generous depreciation allowances, existing tax incentives for the reinvestment of profits would be eliminated. Other important areas of proposed reform for the enterprise profit tax included the capitalization and depreciation over time of expenses on research and development, experimental design and natural resource exploration; and the liberalization of loss carry-forwards from five to ten years. The new enterprise profit tax would be partially integrated with the personal income tax by allowing stockholders to get a credit for the tax on dividends withheld at the enterprise level when paying their personal income tax. The integration of the two taxes would also be facilitated by keeping the enterprise profit tax rate equal to the maximum personal income tax rate, at their existing levels of 30 percent. The special higher rates for some sectors, financial institutions and so on, would be eliminated.

The proposals for the personal income tax were more modest at the beginning of Putin's tenure. They involved cleaning up the numerous existing exemptions, the adoption of a universal standard deduction and several other deductions for property, professional and social reasons. The universal standard deduction would be increased from 300 rubles per month to 1,000 rubles for the disabled, Chernobyl victims and other protected categories of citizens. With respect to the rate structure, the proposal was to keep the existing graduated rates of 12, 20, and 30 percent with indexing of these brackets. The Tax Code required a separate chapter in Part II on contributions to the social funds. In the early Putin years, the proposals here were modest as well and involved a regressive rate schedule pegged to the personal income tax rate structure and future modification in two or three years of all these contributions into a uniform social tax.

On the taxation of natural resources, there were a variety of proposals. The main innovations included an environmental tax, which would substitute for the existing fees for discharging pollutants and disposing of wastes; the introduction of a tax on additional income from hydrocarbon extraction paid only on new deposits; the special tax treatment for product sharing agreements; and a system of taxes on development of unused and low-yielding oil fields.

The most significant proposals on subnational taxes include the following:

- the elimination of the turnover tax for road maintenance, and its substitution with a surtax enterprise profit tax at a rate of 1.5 percent the first year, 0.75 percent the second year, and zero the third year;
- the introduction within a period of three years of a real estate property tax based on market values and in substitution of the three existing property taxes with a proposed maximum rate of 2 percent

and an actual tax base not less than 10-15 percent of the appraised market values;

- keeping the sales tax and making several adjustments in its application; and
- limiting the list of local taxes to five or so main taxes.

Several important issues in tax administration were on the government's agenda for tax reform in the first half of 2000 as well. These required the amendment of Part I of the Tax Code and included highly charged issues in Russia. Many of these amendments had been successfully opposed during the discussion and subsequent passage of Part I of the Tax Code, during the Yeltsin era. These issues included the following: (i) whether to allow the governments to issue interpretive regulations and instructions that clarify and explain the tax law – the winning position in 1999 had been that the Tax Code alone should be the sole source of legal regulations;[9] (ii) whether to repeal the provision in Part I of the Tax Code that the taxpayers should benefit from any ambiguity in the tax laws, which was also fought hard in 1999, and was seen as a way to protect taxpayers' rights against a capricious and often corrupt tax administration; (iii) whether to establish that taxpayers' obligations are not fully discharged until the funds are received in the government accounts, which was seen as necessary because of the fraud associated with claims that taxpayers had deposited the funds in commercial banks for payments of their tax obligations with the banks failing to forward the funds to the treasury; and (iv) whether tax fines could only be collected through court proceedings.

The State Duma did not approve all the proposals on tax reform listed above, and the actual tax measures approved differed at times quite significantly from what was initially proposed. Nevertheless, a major push in the reform of Russia's tax system was accomplished during the summer of 2000. On August 7, 2000, President Putin signed into law the four new chapters of Part II of the Tax Code pertaining to the personal income tax, value added tax, excises, and the consolidated social tax. On August 7, Putin signed into law the bill 'On Enacting Tax Code, Part II' and both of these laws were published on August 10, 2000 and became effective January 1, 2001. A main reason for the reform, broadly recognized at the time, was the personal involvement of President Putin in the process by personally appealing to the Duma to support the measures submitted by the Ministry of Finance and the Ministry of Taxes earlier in 2000.[10] The core of the tax reform in the summer 2000 package was four chapters of Part II of the Tax Code on the personal income tax, the value added tax, excise taxes and social security taxes as well as interim tax legislation. The remaining chapters of Part II of the Tax Code, on the enterprise profit tax and property taxes, were not included. Their fate and current status, as well as the new legislation on the taxation of natural resources, is discussed in greater detail below. The highlights of what is now known as the 'Putin tax reform' included a bold reform of the personal income tax with a flat rate of 13 percent, the substantial reduction and eventual elimination of the subnational turnover taxes,[11] substantial increases in excise taxes and an optional local 'piggyback' enterprise profit tax up to a maximum of 5 percent.[12]

The most significant and also most popular among the new measures was the reform of the personal income tax in 2001.[13] The reform eliminated the existing progressive rate schedule, with rates from 12 percent to 30 percent, and put in place a flat rate of 13 percent.[14] In reality, this meant a significant tax cut for many taxpayers but a 1 percentage point increase for the majority of taxpayers, who through 2000 were paying the lowest rate of 12 percent. The key selling point was improving tax compliance through simplification. Other aspects of the personal income tax were also simplified. The number of deductions was reduced, and deduction levels were expressed in annually indexed amounts of rubles, discontinuing the practice of expressing them as a percent of the minimum wage. In addition, the new personal income tax allowed one-time property-related deductions of the full amount received upon the sale of real estate or land plots, if owned by a taxpayer for more than five years as well as other property owned by a taxpayer for three or more years; up to 1 million rubles for the sale of real estate or land plots, if owned up to five years; 125,000 rubles for the sale of other property, if owned up to three years; 600,000 rubles for the purchase or construction of a home excluding interest paid on mortgage loans obtained for the above purposes; 25,000 for medical expenses and an equal amount for education expenses. Although these deep and radical reforms of the personal income tax had been discussed informally in 1998-99, it was quite a surprise when they were adopted because the early proposals from the Putin administration left this tax pretty much intact.

Also surprising was the early passage of a social tax which unified in a single levy all the contributions to the social funds (pensions, social insurance and medical insurance), thus simplifying taxpayer compliance costs without really impinging on the financial autonomy of the social funds. The reform also reduced significantly the tax burden from payroll taxes. It eliminated the contribution to the employment fund and cut the existing flat rate from 38.5 percent, when all contributions were added together, to a regressive scale of 20 percent for annual payroll amounts in excess of 100,000 rubles but less than 300,000 rubles; 10 percent of amounts in excess of 300,000 rubles but less than 600,000 rubles; and 5 percent for amounts in excess of 600,000 rubles. The 5 percent rate was cut to 2 percent on January 1, 2002. Also, the transfer of the administration and enforcement of the single payroll tax to the Ministry of Taxes and Fees (now back to the State Tax Service) was a significant step taken in conjunction with the introduction of the new social tax. This would economize on the previous duplication of effort in four different agencies. Consolidation of collection into one agency is likely to improve enforcement as it will create the possibility of auditing enterprises for more than one tax and the use of cross-information from different aspects of taxpayers activities. For example, enterprises have an incentive to fully report wages and salaries as a deduction from the enterprise profit tax, but of course this information can be used to check for full compliance with the social tax.

The new chapter on value added tax in Part II of the Tax Code replaced the existing value added tax law, and the new measures became effective on January 1, 2001. Prior to this development, the State Duma had approved in January 2000 an expanded list of foodstuffs and children's goods to be subject to the reduced rate of 10 percent, as opposed to the standard rate of 20 percent, which became effective July 1, 2000 (the standard rate later changed to 18 percent). There was nothing radical in the new value added tax chapter of the Tax Code. The most significant changes included the clarification of the 'place of supply rules', affecting the tax on cross-border services supplied to foreign customers, and the introduction of the concept of 'place of economic activity'. Other changes included the application from July 2001 of zero-rating of sales to Commonwealth of Independent States countries and input value added tax was made creditable on supplies to the Commonwealth of Independent States countries, that is, they would be treated like ordinary exports. This did not, however, apply to oil and gas exports to Commonwealth of Independent States countries, which remained standard rated.

The new chapter on value added tax represented major changes for the construction industry. Beginning in January, 2001, rental of residential premises was exempt from value added tax, irrespective of the owner being a value added tax payer (a company) or not (an individual). Value added tax assessed on self-construction was made recoverable against output value added tax collected on sales rather than capitalized, as was done in the previous regime. Also new at this point was that individual entrepreneurs with turnover exceeding one million rubles became value added tax payers. The value added tax chapter also eased payment requirements by abolishing thrice monthly installments and introduced monthly or quarterly payments depending on turnover. The new chapter also abolished an extensive list of value added tax concessions. Beginning January 1, 2001, the exemptions for patents, copyrights and license payments were abolished, as was the exemption for commercial educational institutions, irrespective of whether they are licensed or accredited. The value added tax exemption for the mass media and on books was abolished on January 1, 2002.

The last new chapter of Part II of the Tax Code approved under Putin in July 2000 was on excises. With respect to existing legislation, the new chapter expanded the list of excisable goods to include a variety of tobacco products, motorcycles, diesel fuel and oil for engines, among others. The most significant changes were increases in tax rates on certain excisable goods, most noticeably the excise tax on gasoline was increased by almost 235 percent for 80 octane gasoline and more than 260 percent for higher octane gasoline and the excise tax on cigarettes to 48 percent. These increases in excise taxes were lower than those proposed by the government at that time and were meant to cover the revenue losses from the elimination or reduction of certain taxes, most conspicuously the turnover taxes.

The other two most important measures adopted in the July 2000 package were the reduction of turnover taxes from 4 to 1 percent and the introduction of an optional 5 percent piggyback surtax on the enterprise profit tax for local governments. The government plans were to eliminate the turnover taxes entirely. Instead, the turnover tax of 2.5 percent was reduced to 1 percent, and the 1.5 percent turnover tax for social infrastructure tax was entirely eliminated. The law on the introduction of the tax reform package allowed for a 1 percent road tax to be in force for two years until 1 January, 2003. The 1 percent turnover tax was kept as a result of political pressure from the regions to fund their highway funds.

While there was no chapter on the enterprise profit tax passed by the State Duma with the July 2000 package, several recent pieces of legislation have been enacted in relation to this tax. For example, the law on the introduction of Part II of the Tax Code reconfirms the right of regional governments to offer reductions in the tax on enterprises for that part of the tax shared with regional governments. In addition, Order 26n of the Ministry of Finance of March 15, 2000 updates the amounts enterprises can deduct for expenses for lobbying, advertising, and training costs. Regulation 420 adopted by the State Duma increases the limits on business deductions for 'voluntary' insurance from 1 percent to 3 percent. A new enterprise profit tax regulation that came into effect on October 16, 2000 defines 'separate subdivisions' with an enterprise and requires the separate subdivisions to pay tax to the regional budgets where they are located. If these subdivisions do not have separate balance sheets and bank accounts, this regulation requires apportionment of net income according to a formula based on fixed assets and payroll. This regulation confirms the ability to carry forward losses for five years but only in installments equal to 1/5th of the loss. It also requires that to qualify for the capital investment allowances, the relevant capital expenditure needs to be actually disbursed. In 2001, Federal Law no. 166FZ amended Chapter 22 on Excises of the Tax Code by introducing the requirement to pay beverage alcohol excises owed to the regional budget according to the place of retail sale of alcohol, when retail sales are located in the territory of a different region. Enterprises are now required to submit a tax return on sales/transfer of goods subject to excise at the place of registration as well as at the place of each branch or other detached subdivision registration.

In April 2001, the State Duma approved on first reading, and by a large majority, the draft of the enterprise profit tax chapter. The other elements of the second phase of the tax reforms are a new tax on natural resource extraction, the real estate property tax, and some other pieces of legislation, such as new regulations on transfer pricing and the elimination of the sales tax on foreign currency purchases. Early in 2001, there were hopes to have all this legislation approved and signed by July 1, before the summer recess of the State Duma, but this did not happen. Complications over passage of other major reforms (personal income tax) pulled the spotlight away from enterprise profit tax reform.

After the big Putin tax reform push of 1999-2001, and around the time of Putin's re-election in 2004, the government adopted two medium-term programs for development and tax reform for 2003-05 and 2006-08. These programs were largely focused on tax administration and a clean up of remaining pieces of the enterprise profit tax, payroll tax reform and continued simplification of the system (via a reduction in special treatment, exemptions and non-standard accounting procedures). As a result of the focus of these programs and Putin's increased political power (with published approval ratings of 85 percent in 2004 and 77 percent in 2006), a number of reforms to the entire system were enacted over the following years.

Regarding the enterprise profit tax, some of the most important changes came in 2004. Several amendments to the enterprise profit tax were adopted on July 29, 2004. Those approved amendments include an increased tax rate of 9 percent for dividends paid by a Russian company to a Russian company and to individuals who are Russian tax residents; a re-allocation of the enterprise profit tax among budgets – 6.5 percent to the federal budget (as opposed to the previous level of 5 percent), 17.5 percent to the regional budgets (instead of 17 percent), a reduction in the rate was allowed to 13.5 percent and the 2 percent share to local budgets was abolished (effective January 2005).

Additional amendments that were proposed in 2004 were not passed into law. These include radical changes in depreciation procedures, grouping assets in a small number of categories and increasing allowances and the abolition of limits on most business-related expenses. One sticking point with the Duma on the draft chapter on the enterprise profit tax submitted by the government was the elimination of the investment allowance and the introduction of accelerated depreciation schedules. Despite the fact that this substitution would have benefited most enterprises, the State Duma refused to accept this part of the draft.[15] Instead, the Duma drafted an alternative, which retains and expands the investment allowance and introduces a more accelerated depreciation schedule. This means that the package will not be revenue neutral, but will instead reduce tax collections by approximately 100 billion rubles. The investment allowance is retained for another five years. Following that period, the investment allowance will be phased out over three years. The draft also introduces accrual accounting for purposes of the enterprise profit tax, but cash accounting will continued to be allowed for small businesses with quarterly sales under one million rubles. Most importantly, the draft bill abolishes all limits on business expenses, with the exception of lobbying expenses, some types of training costs and expenses on the insurance of employees.

The reform of the tax system of the Russian Federation has continued to evolve, sometimes under pressure from the courts. The most significant example of this is the ruling on January 30, 2001 by the Constitutional Court declaring the sales tax, a main source of revenue at the subnational level at that time, as contradicting the Constitution of the Russian Federation. The main issue is that the federal enabling law for the sales tax should have been passed as a separate piece of legislation, as well as providing a clear and concise definition of the fundamental aspects of the structure of the tax.[16] However, the Court established a deadline to amend the tax by January 1, 2002 before it was to be invalidated as of 2004.[17]

Reform does continue. In July 2004, the President signed into law amendments to Part I and Part II of the Tax Code, which became effective on January 1, 2005. Sergei Shatalov, First Deputy Minister of Finance in 2005 declared that the era of tax reform in the Russian Federation was approaching an end. In 2006 a more rational system of capital expensing was introduced for companies and entrepreneurs. The amendments to Part I establish a closed list of ten federal, three regional and two local taxes as well as four special tax regimes – by numbers there are ten federal, three regional and only two local taxes, and four tax regimes. The unified social tax and flat rate income tax significantly reduce the tax burden on labor income, especially for high-income individuals.

Putin's tax legacy may be tax policy based on politics as much as economics. His popularity, especially during his second term, has enabled tax measures to move into place relatively quickly since 2001. The high profile tax case of Yukos and its owners, Mikhail Khodorkovsky and Platon

Lebedev, was seen as a way for the tax administration to show its muscle and keep taxes on the national agenda. Little movement in subnational government revenue instruments – in fact a slight centralization in the system – may also be seen as Putin's way to retain control over the regions.

CONCLUSIONS

The tax system of the Russian Federation still remains a relatively complex system of federal, state, and local taxes, although significant changes have been made over the last 15 years. Major components of reform have taken place since President Putin came into power. In part due to his relatively strong hold over government, the pace of reform since 2001 has exceeded that of the late 1990s. Of course this is also a function of ground work being well laid out when Putin stepped into office.

A continued misperception of the Russian tax system during a good part of the 1990s was that there has been relatively little tax effort in the country. However, the overall level of tax effort – measured as the ratio of tax collections to GDP – has been for most of the transition period quite similar to that of many middle-income countries and higher than in Argentina, Japan, South Africa and the United States. But unlike those countries, the trend in tax effort in Russia has been downward. The main cause appears to be policy changes in tax rates and tax bases for the major taxes rather than overt increases in the rate of tax evasion. Much of this misperception about tax burdens in Russia during this period was due to the fact that the revenue statistics being considered belonged only to the federal government and ignored tax collections at the subnational level as well as contributions to the extra-budgetary funds.

In more recent years, Russia's tax system began to be criticized as being excessively burdensome. As we show in Chapter 4, in fact Russia's overall (or consolidated) tax burden at 37 percent of GDP for 2000 has been above the OECD average and also above the tax burden for most countries in transition. In Chapter 4, we project from international experience that for Russia's level of per capita income its overall tax burden should be around 26 percent. Of course, these comparisons are subject to significant caveats, because actual tax burdens based on collections do not generally reflect differences based solely on differences in statutory rates and special treatments, which in some cases increase and in others decrease tax burdens quite significantly. Because of relatively high statutory rates for most taxes until the recent reforms, tax-compliant firms did indeed face much higher tax burdens than the 36 percent rate indicated by the overall tax burden figure. This phenomenon explains to a large extent the main thrust of current tax policy in Russia: reducing statutory rates while broadening the tax net by controlling tax evasion.

Before the recent reforms under Putin, the vertical distribution of tax burdens under conventional assumptions had been mildly progressive or proportional for the majority of the population, but regressive for the very poor. Relatively high statutory rates, disallowed deductions, widespread tax evasion and uneven enforcement have caused significant horizontal inequities. The complexity of the tax system imposes significant distortions and excess burdens on the use of capital and labor inputs. And like many developing and transition countries, the tax administration is neither trained nor funded to carry out effective administration of the existing system. The recent reforms are not a miracle cure for the many problems that affect the Russian economy. Even if the last two chapters of Part II of the Tax Code are completely passed in the near future, there are still serious problems with weak and often corrupt tax administration, widespread noncompliance with the tax system, corruption, tax arrears and complementary legislation and institutions, such as land reform which jeopardizes the effectiveness of the new tax system.

Before passing final judgment on the trials and tribulations of tax reform in Russia, one needs to put into perspective the enormity of the reform process required in Russia (Aslund, 2000). It was not only the transformation in ideology from Marxism-Leninism and planned socialism to democracy and a market economy, but also the creation of all sorts of new institutions from accounting systems to a modern tax administration. After the initial false start of 1991-92, perhaps it was necessary for Russia to go through the crises of 1994 and 1998 to make progress with institutional reform, and in particular tax reform.

However, reform remains in many ways elusive and fragile. Take, for example, the reform of the energy sector where Unified Energy Systems (UES) and Gazprom still play a monopoly role in the production, transmission, and distribution of electricity, hot water, and natural gas. These are sectors with many problems, characterized by waste, low cost recovery and uneven and at times chaotic regulation by subnational governments. Integral reform with the break up of the current monopolies and the introduction of competition, independent regulation of tariffs and service conditions with full cost recovery has long been awaited. One of the most significant obstacles to reform in recent months has been the opposition by minority shareholders at UES because they fear that its management, which supports the reform, will sell assets to new owners on a closed, non-transparent basis, repeating the privatization abuses of the past (Frank, 2000).

The Putin administration has sought to consolidate power at the federal level, rejecting some recent reforms to decentralize government. This approach seems to have helped the government move their tax policy agenda forward. The changes in subnational taxation in the form of property and sales taxes seem to have taken a backseat to changes in federal taxes. To be fair, Putin has been willing to tackle very difficult issues facing Russia. For example, Putin moved to significantly reduce the power of the regional governors. He also moved to curtail the influence and power of the oligarchs who had gained ascendancy in the loans for shares scheme. Putin also has shown a willingness to address other sacred cows of Russian politics, such as military and land reforms. But other policies may not have been as supportive of market reforms and, in particular, the strengthening of democratic institutions. For example, Putin's administration has re-established state control over the mass media.

The direction for further tax reform in Russia is clear. The basic goal of a tax system is to collect revenue to operate the government at levels adequate to provide the services necessary for a good quality of life and build and maintain the infrastructure required for economic development. The objective is to raise this level of revenue without unduly distorting the economy. Of course, no country does this completely 'right' because pre-existing distortions in the economy may call for discriminatory taxes. Furthermore, policymakers often find it difficult to resist the temptation to use the tax system as a lever to influence economic decisions, and politics often influence tax policy.

Many market economies subjected their tax systems to significant reforms during the 1980s. The reasons for and objectives of these reforms still contain important lessons for the process of tax reform in the Russian Federation. The general thrust of tax reform in market economies has been threefold: to simplify the income tax by flattening rates and broadening the tax base; to introduce broad-based value added taxes on the consumption of most goods and services; and to reduce tariffs on imports. The broadest tax policy objectives were invariably to reduce economic distortions, equalize conditions among economic agents and simplify the tax system. This worldwide reform movement resulted from the practice in the 1960s and 1970s of policymakers attempting to use the tax code, among other policy levers, to pick winners.

Russia has gone a long way in the pursuit of these objectives. Defining the 'right' tax structure in a transition economy, like Russia, still requires more care than in market economies or even in developing countries. Significant distortions still exist in the pricing system; labor and housing markets are still in the process of development; the social safety net remains weak and still not fully in place; the roles of enterprises and governments have been considerably disentangled (although progress in this regard have been reversed in recent years by renationalization of companies) but remain unclear; and most important, there is still a great deal of investor uncertainty. Two other complicating factors are that the fiscal relationships between the center and the regional governments are still being defined and the tax administration system is not very far along in the modernization process.

Where does all this leave Russia's tax reform effort for the future? We believe that the Russian context calls for different emphasis in the traditional principles for 'good' tax policy as follows. There is a need now more than ever to realize that tax reform must be a process – not an event – and a process that evolves over time. The rate of change in the economy is (or at least should be) faster in a transition country than in a mature market economy and, therefore, there will be a continuous need to adapt the tax sysstem to changing circumstances. There is a need to remain focused on the ability of the tax system to raise a target amount of revenues to keep the budget balanced and maintain macroeconomic stability during periods of low international oil prices. There will also be a need to ensure that revenue growth keeps up with the growth in expenditure needs over time.

Despite the significant steps taken recently, there is still a need for simplification of the tax system. Russia's tax system still gets a low grade for horizontal fairness: treating those with similar incomes the same. The fact is that individuals and businesses in the same circumstances are not being treated in the same way by the tax system. The system should relieve government officials of the responsibility for 'picking winners'. Certainty and stability of the tax system must remain a high priority for Russia. To attract foreign and domestic capital for new businesses and expansion of existing businesses, the government must offer investors greater certainty about their tax liabilities in the immediate future. Investors who plan for a particular rate of return are more likely to invest in countries with stable tax systems. Although investment in the Russian economy may offer a potentially higher rate of return than does investment in other countries, an uncertain tax environment can negate this advantage. The objective of certainty and stability is in open contradiction with the need to continue to fine-tune the tax system. Thus, a balance needs to be reached between these two objectives: fine tuning the tax system and stability of the tax system. A possible way to achieve this balance is to bunch changes and innovations at long intervals and produce sufficient information for taxpayers on what changes are being contemplated for the future. Last, structural reform of Russia's tax system still needs to be planned together with reform and modernization of the tax administration system and further reform of intergovernmental fiscal relations.

The next four chapters of this book analyze many of the problems that plague the effectiveness of the tax system in the Russian Federation. Many of these problems exist in a number of transition countries, including those that have sponsored earlier successful tax reforms. These chapters cover the major taxes including the enterprise profit tax, value added tax, personal income tax, excise taxes and property taxes. An additional chapter focuses on the issue of tax administration, and another chapter considers the overlap between tax reform and reform of the system of intergovernmental fiscal relations. In the eyes of many observers, the biggest challenge for effective reform of the tax system and elsewhere in the economy continues to be a corrupt and inefficient bureaucracy. Thus, the reform of tax administration remains a significant challenge for that reason.

Despite an improving economy and the Putin tax reforms, corruption and organized crime are extending to the judicial system and as widespread as ever. As the common saying goes in Russia, 'up to now not one person in Russia has been arrested for corruption in or outside government'.

The final chapter reflects on the enormous changes to Russia's tax system. It also focuses on the remaining shortcomings of the tax system in the Russian Federation. We also consider potential reforms, taking into account Russia's economic, demographic and intergovernmental landscape.

NOTES

1.   To a large extent opposition in the Duma to comprehensive tax reform during the Yeltsin years was old-fashioned partisan politics and opportunistic obstructionism led by the opposition forces dominated by the Communist party but also by others quite happy to play along, such as the liberal Yabloko party. The December 1999 elections still left the Communists holding the largest one-party share of Duma deputies, but the pro-Kremlin Edinstvo party, the second largest group of deputies, has been able to put together majority coalitions in support of President's Putin policies. The elections of December 1999 were heralded in many quarters as a fundamental change for Russian society. As Aslund (2000) remarked, even the Communist Party retracted its anti-market stand before these elections, raising hopes that a new reform consensus has emerged in Russia.

2.   The most serious counterproposals came from the Yabloko party. The main goal of the Yabloko proposal was to reduce the tax burden. This would be accomplished by: (i) allowing full deduction for most business costs including investment, advertisement, insurance, education and training, transportation, catering and the use of accelerated depreciation under the enterprise profit tax; (ii) allowing deductions for health and recreation in Russia, education expenses, purchase, construction and repair of housing, assistance to dependent parents, voluntary pension contributions and charity contributions under the personal income tax; (iii) rolling the payroll taxes into one tax to be divided among social funds; (iv) simplifying the excise tax structure; (v) phasing-out the tax on highway users; (vi) replacing the   land and assets tax with a tax on real property; and (vii) revising the law on imputed income tax.

3.   The turnaround in the level of barter has been fueled by better economic conditions, no doubt, but also by the long-time coming refusal by the federal Ministry of Finance and also public utilities, oil companies and the railway ministry to accept anything but cash in payment for the transactions. The key piece of the turnaround has been the

political will of supporting a policy of cutting off supplies to those in arrears or not paying in hard cash.

4. Putin remained quite popular in 2000 among Russian people. In that year he was voted Person of the Year in Russia, receiving 38 percent of the votes, exactly the same proportion he had won in 1999. In contrast, President Clinton and Gennady Zyuganov, the Russian Communist Party leader, got second ranking with 4 percent of the vote each.

5. Another goal, but this time related to intergovernmental fiscal relations, has been to achieve a greater level of centralization of public sector resources.

6. Other important reforms that are ongoing and complement in many cases the tax reforms included the consolidation of the customs tariffs, the updating of bankruptcy laws, the reduction of red tape to facilitate investments, the introduction of a Land Code and the break up of monopolies in the energy and rail transport sectors.

7. Lower rates were also expected to increase compliance. Some of these hopes were pinned on the experience with alcohol taxes in 1999. After the share of the excise tax in total price decreased, legal production of alcoholic products and excise tax receipts experienced pronounced increases. As discussed below, the sharp increase in personal income tax collections during the first half of 2001 is being credited to the drastic cuts in tax rates approved in 2000.

8. This system had also been proposed in the Shatalov Draft Tax Code of 1997.

9. Actually, Part I of the Tax Code (article 4) allows government bodies to issue rulings, regulations and methodological guidelines on the application of the tax legislation. However, the legal status or normative power of the regulations remains questionable.

10. The Duma and the Ministry of Finance had reached an impasse, openly disagreeing on several key issues, and the Duma was accusing the Ministry of Finance of repeatedly changing its position. Putin's intervention clearly stated the Government's objectives and tilted a significant majority of deputies in favor of many of the reforms after compromises in several key issues. Despite the consensus reached between the Duma and the government in pushing through the July 2000 tax reform package, there has been no lack of dissension in and outside the Duma. Some of these criticisms were vented out during the annual conference of the Russian branch of the International Fiscal Association, as reported in the November 23, 2000 issue of the *Moscow Times* (Moscow Times, 2000). For example, Andrei Makarov, a prominent former Duma deputy and now head of the Duma's expert group on taxes, criticized Putin's reform package as lacking any overarching concept of government tax policy. The former Minister of Taxes and Fees, Alexander Pochinok, now labor minister, criticized the tax package as being full of problems and requiring many amendments in the future. Others, such as Vladimir Panskov, with the State Audit Chamber, expressed disappointment with reform, the rushing of drafts through parliament, and the de facto special treatment for large taxpayers, such as Gazprom. Other observers also complained about the fact that businesses' input and viewpoints were still being ignored in the later rounds of reforms.

11. These were the Housing Maintenance Tax and the Road Users Tax.

12. Recall that in 1999 there was a reduction in the overall rate of the Enterprise profit tax from 35 percent to 30 percent (with the regional enterprise profit tax rate reduced from 22 percent to 19 percent).

13. See, for example, Antel (2002).

14. Two exceptions to the flat rate of 13 percent were introduced. First, there was a rate of 35 percent falling on interest earnings from bank deposits or insurance income with returns above some percent of the refinancing rate. This affected alternative employee compensation schemes using bank deposits and insurance policies, which were quite prevalent through 2000. Second, there was a rate of 30 percent falling on dividend income and expatriates' (residents and non-residents) Russia-sourced income.

15. The new more accelerated depreciation system would have saved taxpayers 300 billion rubles in 2001 and by comparison the investment allowance would have saved them 227 billion rubles. See Sergei Shatalov's interview in *Vedomosti*, March 19, 2001.

16. The sales tax in most regions was applicable to legal entities and independent contractors selling taxable goods and services. This sales tax was imposed at the wholesale and retail

levels but only to 'cash sales'. These were defined to exclude bank wire transfers among legal entities, so the Court found that the tax can be discriminatory. In addition the definition of the 'object of taxation' allows the same transaction to be taxed in more than one jurisdiction.

17. See McDonald (2001).

APPENDIX

Table 3A.1 Major Reforms of the Government under Vladimir Putin, as of September 2005

Effort/Legislation	Content	Status
Tax Code, Part II	• Personal Income Tax • Value Added Tax • Unified Social Tax • Excises	• Passed by the State Duma on July 19, 2000 • Approved by the Federation Council on July 26, 2000 • Signed by the Russian Federation President on August 5, 2000 • Came into effect in January 2001
Tax Code, Part II	• Enterprise Profit Tax	• Passed by the State Duma on July 6, 2001 • Approved by the Federation Council on July 20, 2001 • Signed by the Russian Federation President on August 6, 2001 • Came into force in January 2002. • Amended rates in 2003, 2004, 2005
Tax on recovery of mineral resources (Chapter in Part II of the Russian Federation Tax Code)	• Enact tax on recovery of mineral resources	• Passed by the State Duma on July 13, 2001 • Approved by the Federation council on July 20, 2001 • Signed by the Russian Federation President on August 8, 2001 • Came into force in January 2002

Table 3A.1 Major Reforms of the Government under Vladimir Putin, as of September 2005 (continued)

Effort/Legislation	Content	Status
Taxation system for agricultural producers (single tax on agricultural producers) (Chapter in Part II of the Russian Federation Tax Code)		• Passed by the State Duma in April 2001. • Approved by the Federation Council on December 26, 2001 • Signed by the Russian Federation President on December 29, 2001 • Came into force on January 31, 2002
Simplified system of taxation (Chapter in Part II of the Russian Federation Tax Code)		• Passed by the State Duma on July 2002 • Approved by the Federation Council on July 10, 2002 • Signed by the President on July 24, 2002 • Came into effect on January 1, 2003
System of taxation as tax on imputed income for certain types of activities (Chapter in Part II of the Russian Federation Tax Code)		• Passed by the State Duma on July 1, 2002 • Approved by the Federation Council on July 10, 2002 • Signed by the president on July 24, 2002 • Came into effect on January 1, 2003
Sales tax (Chapter in Part II of the Russian Federation Tax Code)	• Eliminated January 1, 2004	• Passed by the State Duma on November 1, 2001 • Approved by the Federation Council on November 14, 2001 • Signed by the Russian Federation President on November 27, 2001

Table 3A.1 Major Reforms of the Government under Vladimir Putin, as of September 2005 (continued)

Effort/Legislation	Content	Status
Sales tax (Chapter in Part II of the Russian Federation Tax Code) (continued)		• Came into force on December 30, 2001 except for certain provisions, which came into effect on January 1, 2002
Elimination of turnover taxes (Bill of Enactment of Tax Code, Part II)	• Reduce Highway users tax by 1.5%, with up to 1% accrue to regional funds (effective January 1, 2001, fully eliminate from January 1, 2003). Rates, reliefs, and exemptions to be established by regional legislation. • Eliminate tax on housing and utilities	• Passed by the State Duma on July 19, 2000 • Approved by the Federation Council on July 26, 2000 • Signed by the Russian Federation President on August 5, 2000 • Came into force on January 1, 2001
Transport tax (Chapter in Part II of the Russian Federation Tax Code)		• Passed by the State Duma on July 1, 2002 • Approved by the Federation Council on July 10, 2002 • Signed by the Russian Federation President on July 24, 2002 • Came into effect on January 1, 2003

Table 3A.1 Major Reforms of the Government under Vladimir Putin, as of September 2005 (continued)

Effort/Legislation	Content	Status
Reduction of the number of taxes (Bill of Enactment of Tax Code, Part II)	To eliminate: • Tax on sales of fuels and lubricants • Tax on purchase of vehicles • Tax on separate types of transport vehicles • Tax on banks incomes • Tax on incomes from insurance activities • Stamp duty • Cross-border duty	• Passed by the State Duma on July 19, 2000 • Approved by the Federation Council on July 26, 2000 • Signed by the Russian Federation President on August 5, 2000 • Came into effect on January 1, 2001
Amendments to Tax Code, Part II	• 44 federal laws have been adopted from August 2002 to September 2004 to introduce various amendments to Part II of the Tax Code	

Table 3A.1 *Major Reforms of the Government under Vladimir Putin, as of September 2005 (continued)*

Effort/Legislation	Content	Status
Introduce gambling tax (as a separate chapter of the Tax Code, Part II)		• Passed by the State Duma on December 11, 2002 • Approved by the Federation Council on December 18, 2002 • Signed by the Russian Federation President on December 27, 2002 • Came into effect on January 1, 2004
Introduce enterprise assets tax (as a separate chapter of the Tax Code, Part II)		• Passed by the State Duma on October 17, 2003 • Approved by the Federation Council on October 29, 2003 • Signed by the Russian Federation President on November 11, 2003 • Came into effect on January 1, 2004
Establish levies for the use of fauna and for the use of aquatic biological resources as a separate chapter of the Tax Code, Part II		• Passed by the State Duma on October 17, 2003 • Approved by the Federation Council on October 29, 2003 • Signed by the RF President on November 11, 2003 • Came into effect on January 1, 2004

Table 3A.1 Major Reforms of the Government under Vladimir Putin, as of September 2005 (continued)

Effort/Legislation	Content	Status
Introduce Taxation system for those executing Production Sharing Agreements as a separate chapter of the Tax Code, Part II		• Passed by the State Duma on May 21, 2003 • Approved by the Federation Council on May 28, 2003 • Signed by the Russian Federation President on June 6, 2003 • Came into effect on June 9, 2003 • New wording came into effect on January 1, 2005
Introduce Water Tax as a separate chapter of the Tax Code, Part II		• Passed by the State Duma on July 10, 2004 • Approved by the Federation Council on July 15, 2004 • Signed by the Russian Federation President on July 28, 2004 • Came into effect on January 1, 2005
Eliminate law on 'Basic principles of taxation', amending Part I of the Tax Code, to establish the list of federal, regional and local taxes, abolish advertising tax	• Federal taxes and levies • Value added tax, • Excises, Personal income tax • Unified Social Tax • PT • Mineral recovery tax • Estate and Gift Tax • Water tax	• Passed by the State Duma on July 9, 2004 • Approved by the Federation Council on July 15, 2004 • Signed by the Russian Federation President on July 29, 2004 • Came into effect on January 1, 2005

Table 3A.1 Major Reforms of the Government under Vladimir Putin, as of September 2005 (continued)

Effort/Legislation	Content	Status
Eliminate law on 'Basic principles of taxation', amending Part I of the Tax Code, to establish the list of federal, regional and local taxes, abolish advertising tax (continued)	• Levies for the use of fauna and for the use of aquatic biological resources • State Duty • Regional taxes • Enterprise assets tax • Gambling tax • Transport tax • Local taxes • Land tax; Assets tax on individuals • Special tax regimes • Single tax on agricultural producers • Simplified system of taxation • Imputed income tax for certain types of activities	

Table 3A.1 Major Reforms of the Government under Vladimir Putin, as of September 2005 (continued)

Effort/Legislation	Content	Status
Eliminate law on 'Basic principles of taxation', amending Part I of the Tax Code, to establish the list of federal, regional and local taxes, abolish advertising tax (continued)	• Taxation system for those executing Production Sharing Agreements	

Sources: Ministry of Finance of the Russian Federation (2005)

4. Performance of the Tax System before and after the Reform

A country's level of taxation is partly a policy decision, but the level of tax also depends on the size and structure of the economy and the attitude of the population toward paying tax. Having said this, a growing and unsustainable budget deficit is often one indication that revenues are not growing adequately relative to government expenditure.[1] We place the Russian Federation's tax effort into context by comparing the level of taxation there with that of other countries. We also examine trends in the Russian Federation's budget deficit for evidence regarding the adequacy of tax revenue. Then, we attempt to gauge the tax effort of the Russian Federation relative to other countries by controlling for features of the economy that are widely believed to influence the level of taxation. Finally, we assess the performance of the Russian Federation's tax system by examining the distribution of tax burdens among the population by income decile and the economic efficiency of the system.

LEVEL OF TAXATION AND TAX EFFORT

Some countries set higher tax rates, use broader tax bases and devote more resources to tax administration than other countries. Economists refer to the influence of such policy choices on the level of taxation in a country as the country's tax effort. Measuring tax effort, however, is difficult because a given set of policy choices in one country may have a very different revenue yield in another country. For example, variation among countries in the structure of the economy or the willingness of the public to pay tax may result in very different realized levels of taxation in two otherwise identical countries with identical tax systems. Thus, a country's realized level of taxation depends not only on its policy choices or tax effort but also on the size and nature of the economy, the willingness of the public to pay tax and so on.

Having said this, and acknowledging from the outset the limitations of this approach, we use the level of taxation as a proxy for a country's tax effort. More specifically, we measure tax effort as the ratio of realized tax collections to gross domestic product (GDP) to gauge the performance of the Russian Federation's tax system relative to that of other countries.

Table 4.1 reports consolidated tax revenue-to-GDP ratios for the Russian Federation and selected countries for the years 2000 through 2004. Since there are inconsistencies in the fiscal data available from the International Monetary Fund (IMF) and World Bank, we should be careful in making intertemporal and cross-country comparisons.[2] Throughout this period, the Russian Federation's tax effort is somewhat less than that of Latvia and Lithuania, but the ratio of all three countries is very similar by 2004. Throughout 2000–04, the Russian Federation's aggregate tax effort is significantly less than that of other former Soviet Republics, the middle income countries of Eastern Europe and the high income countries of Western Europe. On the other hand, Russia's overall level of taxation is similar to that of Australia and the United States.

Table 4.1   Consolidated Tax Revenues-to-GDP ratio for Russia and Select Countries, 2000–04

Country	2000	2001	2002	2003	2004
Australia	25.7	26.8	25.9	26.3	26.5
Croatia	41.7	39.5	41.9	42.0	42.2
Czech Republic	31.2	32.6	32.5	33.7	34.1
Estonia	28.8	29.2	—	—	—
Germany	31.0	30.3	30.2	30.7	29.3
Hungary	39.6	38.4	37.6	37.5	—
Korea	23.3	22.8	—	—	—
Latvia	27.2	27.5	27.0	27.6	29.8
Lithuania	25.9	26.1	29.2	29.0	29.7
Mexico	14.7	—	—	—	—
Poland	—	32.6	33.3	35.0	34.0
Russia	**23.4**	**25.9**	**25.7**	**28.2**	**29.5**
Singapore	27.0	25.8	22.2	20.5	20.1
Sweden	39.9	42.4	38.1	38.5	—
United States	22.5	20.4	18.1	17.3	17.2

Notes: These figures do not include payroll taxes.

Source: World Development Indicators Online, World Bank (2006)

Based simply on the evidence in Table 4.1, it would be highly speculative and potentially misleading to attribute the relatively low level of tax effort in the Russian Federation to an ill conceived and poorly administered tax system. After all, it is commonly believed that the substantial variation in tax effort among high income countries in Table 4.1, such as Australia and the United States on the one hand, and Germany and Sweden on the other, largely reflects differences in national attitudes and traditions about the proper role and scope of government. Likewise, it may be equally misleading to assess the performance of the Russian Federation's tax system simply based on the evidence in Table 4.1.

Table 4.2 shows that the Russian Federation's level of taxation as a share of GDP declined throughout the 1990s, from 26.4 percent of GDP in 1992 (based on adjusted figures) to 19.85 percent in 1998. Since 1998, consolidated revenues as a percentage of GDP have steadily grown to 32.68 percent of GDP in 2005, with the single exception of 2002 when revenues as a share of GDP declined slightly relative to the previous year.

The decline in revenues from 1992 through 1998 reflects a number of problems with the economy, such as the barter economy; wage, pension and inter-enterprise payment arrears; high statutory tax rates; weaknesses in tax administration; and widespread popular resistance to paying tax. In fact, the performance of the tax system in the Russian Federation may be far worse than these figures indicate. During the first few years of the economic transition, commercial enterprises routinely used in-kind payments to settle tax liabilities and tax arrears. For example, the national railroad, electric utility and other large enterprises routinely settled tax obligations by providing the government with goods and services rather than making cash payments. Furthermore, the government often overvalued such in-kind payments. By some estimates, the amount of free cash in the budgets of the Russian Federation during this period was on the order of 25 to 30 percent. The lack of free cash severely constrained the ability of the government to adjust expenditures to reflect national priorities, especially when the government's debt service obligations had to be settled by cash payments.

Tables 4.3 and 4.4 show the levels of tax collections by type of tax for the Russian Federation in nominal and real rubles, respectively. The growth in nominal tax collections from 1992 through 1999 is due to inflation. Figure 4.1 shows that real tax collections fell somewhat between 1992 and 1993, grew slowly until 1997, and then fell precipitously in 1998. The sharp decline in 1998 coincides with the financial crisis of that year. In the following years, tax collections rapidly improved. The trends in revenue growth between 1999 and 2005 coincide with economic recovery after 1998.

Table 4.2   Tax Receipts as a Percentage of GDP: Consolidated Budget

Year	Consolidated tax receipts as a percentage of GDP	Consolidated tax receipts as a percentage of GDP (adjusted for consistency)
1992	29.60	26.40
1993	28.91	23.68
1994	29.04	23.90
1995	22.68	22.68
1996	22.04	22.04
1997	23.10	23.10
1998	19.85	19.85
1999	21.18	21.18
2000	23.39	23.39
2001	25.94	25.94
2002	25.74	25.74
2003	28.20	28.20
2004	29.50	29.50
2005	32.68	32.68

Notes: Prior to 1995, budget receipts were not classified according to tax and non-tax receipts. Column 2 presents the tax receipts-to-GDP estimates using estimates for 1992 through 1994 to provide a series that is consistent with the tax receipts definition after 1994.

Source: Federal Treasury, Ministry of Finance (various years), Goskomstat (2005), and authors' calculations.

Figure 4.2 summarizes the trends in real consolidated tax collections by type of tax from 1992 through 2005. This figure shows that the trends in real tax collections among the major taxes – enterprise profit tax, personal income tax and value added tax – was downward throughout most of the 1990s, but there were also changes in the relative importance of certain taxes. For example, the value added tax overtook the enterprise profit tax as the largest single source of revenue in 1996. The underlying reasons for these specific changes are discussed below, but we briefly discuss some of them here, as well.

In 1998, real collections for all of the major taxes fell dramatically. This is hardly surprising given the severity of the financial crisis of August 1998. The sharp decline in value added tax revenues in 1993, which resulted, at least in part, from the change in tax rate from 28 to 20 percent for most goods, stabilized in 1994 and turned upward thereafter. The value added became the largest single source of revenue in 1996 and remained so until

2005. The importance of the value added tax reflects the precipitous decline in enterprise profit tax collections, which were declining even before the financial crisis of August 1998.

Another way to gauge the performance of a country's tax system is to examine trends in the fiscal balance. Transition economies have had a difficult time offloading the relatively large amount of public expenditures associated with planned socialism; therefore, large budget deficits were characteristic of many transition countries, at least until just recently. In fact, the IMF reports general government fiscal deficits in transition countries running 50 percent higher as a percentage of GDP than for developing and advanced economy countries through 1997. Since 1997, deficits in transition countries are quite similar in magnitude to those in developing countries and approximately double those in advanced economies (World Economic Outlook).

Figure 4.3 reports total general government balance as a percent of GDP. The relatively high deficits in the Russian Federation through 1998 compared to other transition countries and developing nations is particularly striking. The deficit-to-GDP figures prior to 1999 could indicate that taxes were not adequate in the Russian Federation. These figures could just as well indicate that the Russian Federation did not do as well as other transition economies at reducing expenditures. Such controversies were central to the meetings and debates between the International Monetary Fund and the Russian Federation, especially between 1997 and 2000.[3]

Obviously, the deficits from 1992 to 1998 reflect the inability of the government to reach a political consensus to either raise revenues in line with expenditures and/or reduce expenditures in line with revenues. The political stalemate resulted in large fiscal imbalances and the country lurched from one economic and/or political crisis to another throughout most of the 1990s. Examples of such crises include a period of hyperinflation; President Yeltsin's decision to rule largely by decree; and frequent changes in prime ministers.

Recent trends in the Russian Federation are more encouraging. The economy is growing as a result of increases in the world prices of Russia's major exports, particularly crude oil and natural gas and import substitution due to the sharp devaluation of the ruble in 1998. As a result, the role of barter and payment arrears in the economy is substantially reduced if not eliminated altogether. After the 1998 fiscal crisis, the level of expenditures fell dramatically as a share of GDP, and the revenue share increased. The deficit figures from 2000 to 2005 show a rapid improvement in the general government balance, and the government achieved a surplus of 7.7 percent of GDP in 2005.

Table 4.3 Consolidated Nominal Tax Collections: 1992–2005, trillions of rubles

Year	Total collections	Enterprise profit tax (EPT)	Personal income tax (PIT)	Value added Tax (VAT)	Excise	Property	Natural resource taxes	Taxes on foreign operations
1992	4.8	1.6	0.4	2.0	0.2	NA	0.1	NA
1993	43.7	19.8	4.4	12.2	1.8	NA	1.2	NA
1994	146.1	48.8	17.5	37.3	7.4	4.9	3.1	10.5
1995	364.3	117.6	36.6	95.7	24.0	16.9	12.3	24.9
1996	473.0	96.7	56.6	143.9	53.4	36.9	21.2	22.8
1997	594.1	104.9	75.2	182.8	68.1	47.8	37.2	27.2
1998	564.6	99.3	71.5	170.3	72.2	47.7	22.7	34.4
1999	1,007.5	221.0	117.3	288.2	109.1	53.2	45.3	86.2
2000	1,707.6	398.8	174.8	457.3	166.4	64.8	77.6	229.2
2001	2,345.0	513.8	255.8	639.0	243.3	89.6	135.7	331.3
2002	3,136.8	463.3	358.1	752.7	264.1	120.5	330.8	323.4
2003	3,735.3	526.5	455.7	882.1	347.8	137.8	395.8	452.8
2004	4,942.1	867.6	574.5	1,069.7	246.9	146.8	581.0	859.7
2005	7,058.6	1,332.9	707.0	1,472.3	253.8	253.3	1,001.6	1,622.8

Source: Goskmostat (2005), Federal Treasury, Ministry of Finance (various years).

Table 4.4 Consolidated Real Tax Collections: 1992–2005 (adjusted with CPI to 2005 price level, trillions of rubles)

Year	Total collections	Enterprise profit tax (EPT)	Personal income tax (PIT)	Value added Tax (VAT)	Excise	Property	Natural resource taxes	Taxes on foreign operations
1992	2,547	840	231	1,071	113	NA	56	NA
1993	2,493	1,128	251	696	101	NA	66	NA
1994	2,603	870	312	665	132	87	54	187
1995	2,822	911	284	741	186	131	95	193
1996	3,008	615	360	915	340	235	135	145
1997	3,404	601	431	1,047	390	274	213	156
1998	1,754	309	222	529	224	148	71	107
1999	2,294	503	267	656	248	121	103	196
2000	3,234	755	331	866	315	123	147	434
2001	3,745	820	408	1,020	389	143	217	529
2002	4,352	643	497	1,044	366	167	459	449
2003	4,627	652	564	1,093	431	171	490	561
2004	5,481	962	637	1,186	274	163	644	953
2005	7,059	1,333	707	1,472	254	253	1,002	1,623

Source: Federal Treasury, Ministry of Finance (2005), Goskomstat (2005), IMF (2000, 2004, 2005) and World Bank (2006). The budget classification was changed in 1994, so that there are minor inconsistencies in the collections reported for certain categories. These have been adjusted and the adjusted figures are reported in this table. The nominal numbers are adjusted with consumer prices indexes as reported by Goskomstat.

Tax Reform in Russia

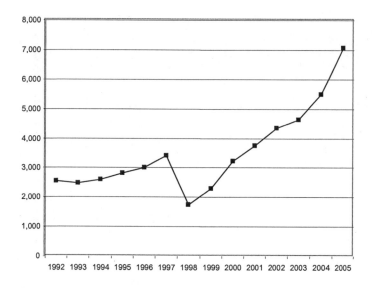

Figure 4.1   Real Tax Collections: Consolidated Budget

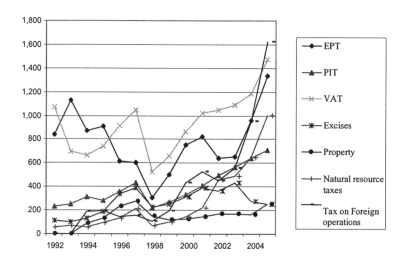

Figure 4.2   Real Tax Collection by Source, trillion rubles in 2005 prices

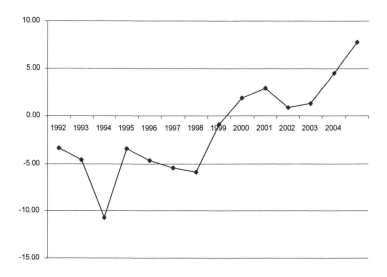

Figure 4.3   Government Balance as Percentage of GDP

The difficulty of raising adequate revenue in the 1990s was also attributable to deficiencies in the tax system. It was overly burdensome for many taxpayers, and the result was widespread resistance to paying tax. In the recent period, however, the federal government has simplified the tax system thus making it easier for taxpayers to comply with the system. Several steps in particular have been taken in this direction. Briefly, recent reforms include a flat rate personal income tax of 13 percent; liberalization of permissible business deductions for purposes of the enterprise profit tax; repeal of certain turnover taxes; and electronic filing of tax returns, to name just a few simplification measures. These reforms reflect genuine progress in creating a more buoyant, efficient and equitable tax system.

The extent to which the decline in the level of taxation after 1992 reflected the inability of the tax administration to enforce a modern tax system; the lack of political will to do so; and resistance to paying tax among the public is certainly a point of considerable controversy. In any event, it took more than half a decade for tax revenues to recover to their 1992 levels in real terms, despite considerable technical assistance for tax policy and administration from the International Monetary Fund, World Bank, United States Agency for International Development and other bilateral donors.

After the 1998 financial crisis, enterprise profit tax collections grew at about the same rate as value added tax revenues in 1999 and 2000, but then the growth in enterprise profit tax revenue slowed in 2001 and decreased in 2002. In 2004 and 2005, enterprise profit tax collections grew very fast, almost catching up with the level of value added tax collections. Excise taxes were the only revenue sources for which collections decreased in 2004 and 2005. The rebound after the 1998 financial crisis was primarily the result of high international oil prices and growth in domestic production due to import substitution resulting from the devaluation of the ruble. These issues are discussed in greater detail below.

Revenue Adequacy: International Comparisons

As previously discussed, simply comparing the aggregate level of taxation among countries is not an entirely satisfactory way to assess the performance of a country's tax system. Tax revenue as a percentage of GDP does not account for differences in demand for public expenditures among countries, nor does it account for differences in economic and demographic circumstances among the countries. The Russian Federation's problems with outstanding debt, barter, payment arrears and weak tax administration are additional issues that may explain, at least in part, the tax revenue trends described above.[4] Nevertheless, the overall level of taxation as a percentage of GDP has long served as a benchmark for cross-country comparisons of tax effort.

However, there are other, more sophisticated measures of tax effort, including regression and representative taxpayer approaches to measuring tax effort. Both of these measures control for some important underlying economic differences among countries and therefore provide a better gauge for cross country comparisons of tax effort.

We begin by estimating the ratio of taxes to GDP for a number of developing and transition countries, after controlling for prominent features of the economies that may influence a country's tax effort. Then, we compare estimated collections to actual collections. We employ a variety of econometric specifications to estimate tax effort. More specifically, we use the following three models:

Model 1: $T/Y = a + b(Yp) + c(Xm) + \varepsilon$;
Model 2: $T/Y = a + b(Min) + c(Ag) + \varepsilon$; and
Model 3: $T/Y = a + b(Yp) + c(Xm) + d(Ag) + \varepsilon$

where:

T/Y = tax collections relative to GDP;
Yp = per capita GDP;

Xm = ratio of the sum of exports plus imports to GDP;
Min = share of mineral and fuel exports in GDP; and
Ag = share of agriculture in GDP.[5]

The independent or right-hand-side variables control for important differences in the tax capacity of a country. The level of per capita GDP controls for the size of the tax base, particularly for income and consumption taxes which are the major sources of revenue in most tax systems. Therefore, the ability of a country to collect tax increases, all other things held constant, as per capita GDP increases. Mineral fuel exports as a share of GDP is a measure of a high value added and easy to tax commodity. The ability of a country to collect tax increases as this share increases, all other things held constant. Agriculture is considered to be a hard to tax sector because there are often large numbers of subsistence farmers that simply are not taxable for all practical purposes. Accordingly, the greater the share of agriculture in GDP, the more difficult it is to collect tax from a given amount of GDP.

The data used for this analysis come from the *Government Finance Statistics* (International Monetary Fund, 2006) and the *World Development Indicators* (World Bank, 2006). The models are estimated with panel data for the years 1992 through 1999, based on a sample of 90 countries in the case of model 1; 80 countries in the case of model 2; and 89 countries in the case of model 3.[6] In each case, the sample is drawn from developing and transition countries.

The predicted values from these regressions are used to rank each country in the sample. The results of the analysis are reported in Table 4.5a. According to this analysis, the Russian Federation ranks at least in the top 20 percent of the countries in the sample. This suggests that relative to many transition and developing countries, even after controlling for prominent features of the economy, the Russian Federation exercises a relative high level of tax effort. Table 4.5b provides the results of similar calculations for the time period after the tax reform (2001–04).

By accounting for the capacity of a country to collect each tax, the representative taxpayer approach is another way to measure tax effort. By applying the average international tax rate to estimates of the respective tax bases of particular countries, we can estimate the total level of tax revenues that would be collected if a country imposed the international average tax rate. Comparing this predicted value to actual collections gives us another measure of tax effort by major tax. Since it is not possible to evaluate the tax base for each country, it is customary to use proxies for a country's tax base by major tax.

To calculate the average international tax rate for each major tax, we estimate regressions for the personal income tax, enterprise profit tax, indirect taxes (including sales and value added taxes), import revenues and export revenues. The level of revenue is expressed as a function of variables measuring the tax base and other control variables. A variety of models are estimated, based on the availability of data from the World Bank and International Monetary Fund (Government Finance Statistics). Final model selection is based on data constraints and overall performance of the equations. The representative tax system approach is used for the following taxes:

Personal income tax revenues = $a + b(GDP) + c(GDPSQ) + \varepsilon$;
Corporate income tax revenues = $a + b(LNGDP) + \varepsilon$;
Total import revenues = $a + b(COMPIMP) + c(COMPISQ) + \varepsilon$;
Total export revenues = $a + b(LNCOMPEXP) + \varepsilon$; and
Indirect tax revenues = $a + b(LNGDP) + \varepsilon$,

where:

GDP = Gross domestic product;
GDPsq = GDP squared;
LNGDP = natural log of GDP;
COMPIMP = Value of commodity imports;
COMPISQ = COMPIMP squared; and
LNCOMPEXP = natural log of the value of commodity exports.[7]

Again we estimate these equations for a number of countries for the periods 1992–99 and 2002–04. Due to a number of missing values, the estimates are based on 61–85 countries for the period 1992–99 and 19–32 countries for the period 2002–04. We report all countries for which we have data, so comparisons of rankings between the tables should be evaluated with care. The results of this analysis are reported in Tables 4.6a and 4.6b and show that Russia's tax effort improved after the introduction of the tax code, especially in the cases of the corporate income tax, import and export tariffs.

Buoyancy and Elasticity of the Tax System

As pointed out above, tax revenues as a percentage of GDP were fluctuating until the sharp fall in 1998, and have been increasing since 1999. A critical issue in these revenue patterns is whether the changes are due to changes in tax structure and voluntary compliance, or the fact that the tax structure

Table 4.5a Index of Tax Effort (Average 1992-99)

	Model 1		Model 2			Model 3		
Rank	Country	Index	Country	Index	Rank	Country	Index	
1	Lithuania	2.833	Lithuania	2.493	1	Lithuania	2.811	
2	Belarus	1.868	Belarus	2.047	2	Burundi	1.963	
3	Gambia, The	1.807	Gambia, The	1.806	3	Gambia, The	1.819	
4	Pakistan	1.793	Lesotho	1.622	4	Belarus	1.759	
5	Grenada	1.741	Dominican Republic	1.609	5	Grenada	1.678	
6	Philippines	1.727	Grenada	1.603	6	Pakistan	1.636	
7	Kyrgyz Republic	1.692	Madagascar	1.589	7	Egypt, Arab Rep.	1.584	
8	Brazil	1.690	Burundi	1.544	8	Peru	1.563	
9	Dominican Republic	1.636	Sudan	1.435	9	Kyrgyz Republic	1.563	
10	Peru	1.612	Bulgaria	1.434	10	Brazil	1.506	
11	Syrian Arab Republic	1.545	Syrian Arab Republic	1.426	11	Lesotho	1.402	
12	Bulgaria	1.461	Philippines	1.420	12	Philippines	1.392	
13	Ukraine	1.396	Peru	1.415	13	Dominican Republic	1.391	
14	Sri Lanka	1.394	Ecuador	1.388	14	Thailand	1.387	
15	Russian Federation	1.367	Pakistan	1.374	15	Bulgaria	1.373	
16	St. Lucia	1.367	Russian Federation	1.371	16	Sudan	1.347	
17	Lesotho	1.316	Oman	1.363	17	Syrian Arab Republic	1.342	
18	St. Vincent and the Grenadines	1.268	Azerbaijan	1.343	18	Russian Federation	1.293	
19	Thailand	1.267	Jordan	1.338	19	Madagascar	1.285	
20	Ecuador	1.250	Lebanon	1.295	20	Jamaica	1.238	

Table 4.5a Index of Tax Effort (Average 1992-99) (continued)

	Model 1			Model 2			Model 3	
Rank	Country	Index	Rank	Country	Index	Rank	Country	Index
21	Sudan	1.231	21	Egypt, Arab Rep.	1.261	21	Sri Lanka	1.230
22	Slovak Republic	1.218	22	Senegal	1.242	22	St. Lucia	1.229
23	Lebanon	1.202	23	St. Lucia	1.202	23	Ecuador	1.216
24	Jamaica	1.164	24	Jamaica	1.170	24	Albania	1.187
25	Algeria	1.154	25	Slovak Republic	1.125	25	Ukraine	1.181
26	Burundi	1.116	26	Brazil	1.120	26	Lebanon	1.169
27	Azerbaijan	1.096	27	Sri Lanka	1.106	27	Argentina	1.167
28	Madagascar	1.073	28	Tajikistan	1.081	28	Jordan	1.159
29	Rwanda	1.068	29	El Salvador	1.077	29	Slovak Republic	1.116
30	Oman	1.051	30	Estonia	1.072	30	Oman	1.115
31	Croatia	1.047	31	Thailand	1.063	31	St. Vincent and the Grenadines	1.096
32	Tajikistan	1.031	32	Tunisia	1.042	32	Azerbaijan	1.077
33	Indonesia	1.014	33	St. Vincent and the Grenadines	1.038	33	Rwanda	1.044
34	Uruguay	1.010	34	Albania	1.021	34	Croatia	1.042
35	Cote d'Ivoire	1.008	35	Cote d'Ivoire	0.997	35	Algeria	1.036
36	Myanmar	0.998	36	Ukraine	0.990	36	Tajikistan	1.015
37	Argentina	0.986	37	Indonesia	0.952	37	Senegal	1.013
38	El Salvador	0.978	38	Mexico	0.952	38	Myanmar	1.003
39	Ghana	0.973	39	Ghana	0.946	39	Cote d'Ivoire	0.976

Table 4.5a Index of Tax Effort (Average 1992-99) (continued)

	Model 1			Model 2			Model 3	
Rank	Country	Index	Rank	Country	Index	Rank	Country	Index
40	Botswana	0.968	40	Myanmar	0.935	40	Romania	0.974
41	Chile	0.966	41	Algeria	0.921	41	Estonia	0.969
42	Senegal	0.950	42	Congo, Rep.	0.908	42	Indonesia	0.965
43	Paraguay	0.948	43	Belize	0.904	43	Fiji	0.957
44	Bolivia	0.947	44	Fiji	0.893	44	El Salvador	0.953
45	Estonia	0.945	45	Uruguay	0.887	45	Chile	0.953
46	Iran, Islamic Rep.	0.941	46	Kenya	0.838	46	Ghana	0.944
47	Nicaragua	0.938	47	Iran, Islamic Rep.	0.836	47	Seychelles	0.943
48	Turkey	0.925	48	Paraguay	0.826	48	Uruguay	0.921
49	Guatemala	0.922	49	Uganda	0.816	49	Georgia	0.919
50	Tunisia	0.919	50	Argentina	0.814	50	Tunisia	0.915
51	Georgia	0.913	51	Croatia	0.804	51	Swaziland	0.906
52	Swaziland	0.911	52	Guatemala	0.802	52	Belize	0.879
53	Albania	0.911	53	Chile	0.798	53	Turkey	0.859
54	Jordan	0.893	54	Maldives	0.790	54	Kenya	0.858
55	Kenya	0.891	55	India	0.778	55	Malawi	0.843
56	Malawi	0.872	56	Nepal	0.773	56	Paraguay	0.837
57	India	0.871	57	Costa Rica	0.763	57	Botswana	0.831
58	Belize	0.836	58	Seychelles	0.763	58	Bolivia	0.819
59	Nepal	0.815	59	Cameroon	0.762	59	Costa Rica	0.818
60	Solomon Islands	0.814	60	Swaziland	0.746	60	Guatemala	0.813

Table 4.5a   Index of Tax Effort (Average 1992-99) (continued)

	Model 1			Model 2			Model 3	
Rank	Country	Index	Rank	Country	Index	Rank	Country	Index
61	Egypt, Arab Rep.	0.806	61	Bolivia	0.721	61	Cameroon	0.803
62	Costa Rica	0.798	62	Trinidad and Tobago	0.711	62	Morocco	0.785
63	Morocco	0.767	63	Solomon Islands	0.704	63	Iran, Islamic Rep.	0.783
64	Maldives	0.761	64	Malawi	0.697	64	Nepal	0.771
65	Czech Republic	0.752	65	Malaysia	0.660	65	Nicaragua	0.770
66	Fiji	0.752	66	Morocco	0.653	66	Maldives	0.745
67	Seychelles	0.743	67	Czech Republic	0.643	67	India	0.739
68	Gabon	0.712	68	Nicaragua	0.617	68	Papua New Guinea	0.734
69	Trinidad and Tobago	0.700	69	Mongolia	0.597	69	Solomon Islands	0.722
70	Mexico	0.676	70	Gabon	0.580	70	Mexico	0.708
71	Papua New Guinea	0.674	71	Ethiopia	0.569	71	Trinidad and Tobago	0.702
72	Cameroon	0.666	72	Hungary	0.543	72	Czech Republic	0.682
73	Colombia	0.658	73	Panama	0.528	73	Gabon	0.663
74	Romania	0.614	74	Bhutan	0.515	74	Mongolia	0.651
75	Sierra Leone	0.609	75	Colombia	0.500	75	Ethiopia	0.617
76	Hungary	0.592	76	Kazakhstan	0.497	76	Sierra Leone	0.614
77	Malaysia	0.552	77	Guinea	0.438	77	Colombia	0.596
78	Kazakhstan	0.551	78	Poland	0.418	78	Kazakhstan	0.577
79	Ethiopia	0.544	79	Mauritius	0.406	79	Panama	0.554
80	Burkina Faso	0.539	80	China	0.393	80	Malaysia	0.552

Table 4.5a Index of Tax Effort (Average 1992-99) (continued)

	Model 1			Model 2			Model 3	
Rank	Country	Index	Rank	Country	Index	Rank	Country	Index
81	Panama	0.533				81	Poland	0.549
82	China	0.528				82	Hungary	0.547
83	Uganda	0.520				83	Burkina Faso	0.536
84	Latvia	0.511				84	Guinea	0.522
85	Guinea	0.507				85	Uganda	0.474
86	Mongolia	0.500				86	China	0.461
87	Congo, Rep.	0.462				87	Bhutan	0.433
88	Poland	0.449				88	Congo, Rep.	0.399
89	Bhutan	0.347				89	Mauritius	0.311
90	Mauritius	0.272						

Source: Calculated using data from *World Development Indicators*, World Bank (2006) and *Government Finance Statistics*, IMF (2006)

Table 4.5b Index of Tax Effort (Average 2002-04)

	Model 1			Model 2			Model 3	
Rank	Country	Index	Rank	Country	Index	Rank	Country	Index
1	Lesotho	1.780	1	Belarus	1.653	1	Lesotho	1.725
2	Belarus	1.616	2	Seychelles	1.407	2	Belarus	1.537
3	South Africa	1.539	3	Croatia	1.349	3	South Africa	1.466
4	Russian Federation	1.406	4	Mongolia	1.345	4	Croatia	1.320
5	Croatia	1.309	5	St. Vincent and the Grenadines	1.264	5	Russian Federation	1.318
6	St. Vincent and the Grenadines	1.270	6	South Africa	1.223	6	St. Vincent and the Grenadines	1.241
7	Seychelles	1.156	7	Hungary	1.196	7	Seychelles	1.151
8	Mongolia	1.146	8	Vietnam	1.188	8	Argentina	1.147
9	Hungary	1.132	9	Moldova	1.172	9	Mongolia	1.130
10	Bolivia	1.129	10	Bulgaria	1.114	10	Bolivia	1.117
11	Kazakhstan	1.119	11	Russian Federation	1.069	11	Hungary	1.107
12	Bulgaria	1.104	12	Albania	1.012	12	India	1.102
13	Vietnam	1.066	13	Ukraine	1.009	13	Albania	1.102
14	Poland	1.059	14	Argentina	0.998	14	Vietnam	1.074
15	Ukraine	1.053	15	Kazakhstan	0.958	15	Bulgaria	1.067
16	India	1.042	16	Lithuania	0.942	16	Kazakhstan	1.056
17	Argentina	1.039	17	Poland	0.934	17	Poland	1.037
18	Moldova	1.014	18	Malaysia	0.928	18	Moldova	1.016

Table 4.5b Index of Tax Effort (Average 2002-04) (continued)

	Model 1			Model 2			Model 3	
Rank	Country	Index	Rank	Country	Index	Rank	Country	Index
19	Albania	1.006	19	Bolivia	0.912	19	Ukraine	1.004
20	Romania	0.987	20	Romania	0.887	20	Romania	0.974
21	Lithuania	0.943	21	Latvia	0.880	21	Lithuania	0.925
22	Latvia	0.928	22	Slovak Republic	0.845	22	Chile	0.907
23	Chile	0.907	23	India	0.836	23	Latvia	0.899
24	Peru	0.854	24	Mauritius	0.824	24	Peru	0.838
25	Georgia	0.814	25	Thailand	0.820	25	Georgia	0.825
26	Mauritius	0.804	26	Chile	0.818	26	Mauritius	0.789
27	Thailand	0.798	27	Georgia	0.762	27	Thailand	0.767
28	Slovak Republic	0.770	28	Costa Rica	0.672	28	Slovak Republic	0.739
29	Malaysia	0.711	29	Peru	0.648	29	Tajikistan	0.707
30	Tajikistan	0.686	30	Iran, Islamic Rep.	0.347	30	Malaysia	0.694
31	Costa Rica	0.679				31	Costa Rica	0.679
32	Maldives	0.650				32	Bhutan	0.636
33	Bhutan	0.549				33	Iran, Islamic Rep.	0.434
34	Iran, Islamic Rep.	0.445				34	Congo, Rep.	0.403
35	Congo, Rep.	0.443						

Source: Calculated using data from *World Development Indicators*, World Bank (2006) and *Government Finance Statistics*, IMF (2006)

Table 4.6a Tax Effort Ranking by Country: Highest to Lowest (Average 1992–99)

	Personal Income Tax		Corporate Income Tax		Indirect Tax		Import		Export
1	China	1	Indonesia	1	Madagascar	1	Russian Federation	1	Brazil
2	Estonia	2	Russian Federation	2	India	2	Guinea	2	Georgia
3	Zambia	3	Malaysia	3	Pakistan	3	Madagascar	3	China
4	Papua New Guinea	4	Venezuela, RB	4	Cote d'Ivoire	4	Cote d'Ivoire	4	Russian Federation
5	South Africa	5	Brazil	5	Botswana	5	Malaysia	5	Mexico
6	Zimbabwe	6	South Africa	6	Morocco	6	Ethiopia	6	India
7	Trinidad and Tobago	7	Thailand	7	Lesotho	7	Belarus	7	Poland
8	Lithuania	8	Colombia	8	Tunisia	8	Ghana	8	Madagascar
9	Madagascar	9	India	9	Egypt, Arab Rep.	9	Azerbaijan	9	Zambia
10	Poland	10	Poland	10	Dominican Republic	10	Papua New Guinea	10	Turkey
11	Latvia	11	Egypt, Arab Rep.	11	Lebanon	11	Sudan	11	Argentina
12	Jamaica	12	China	12	Seychelles	12	Cameroon	12	South Africa
13	Georgia	13	Albania	13	Cameroon	13	Syrian Arab Republic	13	Thailand
14	Hungary	14	Argentina	14	Swaziland	14	Indonesia	14	Chile
15	Turkey	15	Botswana	15	Ethiopia	15	Mauritius	15	Hungary
16	Croatia	16	Turkey	16	Uganda	16	Argentina	16	Indonesia
17	Azerbaijan	17	Iran, Islamic Rep.	17	Philippines	17	Costa Rica	17	Croatia

Table 4.6a Tax Effort Ranking by Country: Highest to Lowest (Average 1992–99) (continued)

	Personal Income Tax		Corporate Income Tax		Indirect Tax		Import		Export
18	Bulgaria	18	Philippines	18	Zimbabwe	18	Fiji	18	Ukraine
19	Romania	19	Pakistan	19	China	19	India	19	Belarus
20	Slovak Republic	20	Papua New Guinea	20	Vietnam	20	Thailand	20	Azerbaijan
21	Senegal	21	Romania	21	Mauritius	21	Nepal	21	Malaysia
22	Indonesia	22	Madagascar	22	Peru	22	Iran, Islamic Rep.	22	Morocco
23	Mauritius	23	Trinidad and Tobago	23	Sudan	23	Panama	23	Peru
24	Argentina	24	Oman	24	Papua New Guinea	24	Tunisia	24	Estonia
25	Botswana	25	Vietnam	25	Jordan	25	Peru	25	Colombia
26	Ukraine	26	Slovak Republic	26	Guinea	26	Sri Lanka	26	Venezuela, RB
27	Belarus	27	Peru	27	Kenya	27	Lithuania	27	Slovak Republic
28	Morocco	28	Belarus	28	Brazil	28	Uruguay	28	Mauritius
29	Tunisia	29	Hungary	29	Thailand	29	Mexico	29	Philippines
30	Russian Federation	30	Morocco	30	Poland	30	Zambia	30	Romania
31	Guinea	31	Zimbabwe	31	Venezuela, RB	31	Bulgaria	31	Latvia
32	Malaysia	32	Bulgaria	32	Ghana	32	Nicaragua	32	Uruguay
33	Philippines	33	Azerbaijan	33	Zambia	33	Uganda	33	Lithuania
34	Thailand	34	Algeria	34	Argentina	34	Brazil	34	Pakistan
35	Yemen, Rep.	35	Yemen, Rep.	35	Sri Lanka	35	Morocco	35	Sri Lanka
36	Kazakhstan	36	Zambia	36	Croatia			36	Egypt, Arab Rep.

Table 4.6a Tax Effort Ranking by Country: Highest to Lowest (Average 1992–99) (continued)

	Personal Income Tax		Corporate Income Tax		Indirect Tax	Import		Export
37	India	37	Estonia	37	Iran, Islamic Rep.		37	Jamaica
38	Cote d'Ivoire	38	Ukraine	38	Belize		38	Bulgaria
39	Cameroon	39	Jamaica	39	Hungary		39	Trinidad and Tobago
40	Ethiopia	40	Uruguay	40	Mexico		40	Tunisia
41	Dominican Republic	41	Tunisia	41	Fiji		41	Bolivia
42	Ghana	42	Ethiopia	42	Nepal		42	Vietnam
43	Algeria	43	Latvia	43	Rwanda		43	Kenya
44	Jordan	44	Cote d'Ivoire	44	Guatemala		44	Guinea
45	Uruguay	45	Paraguay	45	Colombia		45	Kazakhstan
46	Iran, Islamic Rep.	46	Jordan	46	Syrian Arab Republic		46	Costa Rica
47	Uganda	47	Mauritius	47	Yemen, Rep.		47	Jordan
48	Sri Lanka	48	Costa Rica	48	Albania		48	Senegal
49	Brazil	49	Sri Lanka	49	Russian Federation		49	Algeria
50	Peru	50	Kazakhstan	50	Romania		50	Syrian Arab Republic
51	Nepal	51	Lithuania	51	Malaysia		51	Zimbabwe
52	Pakistan	52	Croatia	52	Sierra Leone		52	Iran, Islamic Rep.
53	Egypt, Arab Rep.	53	Panama	53	Uruguay		53	Uganda

Table 4.6a   Tax Effort Ranking by Country: Highest to Lowest (Average 1992–99) (continued)

	Personal Income Tax		Corporate Income Tax		Import		Indirect Tax		Export
54	Sudan	54	Cameroon			54	St. Vincent and the Grenadines	54	Nepal
55	Costa Rica	55	Guatemala			55	Congo, Rep.	55	Dominican Republic
56	Vietnam	56	Senegal			56	Gambia, The	56	Guatemala
57	Bolivia	57	Ghana			57	Jamaica	57	Ghana
58	Panama	58	Dominican Republic			58	Maldives	58	Paraguay
59	Colombia	59	Guinea			59	Paraguay	59	Panama
60	Guatemala	60	Bolivia			60	South Africa	60	Cote d'Ivoire
61	Venezuela, RB	61	Sudan			61	Costa Rica	61	Cameroon
		62	Nepal			62	Bulgaria	62	Papua New Guinea
		63	Georgia			63	Nicaragua	63	Ethiopia
		64	Uganda			64	Vanuatu	64	Sudan
						65	Trinidad and Tobago	65	Botswana
						66	Burundi	66	Yemen, Rep.
						67	Indonesia	67	Lebanon
						68	Bolivia	68	Oman
						69	Turkey		
						70	Slovak Republic		
						71	Oman		
						72	Azerbaijan		

Table 4.6a Tax Effort Ranking by Country: Highest to Lowest (Average 1992–99) (continued)

Personal Income Tax	Corporate Income Tax	Indirect Tax		Import	Export
		73	Panama		
		74	Ukraine		
		75	Georgia		
		76	Grenada		
		77	Belarus		
		78	Mongolia		
		79	Tajikistan		
		80	Lithuania		
		81	Latvia		
		82	Kazakhstan		
		83	Moldova		
		84	Estonia		
		85	Bhutan		

Source: Calculated using data from *World Development Indicators*, World Bank (2006) and *Government Finance Statistics*, IMF (2006)

Table 4.6b Tax Effort Ranking by Country: Highest to Lowest (Average 2002 – 04)

	Personal Income Tax		Corporate Income Tax		Indirect Tax		Import		Export
1	Latvia	1	Russian Federation	1	Iran, Islamic Rep.	1	Russian Federation	1	Russian Federation
2	Lithuania	2	South Africa	2	Peru	2	Argentina	2	India
3	South Africa	3	India	3	Argentina	3	Romania	3	Poland
4	Hungary	4	Thailand	4	Lesotho	4	Belarus	4	South Africa
5	Russian Federation	5	Vietnam	5	Mauritius	5	Ukraine	5	Hungary
6	Poland	6	Argentina	6	Jamaica	6	Thailand	6	Argentina
7	Ukraine	7	Poland	7	Belarus	7	Kazakhstan	7	Thailand
8	Croatia	8	Ukraine	8	Russia Federation	8	Costa Rica	8	Chile
9	Bulgaria	9	Kazakhstan	9	Chile	9	South Africa	9	Croatia
10	Belarus	10	Iran, Islamic Rep.	10	Ukraine			10	Belarus
11	Slovak Republic	11	Hungary	11	South Africa			11	Romania
12	Romania	12	Peru	12	Croatia			12	Slovak Republic
13	India	13	Romania	13	Thailand			13	Peru
14	Kazakhstan	14	Belarus	14	Kazakhstan			14	Bulgaria
15	Thailand	15	Slovak Republic	15	Costa Rica			15	Ukraine
16	Peru	16	Croatia	16	Albania			16	Vietnam
17	Argentina	17	Bulgaria	17	Bulgaria			17	Lithuania
18	Iran, Islamic Rep.	18	Albania	18	Bolivia			18	Albania
19	Vietnam	19	Georgia	19	Congo, Rep.			19	Kazakhstan
		20	Jamaica	20	Hungary			20	Georgia
		21	Bolivia	21	Seychelles			21	Congo, Rep.
		22	Latvia	22	Maldives			22	Costa Rica
		23	Lithuania	23	Georgia			23	Latvia
		24	Mauritius	24	St. Vincent and the Grenadines			24	Bolivia

Table 4.6b   Tax Effort Ranking by Country: Highest to Lowest (Average 2002 – 04) (continued)

Personal Income Tax	Corporate Income Tax	Indirect Tax		Import	Export	
		25	Poland		25	Mauritius
		26	Tajikistan		26	Iran, Islamic Rep.
		27	Moldova			
		28	Slovak Republic			
		29	Lithuania			
		30	Latvia			
		31	Mongolia			
		32	Romania			

Source: Calculated using data from *World Development Indicators*, World Bank (2006) and *Government Finance Statistics*, IMF (2006)

does not capture natural growth (decline) in the economy. It is important to understand the dynamic relationship between the tax system and GDP over time. A benchmark for a tax system's dynamic performance is whether the growth in revenue yield is keeping pace with the growth in GDP.

The buoyancy of a tax system is a straightforward measure of the relationship between revenue yield and GDP growth. This measure tells us whether tax receipts are keeping up with growth in the economy, as measured by the growth in observed GDP. A buoyancy (elasticity) estimate of 1.0 or greater means that tax receipts are growing at least as fast as GDP; an estimate of less than 1.0 means that receipts are not growing as fast as GDP.

Buoyancy estimates can be misleading because they do not account for legislative changes in tax rates and tax bases. For example, tax receipts may be increasing (decreasing) due to economic growth (contraction), or they may be growing (declining) due to increases (decreases) in tax rates. In contrast, elasticity estimates describe the effect of economic growth on the level of revenue, after controlling for any changes in tax rates, tax bases and tax administration.

If expanding sectors of the economy are in the tax net, then government revenues will tend to grow as the economy grows, without policy interventions to increase tax rates or resort to deficit financing. Since people tend to demand more government services as their incomes increase, a growing economy implies that there may be popular pressure to increase government expenditures. Unless the tax elasticity is greater than 1.0, the government will face difficult policy choices to either increase tax revenue through legislative changes in tax rates or tax bases, allow popular demand for growth in public expenditures to go unsatisfied, or allow budget deficits to grow.

This is precisely the dilemma facing many developed countries. In the United States, for example, services are the fastest growing sector of the economy. However, the tax system of the United States, which relies heavily on sales taxes as a source of revenue at the subnational level, does a poor job of bringing services into the tax net. As a result, the growth of state tax revenues is not keeping pace with growing demands for state expenditures. Since the US states must balance their operating budgets, the result is growing pressure on state budgets and increasing pressure by the states for larger transfers from the federal government. Another important example of a potentially shrinking tax base is due to globalization and the high mobility of capital across national borders in the form of foreign portfolio and direct investment.

Buoyancy estimates are reported in Table 4.7 and are based on monthly tax collections and GDP figures for three time periods: 1994–98, which is the period before the biggest tax reform changes; 1999–2001, which is the period immediately following the adoption of Part I of the Tax Code; and 2002–05, which is the period after tax reform was introduced. The estimates are based on ordinary least squares (OLS) estimation of a double-log functional form.

The estimates in Table 4.7 show that total real collections grew faster than GDP for all time periods. More specifically, the buoyancy estimates for total tax receipts is 1.26 in 1994–98; 1.94 in 1999–2001; and 1.32 in 2002–05. In other words, for the period 1994–98, tax receipts increased by 1.26 percent for every 1 percent increase GDP; 1.94 percent for each 1 percent increase in GDP between 1999 and 2001; and 1.32 percent for 2002–05. The increase in the buoyancy of the tax system between 1999 through 2001 was followed by a decline in buoyancy between 2002 through 2005. This pattern could be due to a variety of factors:

- The tax base is defined in such a way that expanding sectors of the economy are fully taxed so that as these sectors grow (decline), the tax revenue grows (declines) as well.
- The compliance rate is evolving at a slower rate than changes in GDP.
- Tax rates may be increasing over time.
- Tax exemptions and deductions may be decreasing over time.
- There are outliers in the collections data that are influencing the regression estimates.[8]

It is interesting to note that for most of the specific taxes, the buoyancy estimates are approximately equal to or greater than 1.0 for all three time periods. The buoyancy of the enterprise profit tax sticks out in this analysis, with an estimate of 2.62 for the 1994–98 period. As discussed in greater detail below, this is due to the large number of outliers in this series, which are associated with payments by some of the largest firms to settle tax arrears. The buoyancy of the personal income tax is close to 1.0 for the two periods 1994–98 and 2002–05, and it increases to 1.68 in 1999–2001. The buoyancy of excise taxes is surprisingly close to –1.0 for the time periods before and after the reform, but have large positive values in 1999–2001. Nominal buoyancy estimates seem to be more robust: they have smaller absolute values and are always greater than zero. The small coefficient for nominal excise tax revenues may be a function of the unindexed specific rates applied to many excisable goods.

A more detailed analysis of the relationship between revenue and GDP can be conducted by controlling for major changes in tax policy and obvious collection patterns that are influenced by the realities of

Table 4.7   Buoyancy 1994–2005

Revenue Source	Real			Nominal		
	1994– 1998	1999– 2001	2002– 2005	1994– 1998	1999– 2001	2002– 2005
Value added tax	0.86	1.75	0.94	1.03	1.26	0.90
Excises	−1.02	1.77	−1.05	1.31	1.27	0.05
Enterprise profit tax	2.62	1.94	1.96	0.55	1.33	1.10
Personal income tax	1.13	1.68	0.97	0.97	1.24	1.02
Total collections	1.26	1.94	1.32	0.95	1.33	1.12

Source: Calculated using tax revenue from Table 4.2 and GDP data from *World Development Indicators*, World Bank (2006). Calculation for real terms uses CPI (CPI 2000=100) as a deflator for tax revenues and GDP.

tax payments in Russia. In the Russian Federation, as in many countries, the tax structure has undergone significant change from year to year, including tax rates and bases. The history of these changes and the current structure of the main taxes are described in detail in subsequent chapters. Suffice it to say, for the moment, that in each year, every major tax underwent a structural change, but some of these changes were more significant than others.

To provide a more useful estimate of the relationship between revenue yield and GDP growth, we estimate tax elasticities for each of the four major taxes by controlling for significant rate and/or base changes and for obvious payment behavior not associated with changes in the economy. In this manner, we can isolate the effect of changes in GDP on tax receipts from legislative and administrative changes. We refer to these estimates as arc elasticity estimates to distinguish them from the buoyancy estimates, described above.

The elasticity estimates are reported in Table 4.8 and are even larger in absolute value for several taxes than the corresponding buoyancy estimates.[9] Even after controlling for the influence of structural changes in tax policy and the presence of very large tax payments associated with large enterprises settling tax arrears, the elasticity of real enterprise profit tax stands out with really high estimates; suggesting that enterprise profit tax revenues have been growing at least twice as fast as GDP. These estimates are even larger that the buoyancy estimates for two out of three time periods.

Table 4.8   Arc Elasticity, 1994–2005

Revenue Source	Real			Nominal		
	1994–1998	1999–2001	2002–2005	1994–1998	1999–2001	2002–2005
Value added tax	0.88	1.94	0.93	1.08	1.42	0.96
Excises	−1.54	1.97	−0.73	2.64	1.44	−0.04
Enterprise profit tax	2.06	2.21	2.47	0.31	1.55	1.88
Personal income tax	1.10	1.84	0.96	0.93	1.38	0.98

Source: Calculated using tax revenue from Table 4.2 and GDP data from *World Development Indicators*, World Bank (2006). Calculation for real terms uses CPI (CPI 2000=100) as a deflator for tax revenues and GDP.

Further analysis suggests that this is due, in part, to the changing number of profitable firms. In the early years of the transition, the number of firms with losses grew more quickly than those that were profitable. GDP estimates account for negative value added (losses), while enterprise profit tax receipts do not because enterprises are not able to claim a refund for advanced tax payments made in a loss-making year, and the tax code does not provide for loss carry backs, only loss carry forwards. As GDP declined from 1992 through 1998, the number of loss-making enterprises increased and the number of profitable and therefore taxpaying enterprises decreased. This dynamic induces a strong positive correlation between GDP and enterprise profit tax receipts and thus the large elasticities observed in Table 4.8.

Goskomstat figures provide some support for this hypothesis. In 1994, loss-making firms accounted for 32.5 percent of all firms. In 1998 the proportion was 48.3 percent of the total. Most likely a similar story occurred when the economy began to recover after the 1998 financial crisis. More specifically, the number of profitable and therefore taxpaying enterprises increased, inducing a correlation between GDP and enterprise profit tax receipts and boosting its elasticity. Unfortunately, information is not available that would allow us to control for the growth in loss-making firms.

These results suggest that legislative changes in tax policy can be used to help stabilize revenue. If compliance rates remain approximately equal over this time period, their influence could not account for changing elasticity estimates among the time periods analyzed. In contrast, if compliance rates are correlated with GDP, changing compliance rates would be reflected in the elasticity estimates. Changes in compliance rates due to other factors, such as low taxpayer morale and the like, are likely to be reflected in the error term of the regressions.[10]

This analysis shows that structural changes in the major taxes are significant factors in the observed real revenue growth (decline) with respect to GDP. While this is not surprising, it is often overlooked. The information we have presented thus far should dispel some of the misconceptions about the Russian tax system. In particular, tax effort in the Russian Federation is in line with that of many countries, and the elasticity of the major taxes is reasonable, even after accounting for tax policy changes and anomalous tax payments. In order to address the remaining criticisms of taxation in the Russian Federation, it is important to examine the specific structure of the tax system.

Tax Structure Composition

Since 1992, the tax system of the Russia Federation has depended heavily on four basic taxes: the value added tax, enterprise profit tax, personal income tax, and excise taxes. In addition, there are many other federal and regional taxes, but these four taxes contribute most of the revenue to the government.[11] Tables 4.9 and 4.10 report the shares of these taxes in total tax collections and as a percentage of GDP for the period 1992–2005. As these tables show, at the beginning of the transition, the value added tax and enterprise profit tax comprise 75 percent of total tax collections. As the value added tax and enterprise profit tax rates are lowered and enterprise profit tax exemptions grow over time, these tax sources, while remaining the most important sources of government revenue, become smaller percentages of total revenue. By 1998, they comprise only 47 percent of total tax revenues.

The personal income tax and excise taxes have slowly grown in importance as sources of consolidated revenues. From 1998 to 1999, excise tax rates have fallen way behind price increases, but attempts to index most excise tax rates have failed. Property and natural resource taxes thus far account for only a relatively small share of total revenues.

As discussed in a greater detail in a subsequent chapter, the Russian Federation's tax system is quite unique in that regional governments receive upwards of 50 percent of consolidated revenues, mostly through a revenue-sharing arrangement. This means that federal tax policy has a substantial influence on subnational tax policy as well.

Table 4.11 provides the actual revenue split for total tax collections between the federal and subnational budgets for the period from 1992 to 2005. Beginning in 1992–97 subnational governments received a slightly growing share of total tax collections. This trend stopped in 1998 and was

Table 4.9 Nominal Tax Collections as a Percentage of Total Consolidated Collections

Year	Total collections	Enterprise profit tax (EPT)	Personal income tax (PIT)	Value added tax (VAT)	Excise taxes	Property taxes	Natural resource taxes	Taxes on foreign operations
1992	100	32.97	9.08	42.06	4.45	NA	2.20	NA
1993	100	38.39	10.05	27.93	4.07	NA	2.65	NA
1994	100	33.42	11.99	25.56	5.08	3.33	2.09	6.21
1995	100	32.50	10.13	26.50	6.74	4.68	3.42	6.73
1996	100	20.44	11.96	30.41	11.29	7.81	4.48	4.83
1997	100	17.85	13.12	29.85	10.97	8.30	6.22	4.86
1998	100	17.71	13.09	28.77	12.46	8.62	4.09	6.72
1999	100	21.94	11.64	28.60	10.82	5.29	4.49	8.56
2000	100	23.38	10.23	26.76	9.58	3.79	4.55	13.42
2001	100	21.93	10.90	27.34	10.37	3.82	5.51	14.14
2002	100	16.55	12.77	26.92	9.28	4.30	11.95	11.56
2003	100	14.10	12.20	23.61	9.19	3.69	10.60	12.12
2004	100	19.32	12.79	23.82	5.44	3.27	12.90	19.14
2005	100	18.88	10.02	20.86	3.60	3.59	14.19	22.99

Source: Federal Treasury, Ministry of Finance (2005), authors' calculations, IMF (2000, 2004, 2005) and World Bank (2006). The budget classification was changed in 1994, so that there are minor inconsistencies in the collections reported for certain categories as noted in Table 2.2. These have been adjusted and the adjusted figures are reported in this table.

Table 4.10 Consolidated Tax Collections as a Percentage of GDP

Year	Total collections	Enterprise profit tax (EPT)	Personal income tax (PIT)	Value added tax (VAT)	Excise taxes	Property taxes	Natural resource taxes	Taxes on foreign operations
1992	26.40	8.70	2.40	11.11	1.18	NA	0.58	NA
1993	23.68	11.50	2.55	7.10	1.03	NA	0.67	NA
1994	23.90	7.99	2.87	6.11	1.22	0.80	0.50	1.57
1995	22.68	7.37	2.30	6.01	1.53	1.06	0.78	1.53
1996	22.04	4.50	2.64	6.70	2.49	1.72	0.99	1.06
1997	23.10	4.12	3.03	6.90	2.53	1.92	1.44	1.12
1998	19.85	3.52	2.60	5.71	2.47	1.71	0.81	1.33
1999	21.18	4.65	2.46	6.06	2.29	1.12	0.95	1.81
2000	23.39	5.47	2.39	6.26	2.24	0.89	1.06	3.14
2001	25.94	5.69	2.83	7.09	2.69	0.99	1.43	3.67
2002	25.74	4.26	3.29	4.17	2.39	1.11	3.08	2.98
2003	34.94	4.93	4.26	8.25	3.21	1.29	3.70	4.24
2004	29.74	5.74	3.80	7.08	1.62	0.97	3.84	5.69
2005	32.68	6.17	3.27	6.82	1.17	1.17	4.64	7.51

Source: Federal Treasury, Ministry of Finance (2005), authors' calculations, IMF (2000, 2004, 2005) and World Bank (2006). The budget classification was changed in 1994, so that there are minor inconsistencies in the collections reported for certain categories as noted in Table 2.2. These have been adjusted and the adjusted figures are reported in this table.

Table 4.11   Distribution of Total Tax Collections (percentage of Consolidated Budget Tax Revenues)

Year	Federal	Regional
1992	58.45	41.55
1993	49.28	50.72
1994	45.91	54.09
1995	47.42	52.58
1996	46.24	53.76
1997	42.54	57.46
1998	43.37	56.63
1999	50.59	49.41
2000	56.54	43.46
2001	62.64	37.36
2002	49.35	50.65
2003	64.10	35.90
2004	60.38	39.62
2005	68.16	31.84

Source: Federal Treasury, Ministry of Finance (2005), authors' calculations, and IMF (2000, 2004, 2005) estimates. For 1992–94, the distribution is based on IMF estimates of the division between federal and regional (including local) tax revenues. For the period 1995–98, the sharing rates are based on the actual distribution of collections based on data from the Ministry of Finance.

reversed through 2005, with the exception of 2002. The reversal in this trend may reflect the consolidation of power in the center by Putin's administration. These figures demonstrate the importance of subnational governments in the Russia Federation.[12]

By law, the value added tax, enterprise profit tax, personal income tax and excise taxes are federal taxes, but the revenues from these so-called regulating taxes have been shared with regional governments. Early on these regulating taxes were meant to address horizontal imbalances among the regions and later, after the introduction of an explicit equalization grant system, to address vertical imbalances between the federal government and the regions. Although there have been some important changes in the sharing schemes for the major taxes over the years, the data on actual shares by type of tax are relatively stable. More specifically, the value added tax share to the subnational governments increased somewhat between 1995 and 1998, but it was reduced in 1999. The personal income tax share was also reduced in 1999 as the federal government established a piggyback system whereby the first 3 percent of the tax is a federal revenue source.

These taxes are shared on a derivation basis that is based on where the tax is collected. This has led to some difficulties, particularly in the scheme of value added tax crediting. In 2000, domestic value added tax was shared 85-15 percent between the federal and regional government, respectively. In contrast, 100 percent of the revenue from value added tax on imports went to the federal government. Since 2001, 100 percent of the value added tax, irrespective of source, goes to the federal government.

In 2000, the enterprise profit tax was shared through a piggyback scheme whereby the federal government taxes profits at 11 percent and regional governments are permitted to levy a tax on profits of normal business at a rate up to 19 percent, for a total levy of 30 percent. In 2001, the regional share of enterprise profit tax grew from 19 to 24 percent as a result of the introduction of a 5 percent local option piggyback tax. Since 2002, the federal enterprise profit tax rate was 7.5 percent; the regional rate was 14.5 percent; and a local rate was 2 percent. In 2003, the enterprise profit tax was shared. The federal rate was 6 percent; the regional rate was 16 percent; and a local rate was 2 percent. In 2004, the enterprise profit tax was shared, with a federal rate of 5 percent; a regional rate of 17 percent; and a local rate of 2 percent. Finally, in 2005, the federal enterprise profit tax rate was 6.5 percent; the regional rate was 17.5 percent; and the local rate was abolished.

In 1999, the personal income tax sharing scheme was changed to a piggyback tax. The federal government levied a rate of 3 percent on all income, and the regions levied an additional rate up to a total levy of 35 percent. Prior to this change, the tax was shared 100 percent with the regional governments. Since 2000, the personal income tax sharing scheme was changed to 16 percent federal and 84 percent regional. The regional personal income tax rates are set by the federal law whereas the regional governments have discretion over the maximum rates for the enterprise profit tax. In 2001, the new personal income tax legislation established a 13 percent flat rate on all income, except for those of non-residents, bank interest and dividends. The revenues were shared 1 percent to the federal government and 99 percent to regional governments. From 2002 to 2004, 100 percent of the personal income tax was shared with regional governments.

The Distribution of Tax Burdens

Many tax policy experts as well as politicians believe that fairness is an important attribute of a tax system. In particular, there is the notion of horizontal equity which is the belief that a tax system should impose similar tax burdens on similarly situated people. A perhaps more familiar concept of fairness is the ability to pay concept, or vertical equity, which is the belief that tax burdens should increase as the ability to pay tax increases. Typically, ability to pay tax is believed to be positively correlated with income. Thus, the ability to pay principle is an often used justification for a progressive income tax. Currently, little is known about the actual distribution of tax burdens in the Russia Federation before or after the tax reforms of the 1990s and 2000s. There are good reasons to believe that problems with horizontal equity arise because of wide differences in the ability to evade taxes by source of income and the preferential treatment of capital income. Furthermore, the personal income tax is largely paid by withholding at source, so that it falls more heavily on wage earners in the formal economy.

We provide a detailed analysis of the distribution of the Russian tax system under the 1996 tax code, using data from the Russian Longitudinal Monitoring Survey (RLMS-VII). Analyzing this distribution is helpful to understanding the underlying tax burden conditions that may have been a force for reform. The RLMS data contain the responses to detailed questionnaires obtained from face-to-face interviews of every adult household member in the sample and includes extensive information on the income and expenditure characteristics of the household members. The analysis is based on the RLMS comprehensive measure of total household income, specifically the sum of after-tax wages and salary, pension income, capital investment income, rental income, income from home production, insurance payouts, property sales, alimony, help from family and friends, government transfers, help from organizations and other income. For purposes of this analysis, we assume that households ultimately pay all taxes. The incidence of taxes is based on simple rules of thumb for each major tax.

The results are in Table 4.12. The distribution of tax burdens is arranged by deciles, with the same number of households in each of the ten income strata. Note that household income ranges are reported in terms of monthly total income, but the allocation of taxes and the percentage of taxes paid are distributed on the basis of annualized household incomes. With the exception of the bottom two deciles, the overall distribution of tax burdens was progressive in 1997. This general result is due to the combination of progressive distribution of tax burdens for direct taxes and a mildly regressive distribution of indirect taxes. These results suggest that the tax burden on low income groups may be high due to the share of indirect taxes in Russia's tax system in 1997, and remains true today

If these estimates are to be believed, then Russia's pre-reform tax system had a U-shaped vertical distribution of tax burdens: highly regressive at the bottom and quite progressive at the top of the income distribution. While this analysis is interesting, these results should be viewed as illustrative of tax burden analysis. The computed tax burdens on the first two deciles at the bottom of the income distribution are quite high and thus somewhat dubious. There are reasons to question the validity of the RLMS data. For example, there are large disparities between reported income and reported consumption in the data. At the very least, this preliminary effort at measuring the distribution of tax burdens in Russia provides some interesting evidence of the impact that the tax system may have on the behavior of individuals. The overall burden on individuals may be a force driving tax reform as individuals seek to adjust their behavior to minimize the tax burden. That is the issue to which we turn next.

Economic Efficiency of the Tax System

Taxes divert resources from private to public uses. As such, taxes influence the resources available to households for consumption and saving. Consequently, taxes may influence the distribution of income. In addition to such distributional effects, taxes also may induce behavioral responses by taxpayers. It would be impossible to report all of the myriad distortions induced by the tax system; therefore, we concentrate here on two prominent features of the tax code that are likely to impose the greatest costs on the economy: the high marginal tax rates on labor income and the differential tax treatment of capital income. We begin, however, by briefly explaining how taxes influence economic efficiency.

Taxes on labor income influence labor supply decisions: how many hours a person works per year; how many years a person works before retirement; how hard they work and so on. In addition, taxes may affect the productivity of labor. When the rewards for one's efforts are reduced by a tax on labor income, people may devote less time to activities, such as education and training, which may influence the productivity of their labor. Through their effects on labor supply and labor productivity, taxes on labor income alter production costs. Since labor is such a large component of the total factor costs of production, taxes on labor income influence pricing decisions, output, gross sales, and thus the rate of return to capital. In general, the higher is the tax on labor income, the lower the rate of return to capital and vice versa.

By influencing the relative rates of return to capital and labor, differences among countries in the taxation of income play an important role in determining international financial flows. If potential investors anticipate high rates of return in a given country, in part, perhaps, as a result of moderate levels of tax, holding all other things constant, that country may be a more attractive location for foreign direct investment. Also, high rates

Table 4.12 Distribution of Tax Burdens as a Percentage of Gross-of-Tax Household Income (1997 Tax Law)

Income Range	Household Income[1]	PIT[2]	EPT[3]	SF[2]	VAT[4]	Excise[5]	NR[3]	Duty[4]	Prop[3]	Indirect[6]	Total
<100	0.6	12.6	1.1	79.0	58.6	20.0	0.4	9.5	0.005	167.6	181.4
100-300	2.0	3.7	0.4	20.1	16.5	5.2	0.1	2.7	0.002	44.7	48.7
301-426	2.9	3.0	1.6	13.3	10.8	2.9	0.5	1.8	0.007	29.3	33.8
427-600	4.3	2.3	0.5	14.4	9.8	3.0	0.2	1.6	0.003	29.0	31.8
601-789	5.4	1.8	1.0	12.2	7.4	2.1	0.4	1.2	0.005	23.2	26.0
790-1,012	7.1	1.8	1.8	9.5	8.2	3.2	0.6	1.3	0.008	22.9	26.5
1,013-1,300	9.7	1.9	2.6	12.7	6.8	2.5	0.9	1.1	0.012	24.0	28.6
1,301-1,768	11.9	2.5	2.4	8.7	7.0	2.4	0.8	1.1	0.011	20.1	25.0
1,769-2,697	16.7	2.9	1.5	7.6	6.0	2.6	0.5	1.0	0.007	17.6	22.1
≥2,698	39.3	3.3	7.1	6.2	3.9	1.6	2.5	0.6	0.033	14.9	25.2
All	100	2.8	3.9	7.1	6.4	2.4	1.3	1.0	0.018	18.3	24.9

Notes:

[1] This column shows the distribution of total gross-of-tax household income by decile. The figures reported in this table are based on the authors' calculations. For this purpose, we used household level data from Round VII (1996) of the Russian Longitudinal Monitoring Survey (RLMS). Additional detail on calculations can be found in USGTA (1999b).

[2] A detailed tax calculator was used to impute the personal income tax (PIT) and social fund (SF) liabilities to each household in the sample. Actual tax receipts from the PIT and SF were distributed according to a decile's share of total PIT and SF liabilities in the sample. Thus, we implicitly assume that the rate of tax compliance is uniform throughout the income distribution. Obviously, high income households have a greater scope to conceal income than low income households. Thus, the assumption of a uniform rate of tax compliance may overstate the progressivity of the PIT and SF.

[3] Actual tax receipts from the enterprise profit tax (EPT), property tax (Prop) and natural resource taxes (NR) are distributed according to a decile's share of total capital income. Alternative incidence assumptions are equally plausible.

[4] Tax receipts from the value added tax (VAT) and customs duties (Duty) are distributed according to a decile's share of total household expenditure on taxable goods. The high shares of value added tax and Duty as a proportion of income attributed to the low income decile points to the discrepancy between reported income and expenditures in the RLMS. Whether this truly reflects consumption out of savings by low income households or misreporting of income and/or expenditure is not known.

[5] Tax receipts from excise taxes (Excise) are distributed according to a decile's share of total household expenditure on excisable goods, specifically beverage alcohol, tobacco and automobile fuels.

[6] Indirect taxes (Indirect) = social fund taxes, value added taxes, excise taxes, natural resources taxes, property taxes and customs duties.

of return at home mean domestic savings are more likely to be invested at home rather than abroad. Finally, investments in plant and equipment increase the productivity of labor, which helps determine the international competitiveness of domestically produced goods and services. The productivity of labor, the rate of return to capital and international competitiveness are fundamental factors determining the willingness of firms to expand production by hiring workers and purchasing plant and equipment, and this willingness to hire and invest is the foundation of economic growth. To complete this circle, the productivity of labor, the return to capital and economic growth, in turn, affect the distribution of income. In short, the taxation of labor and capital income has important implications for the distribution of income as well as economic efficiency.

Economic Efficiency and the Taxation of Labor Income

We proceed below by comparing the statutory marginal tax rates on labor income in the Russian Federation to that in a number of other countries in 1996-97 – shortly before the major reforms in personal income tax and social taxes. In most countries, including the Russian Federation, two taxes are levied on labor income: (1) a personal income tax and (2) a payroll tax. Russia continues to levy both taxes in 2007, but at lower marginal rates. The shares of these taxes in GDP for the Russian Federation and six member countries of the Organization for Economic Cooperation and Development (OECD) are provided in the upper part of Table 4.13. For example, this table shows that 2.8 percent of GDP was collected through the PIT in Russia for 1997, and social fund payroll taxes collected approximately 7.5 percent of GDP. Thus, in 1997, according to this measure, the tax burden on labor income in the Russian Federation was 10.3 percent of GDP. This measure of burden is useful because it shows the reduction in household income available for consumption and saving.

As important as it is, this measure does not tell the whole story regarding the effect of taxes on behavior. For example, if workers respond to a tax on labor income by working less, or employers respond by reducing their demand for labor, the resulting decrease in earnings should be counted as part of the total tax burden. Furthermore, taxes impose compliance burdens on individuals and enterprises due to the time and expense required to understand the tax system, obtain the necessary tax forms, complete and file them. The administration and enforcement of taxes also require resources. In fact, the tax system of the Russian Federation became overly complex in the 1990s, but it has been somewhat simplified in more recent years. Nevertheless, the tax system remains complicated and thus imposes significant compliance and administrative costs. Both the substitution effects resulting from tax induced changes in relative prices as well as compliance and administrative costs add to the total burden of taxation. The burden of a tax in excess of the revenue burden is called the excess burden of taxation.

As is evident from these considerations, the concept of tax burden is more complex than suggested by a simple formulation in which revenue and burden are assumed equal. To measure the total burden of a tax requires accounting for the entirety of its effects which is an enormously complicated task. Fortunately, there is a convenient rule of thumb that allows us to estimate the excess burden of taxation.

If we assume for expositional purposes that the compliance and administration costs of taxation are equal to zero, then the excess burden of a tax is equal to the economic distortions that result from tax-induced changes in relative prices. For example, an income tax with preferential rates for capital income changes the after-tax returns to factors of production, such as land, labor and physical capital. In this example, the preferential rate on capital income may cause firms to substitute physical capital for labor in the production process. But this new combination of capital and labor cannot be the most efficient one; otherwise a profit-maximizing firm would have chosen this combination in the first place. The resulting increase in the cost of production from substituting capital for labor induced by the tax corresponds to the excess burden of taxation and is referred to as the substitution effect of a tax.

The larger the substitution effect, the larger is the excess burden of the tax, and the substitution effect depends upon the tax-induced change in relative factor prices and the technical ability of enterprises to substitute factors of production. In short, the change in relative prices is proportional to the marginal tax rate on labor income.

Thus far our discussion of the total burden of taxation has ignored several important complicating factors. First, the statutory incidence of a tax tells us nothing about the economic incidence of a tax. A tax statutorily placed on the employer, such as the employer's contribution to the social funds in the Russian Federation, may not be borne entirely by the employer. The employer's demand for labor depends upon the total cost of hiring an additional employee, including any taxes associated with that employee. The employer may be able to shift the burden of payroll taxes forward onto consumers by increasing output prices or backward onto labor through lower wages. For purposes of this study, we assume that the burden of the PIT and the employee and employer's contributions to the social funds are entirely paid by the employee. This assumption is consistent with international evidence on tax incidence.

Table 4.13 International Comparisons of Tax Burdens on Labor Income (in percent)

	Russia	Czech R	France	Germany	Poland	Turkey	USA
	1997	1996	1996	1995	1995	1995	1995
Tax Receipts From Labor Income As a Share of GDP							
Personal income taxes	2.8	5.7	6.6	10.0	9.7	4.2	10.0
Social fund taxes	7.5	16.0	17.9	15.4	10.3	–	6.8
Total tax receipts from labor income	10.3	21.7	24.5	25.4	20.0	4.2	16.8
	1998	1996	1996	1996	1996	199	1996
Statutory Tax Rates on Labor Income							
Average rates							
Individual's total average tax	9.2	17.9	21.7	21.8	15.9	29.1	12.6
Total average tax wedge	44.1	39.2	45.4	35.0	43.3	35.7	23.9
Marginal rates							
Individual's total marginal tax	12.9	25.6	21.7	47.4	21.0	25.5	51.0
Total marginal tax wedge	46.4	44.9	45.4	56.2	46.7	25.5	54.4

Source: USGTA (1998a)

Second, as previously discussed, the excess burden of taxes is proportional to the effective marginal tax rate. If labor income is under-reported to the tax authorities, then the effective tax rate is less than the statutory rate. For purposes of this discussion, we assume that the effective marginal tax rate and the statutory marginal tax rate on labor income are the same. At first blush, this assumption may seem unsatisfactory because there is a significant amount of noncompliance with the tax system in the Russian Federation, especially with the taxes on labor income. However, there is a substantial body of evidence that tax evasion depends, at least in part, upon statutory marginal tax rates.

We argue below that tax evasion is one of the undesirable consequences of the relatively high statutory marginal tax rates in the Russian Federation. Therefore, for our purposes here, the assumption that effective and statutory marginal tax rates are unequal may not be as misleading as it may first appear. Nevertheless, it is important to keep in mind that under-reporting labor income reduces the effective marginal tax rate on labor income and thus also reduces the excess burden of a tax.

In the lower part of Table 4.13, we report two measures of the marginal tax rate on labor income in the Russian Federation and six OECD countries: the individual's total marginal tax rate and the individual's total marginal tax wedge for 1995-97. The essential difference between these two measures is that the former does not account for employer contributions to a tax on wages, whereas the latter does. For example, as provided in Table 4.13, the individual's statutory total marginal tax rate in the Russian Federation is 12.9 percent, while the total marginal tax wedge is 46.4 percent. The difference between the two reflects the effect of the employer contribution to the social funds on after-tax income.

Table 4.13 shows that the Russian Federation collected only 2.8 percent of Gross Domestic Product (GDP) through the personal income tax. This is the lowest rate among the seven countries considered for this study. Social fund tax collections in the Russian Federation accounted for 7.5 percent of GDP, which is also at the lower end of the range observed in these countries. Among these seven countries, only the US and Turkey devoted a smaller share of GDP to social funds. Table 4.13 also shows that total tax receipts from labor income as a share of GDP were lower in the Russian Federation than in all six OECD countries except Turkey. Turkey collected only 4.2 percent of GDP, while Russia collected approximately 10.3 percent. Germany collected the highest share of GDP among these seven countries, 25.4 percent.

The shares reported above are based upon actual tax receipts and seem to indicate that labor income is lightly taxed in the Russia Federation as compared to other countries in the table during the pre-reform period.

These shares provide important but incomplete information on the tax burden on labor income. Low rates of tax collection could be the result of either low tax compliance or low statutory tax rates. To get a more complete picture one must also examine the statutory tax burden on labor income, that is, the tax burden on labor income which is not earned through employment in the shadow economy.

Accordingly, in the lower part of Table 4.13 we report the individual's total average tax rate and total average tax wedge on labor income faced by the average production worker (APW) in each of these seven countries. The evidence in Table 4.13 suggests that there was a compliance problem in Russia. The difference between the total average tax wedge and the share of GDP collected by the government on labor taxes is attributable, at least in part, to the rate of tax compliance. In Russia this difference was equal to 33.8 (44.1 − 10.3). This is the highest difference among the countries reported in Table 4.13. Turkey was the second highest with a difference of 31.5, followed by Poland (23.3). The US was lowest with a difference of 7.1.

All taxes on labor income drive a wedge between what an employer pays a worker and what the worker receives in his pocket and, thereby, reduce the reward received from work. The larger the total marginal tax wedge the less likely that a legal agreement will be reached between an employer and an employee and the more likely that they will try to avoid taxation by joining the shadow economy. But, tax compliance problems and the growth of the shadow economy are not the only reasons to avoid high statutory burdens. It is also important to recognize that high tax rates on labor income can be harmful to an economy even if all individuals carefully obey the tax code. Taxes on labor income may influence the number of hours individuals spend working as well as the level of effort they devote to entrepreneurial activities, education and training.

As previously discussed, the excess burden of taxation is proportional to the total marginal tax wedge. According to Table 4.13, the excess burden of taxation was high in Russia relative to the amount of taxes collected. At 46.4 percent, the total marginal tax wedge in Russia was among the highest observed in Table 4.13, exceeded only by Germany (56.2 percent), the US (54.4 percent) and Poland (46.7 percent). In other words,   Russia collected a smaller share of GDP with higher statutory tax rates that impose relatively high excess burdens.

Finally, Table 4.13 shows that the individual's average total tax rate in the Russian Federation was the lowest among the countries selected for this study, while the individual's total average tax wedge was among the highest. This discrepancy arises because the total average tax wedge takes into account the employer's share of social fund taxes; while the individual's total average tax rate does not. In other words, in the Russian Federation the employer's contribution rate to the social funds (38.5 percent) was much higher than the employee's contribution rate (1 percent). In many countries, the employer does not bear such a disproportionate share of the statutory burden for social fund contributions. For example, in the US the sharing rate is 50 percent to the employer and 50 percent to the employee.

Excess Burden and the Taxation of Capital Income

Another obvious tax distortion arises from the differential tax treatment of capital income, not only relative to wage and salary income but also by type of capital income. Such tax differentials not only compromise the horizontal and vertical equity of the tax system but also give rise to excess burdens. Taxing income at different rates depending on the source of income changes net-of-tax relative factor prices. This leads to behavioral responses and thus tax induced excess burdens or a less efficient tax system.

Consider the information in Table 4.14, which summarizes the treatment of capital income under current law (USGTA 1999c). The treatment is different depending on who is paying interest and dividends and to whom they are being paid. To begin, dividends are paid out of net profits, while interest is deductible. By law, dividends paid to individuals are subject to the regular PIT rates, unless they are reinvested, which means a rate of up to 35 percent. However, dividends paid to a Russian entity are taxed at a 15 percent rate. Interest paid by a Russian entity to a Russian entity is taxed at a rate of 30 percent and 39 percent in the case of banks and insurance companies. Interest paid by an entity to an individual is taxed as regular income, up to a rate of 35 percent. Interest and dividends paid to a foreign entity or individual are taxed at a rate of 15 percent in the case of foreign entities and 20 percent in the case of a foreign individual. While there are no data on total issues of stocks and bonds and holders of those issues, it is probable that the double taxation of dividends outweighs benefit of the preferential rate for dividends paid to Russian entities.

How important is this differential treatment in the Russian Federation? The notorious lack of capital financing for enterprises suggests that this distortion may not currently be imposing high welfare costs. In the long run, however, the welfare costs associated with this distortion may become more important. A large number of securities were issued during the privatization of numerous Soviet-era enterprises. The decision to issue shares was not the result of managers weighing the costs and benefits of alternative sources of financing according to the dictates of market forces. Instead, stock

Table 4.14   Summary of the Differential Tax Treatment of Capital Income

A. Dividends	Current Law
1. Paid by a Russian entity to:	
a. Russian entity	6% 112 scheduler tax
b. Russian individual	Up to 6%
c. Foreign entity	15% 112 scheduler tax
d. Foreign individual	30% 112 scheduler tax
2. Paid by a Foreign Entity to:	
a. Russian entity	15%
b. Russian individual	Up to 6%

B. Interest	Current Law
1. Paid by Russian government to:	
a. Russian entity	15%
	0% on certain issues of bonds, defined by the law
b. Russian individual	Not defined in law
c. Foreign entity	15%
d. Foreign individual	30%
2. Paid by a Russian bank on deposit account to:	
a. Russian entity	Up to 24% (38% for banks, insurance companies and intermediaries)
b. Russian individual	Not taxable if interest rate does not exceed CB refinancing rate, in case of ruble deposits or 9% in case of foreign currency deposits; if in excess – taxed at 35%
c. Foreign entity	15%
d. Foreign individual	30%
3. Paid by a Russian entity borrower to:	
a. Russian entity	Up to 30% (38% for banks, insurance companies and intermediaries)

Table 4.14   Summary of the Differential Tax Treatment of Capital Income (continued)

B. Interest	Current Law
3. Paid by a Russian entity borrower to:	
b. Russian individual	Up to 35%. (the rate is 35%, if the gain exceeds ¾ CB rate for RUR denominated agreements, and 9% for foreign currency denominated agreements)
c. Foreign entity	15%
d. Foreign individual	30%
4. Paid by a foreign borrower to:	
a. Russian entity	24% (38% for banks, insurance companies and intermediaries)
b. Russian individual	Up to 35%. (the rate is 35%, if the gain exceeds ¾ CB rate for RUR denominated agreements, and 9% for foreign currency denominated agreements)
5. Paid by a foreign bank on deposit to:	
a. Russian entity	24% (38% for banks, insurance companies and intermediaries)
b. Russian individual	Up to 35% (the rate is 35%, if the gain exceeds ¾ CB rate for RUR denominated agreements, and 9% for foreign currency denominated agreements)
C. Capital Gains	Current Law 2004
1. On sale of Russian securities by:	
a. Russian entity	24%
b. Russian individual	Up to 13%
c. Foreign entity	15% schedular tax
d. Foreign individual	30% schedular tax

certificates were issued as a means to privatize industry and not as a source of new capital financing.

As the market in Russia matures, the cost of alternative means of financing will eventually become more important. If the tax system treats equity and debt financing differently, the tax system encourages one form of financing over another. This in effect penalizes certain enterprises and industries as against others. For example, consider the case of a closely-held enterprise with little legal option to issue stock. If the tax system treats equity more favorably than debt, then this hypothetical firm would face higher financing costs simply because of the manner of ownership and differences in the tax treatment of interest and dividends.

Realized capital gains from the sale of other than government securities are taxed at regular rates: 30 percent for enterprises and up to 35 percent for individuals. As in many countries, government securities are given a preferential tax treatment in part to encourage purchases of them. Realized capital gains on the sale of other assets are taxed at regular rates. There is a lack of consensus on the effect of taxation on realized capital gains. However, the taxation of realized capital gains may create a lock-in effect, whereby investors hold on to assets longer than they would in the absence of the tax. Consequently, investors may not adjust their portfolios in an optimal manner in order to avoid paying tax on transactions. The difference in rates between capital gains, interest and dividends would certainly encourage investors to prefer some instruments as opposed to others. The 1998 Draft Tax Code would not have equalized the taxation of realized capital gains with other forms of income from capital. In the draft version of the tax code, income from realized capital gains would have been subject to regular tax rates under the personal income and enterprise profit taxes, but interest and dividends would be taxed separately under the capital tax.

Interest income on ruble-denominated bank deposits paid to individuals is tax free for interest rates up to the Central Bank financing rate. The basically tax-free treatment of interest income at the individual level has given rise to an interesting tax avoidance practice in the Russian Federation. According to anecdotal evidence, companies give loans to their employees in the form of deposits in banks. Employees are then paid their salary from the interest distributions associated with these deposits. Interest income to the employee is tax-free; no social fund payments are made; and, in certain circumstances, the company can deduct the loan made to the individuals. The tax avoidance scheme is not as widely used since the collapse of the banking system, but this scheme is the direct consequence of the differential tax treatment of labor versus interest income.

The differential treatment of income from interest and dividends is not unique to Russia. In fact, many countries struggle with the appropriate treatment of interest and dividend income and the integration of the taxation of dividends under the enterprise profit tax and personal income tax. Integration of the corporate and personal income tax eliminates the double taxation of dividends that occurs in a classical income tax system: once under the enterprise profit tax and again when they are distributed to individual under the personal income tax. The 1998 Draft Tax Code included provisions to reduce the double taxation of dividends. However, the current enterprise profit tax does not eliminate the double taxation of interest income.

The current enterprise profit tax introduces a number of additional distortions into the system through special exemptions for certain types of profits and a reduction in the level of deductions for certain normal business expenses. However, the newly enacted enterprise profit tax chapter expands the previously limited list of deductions for normal business expenses. Another distortion is induced by a provision that exempts from taxation the profits of firms for which not less than 50 percent of the total number of employees is handicapped and the salaries of the handicapped employees account for not less than 25 percent of total salaries. A similar provision applies to value added tax on outputs from such firms. This provision encourages firms to hire disabled employees. However, it is apparent that such employees are largely hired on a very part-time basis so that the enterprise can take advantage of the exemption. This provision obviously distorts employment decisions by firms. Furthermore, it creates an opportunity for firms to avoid taxes by falsely claiming to hire handicapped employees or exaggerating the number hired. Thus, the tax authorities must monitor compliance with companies using this provision, which is a wasteful use of limited tax administration resources.

Within every tax, there are numerous exemptions and deductions which may alter behavior. For example, the value added tax exempts imports from member countries of the Commonwealth of Independent States through 2001 July 1. For a number of years, importers took advantage of this exemption and weak tax administrations in other countries to import into Russia through other member countries of the Commonwealth of Independent States rather than directly into Russia. One famous example was an automobile import business being run through Belarus. Another example of a scheme to avoid paying domestic value added tax results from the differential value added tax treatment of goods to and from member countries of the Commonwealth of Independent States and goods to and from non-member countries of the Commonwealth of Independent States or from far abroad. Exports to the far abroad were exempt from value added tax, while imports from member countries of the Commonwealth of Independent States were exempt from value added tax. Russian companies would load domestically produced goods on to a cargo ship with a bill of lading showing the destination to be far abroad and thus exempt from value added tax. The cargo ship would sail about the Baltic Sea and return to a different Russian port and eventually offload the locally produced goods with a bill of lading indicating that they were being imported from a member country of the Commonwealth of Independent States and thus exempt from value added tax. In this manner a company could avoid domestic value added tax on its manufactures. Over time, some of this activity has been stemmed by greater cooperation among the member countries of the Commonwealth of Independent States and tighter rules on point of importation.

The extent of differential treatment in the tax code of different industries is an important source of distortion. The most important consequence of the differential treatment is that the marginal effective tax rate on the investment in different assets and different industries may oscillate from being so high as to be almost confiscatory to actually being a negative marginal rate, meaning that those investments are actually subsidized by the government. These potentially large differences in the after-tax rate of return to different investments clearly distort investment decisions, attracting too much investment to some sectors and too little to others, as compared to the result that would arise with an equal tax treatment across economic sectors. Even within the same sector, the distortions to production and investment decisions, and therefore the real costs of production, can be significant when certain types of assets are favored over others by the tax system.

Another important set of distortions arises from cascading effects in the economy. Before 2003, there were two turnover taxes, which were levied based on the level of turnover. These turnover taxes encouraged vertical integration of industry as a means to reduce tax liabilities and the price effects of the turnover taxes. Industries which were not vertically integrated were at a competitive disadvantage relative to imports and other substitute goods. Business purchases by entrepreneurs were not exempt from sales taxes unless they were small entrepreneurs, with sales turnover lower that 1 million rubles for three consecutive months, nor were business purchases made by cash. Value added tax also created distortions in the production process as there are situations in which the value added tax on some inputs was not creditable. Since many of the transactions among enterprises also have been in the form of barter, the credit mechanism in the value added tax probably does not work well in these cases. The result is that the value added tax distorts the production process, increasing the price of certain goods relative to others.

A number of exemptions for certain industries yields higher or lower effective tax rates in some industries vis-à-vis other industries. If we consider the following taxes, it is possible to calculate the effective tax rate in different industries, considering the special treatment that is part of the tax code: enterprise profit tax, tax on property, payroll taxes, motorway use

fees, housing maintenance tax (turnover taxes), education and police fees
and payments for use of natural resources. By applying the statutory tax law
to hypothetical firms in these industries, we are able to estimate the
effective tax rate – measured as taxes paid divided by operating income – in
each industry.

Marginal effective tax rates by industrial sector are reported in Table
4.15. As the figures in this table show, the tax code in effect makes
investment in certain industries more attractive than in others. In addition,
the distortions imposed on production in certain industries carries over to
output prices in industries as well, although the net effect on prices depends
on substitutability in consumption, the availability of imports and tax
compliance.

Table 4.15   Marginal Effective Tax Rates by Industrial Sector

Industry	Effective Tax Rate (%)
Electricity	51
Fuels	53
Machine Tools	52
Chemicals	50
Construction Materials	57
Food Processing	62
Transport	61
Communications	52
Construction	62
Trade	68
Light Industry	57
Agriculture	54
Wood, Paper, Pulp	50

Source: Authors' calculations

For example, it is ironic that the income from food processing is taxed
relatively heavily in production, but food consumption is taxed at a lower
value added tax rate. If the government wishes to support lower tax rates on
food consumption, it may be able to accomplish this through more equal
treatment of the food processing industry. Also, if a goal of the government
is to become more competitive internationally, picking winners and losers
through the domestic tax system generally reduces the ability of industries
to compete on the international market because often bureaucratic guesses
are off the mark as to where international markets are moving, and the

distortions created by discriminatory treatment often ends up in producing higher production costs for potential exporters. A lower and more uniform treatment of all sectors is more likely to increase the competitiveness of domestic industries.

CONCLUSIONS

This chapter provides a series of empirical analyses of the performance of the tax system of the Russian Federation before and after the major tax reforms through 2005. While there are some mixed messages that come through the analyses, it does appear that the system was quite unstable prior to the reforms of 2000 and beyond. However, important issues such as the distribution of the tax burden and the wedge between gross and net returns on factors such as labor remain troubling (although less so for the most part than prior to 2000). The tax system has changed rapidly over the period from 1996 to 2005, with larger revenues coming from taxes on foreign operations and natural resources, and with a concentration of revenues at the central government level. In the next chapter, we provide a detailed look at the structure of the major taxes, which sheds additional light on the changes in the performance of the overall system.

NOTES

1. As noted by Tanzi and Zee (2001) and others, theory has more to say about the composition of taxes and less to say about the appropriate level of taxation.
2. A word of caution must be raised when analyzing these statistics. While all countries have problems reconciling aggregate data such as GDP and total budgetary revenues and expenditures, in Russia the problem is compounded by government set wages and expenditure norms. While there should be a correspondence between the budget and GDP numbers for inputs such as labor costs, there may be some discrepancies between the two.
3. The issue of the government balance is discussed in the IMF Program memorandum, July 1998.
4. Also the distribution of tax revenues between the central and subnational governments in Russia is quite different from that in most countries. The central/subnational revenue split in Russia is very roughly 50/50 (depending on the year), while in most countries, subnational government revenues are a much smaller portion of total revenues. This results in a situation in which Russia's central government revenue-to-GDP ratio is more in line with that of lower middle income countries, while that of the subnational governments in Russia is similar to that of high income OECD countries.
5. These models are discussed in detail in Lotz and Morss (1967), Bahl (1971), Chelliah (1971), Tait et al. (1979), and Bahl et al. (1996).
6. Model 2 is estimated with fewer countries since the statistics on mineral and fuel exports were not available for all countries.
7. Bahl (1971) developed this method for making inter-country comparisons that related the tax effort index to the intensity of use of specific types of taxes. In the equations run here, we use a fixed effects model and control for both year and country.

8.   We present these average buoyancy estimates versus the year-to-year estimates as the latter show significant fluctuation in most periods. This is an important finding, but we concentrate on the general trend in this analysis.

9.   The CPI was used to create real variables. It would have been preferable to use the CPI deflator for the tax collections and the GDP deflator to deflate GDP, but that deflator is not available on a monthly basis. The bias introduced by smoothing this deflator seemed more problematic than the use of the CPI deflator.

10. The explained variation (percent) for each tax is as follows: enterprise profit tax: 61, personal income tax: 69, value added tax: 72, Excises: 24.

11. In 1998, these four taxes constituted 71.5 percent of total tax collections of the consolidated budget.

12. The subnational governments have little discretion over the major taxes, as the bases and rates are largely set by the federal government. Additionally, this analysis does not refer to the expenditure side of the equation where there have been some shifts in the de facto responsibilities for the different levels of government.

5. The Structure of Taxes

Tax policy is often the art of the possible rather than the pursuit of the optimal.
(Tanzi and Zee, 2001)

On paper, the tax structure of the Russian Federation quickly evolved from a Soviet-style system of hidden taxes to a modern tax system with a value added tax as the core revenue producer. The turnover tax of the pre-1991 system was abolished; more modern personal and corporate income taxes replaced wage taxes and inter-enterprise price adjustments; and excise taxes and import duties were rationalized to a degree. However, no system undergoes even minor reform smoothly. Over the course of a single decade, the Russian Federation witnessed a major overhaul of its tax structure and continues to make major adjustments. This chapter presents a detailed look at the specific structure of all major taxes and provides an analysis of changes and discussion of policy issues that remain unresolved.

PERSONAL INCOME TAX (PIT)

Personal income taxes are more heavily used in developed than in developing countries.[1] In transition countries, the combination of payroll taxes and a personal income tax is an important part of the tax structure. In 2005, this combination accounted for approximately 24 percent of consolidated government revenue in the Russian Federation.

In many countries, the majority of the personal income tax comes from a system of income tax withholding at the place of employment. In simple cases (a single job and one employer), this form of tax administration can be quite effective at raising substantial amounts of revenue without imposing undue compliance or administrative burdens. In those cases in which individuals have multiple jobs with multiple employers, however, the withholding system can be more difficult to administer, especially in the case of a system with graduated tax rates, multiple exemptions for family size and other special features.

Until very recently, little effort was made to enforce taxes accruing from secondary sources of employment in the Russian Federation. Furthermore, as discussed in greater detail below, the marginal tax rates on labor income in the Russia Federation were high by any standard. The result was that sources of income subject to lower rates of tax or that are more difficult to monitor, such as housing subsidies, credits within large firms and in-kind payments, were used in place of cash wages to compensate employees. As discussed in greater details below, such tax distortions led the Russian Federation to adopt major reforms of the personal income tax in 2000. We proceed below with a discussion of the major design issues of a personal income tax to set the stage for a detailed discussion of the evolution of the Russian Federation's personal income tax.

As previously mentioned, the personal income tax can be very productive at raising revenue and is often a major element of the tax structure of many countries. In addition, the personal income tax is a wonderfully flexible instrument that is often used to pursue a variety of societal and economic goals. The general use of a personal income tax is often justified on equity grounds. The justification for progressive taxation of income is that such a tax is consistent with the ability to pay principle. This principle requires that people with a greater ability to pay tax should bear a greater tax burden than those with less ability to pay tax. Generally speaking, the ability to pay tax should be positively correlated with income. Therefore, a progressive income tax with marginal tax rates that increase with income satisfies the ability to pay principle. Furthermore, the personal income tax can be adjusted to account for particular situations that also may reflect the ability to pay principle, such as deductions for the number of dependents, medical expenses and so on (Goode, 1984). The most widely used exemptions are for family size and age, as when pension income is exempt from income tax. In some countries, there may be exemptions for war veterans, the handicapped, artists and teachers; those living in high cost areas; those living in environmentally degraded areas; and so on.

Governments often pursue other societal and economic goals by providing exemptions, deductions, credits and concessionary rates for favored causes. This changes relative prices. For illustrative purposes, suppose an individual is subject to a 25 percent marginal tax rate and is allowed to deduct charitable contributions means. In this case, the out of pocket cost of a $100 donation is $75. In other words, the deduction has lowered the price of donations relative to other uses of income such as consumption and investment. If individuals are responsive to such changes in relative prices, then the personal income tax can be used successfully to pursue a wide variety of societal and economic goals. In many countries, for example, capital income is subject to concessionary rates. This changes the net-of-tax price of investment. The idea is that by reducing the relative price of investment, this encourages entrepreneurs to consume less and invest more. The effectiveness of such an approach depends on the elasticity of substitution between the uses of these two uses of income.

Although the personal income tax is a very flexible tax, using it to pursue societal and economic goals may come at a cost in terms of a potentially less buoyant tax; increased administrative and compliance burdens; a lack of horizontal equity; and a less efficient tax.

A well designed and properly administered personal income tax is a potentially buoyant tax, where buoyancy describes the relationship between the revenue yield of a tax and changes in national income or gross domestic product (GDP). If the tax base of the personal income tax is sufficiently comprehensive, it should grow at about the same rate as national income. Furthermore, as nominal incomes grow over time due to inflation, individuals will be pushed into higher tax brackets, assuming of course that the tax brackets and other features of the tax are not indexed for inflation. This phenomenon is referred to as bracket creep. Consequently, the revenue yield of a well administered personal income tax with a comprehensive tax base and without indexing would grow faster than national income. In contrast, a personal income tax is less buoyant when exempt sources of income grow faster than taxable sources. Similarly, indexing tax brackets for inflation eliminates bracket creep, and consequently an indexed personal income tax is less buoyant than one that is not indexed.

Another potential consequence of generous exemptions, deductions, credits and concessionary rates may be a less progressive personal income tax. For example, granting concessionary tax rates to capital income reduces the progressivity of the personal income tax because high income individuals tend to receive a larger fraction of total income from capital than low and middle income individuals.

Numerous special treatments of income also increase the complexity of a tax which in turn adds to the administrative and compliance burdens. Furthermore, concessionary tax rates and other special treatments may violate the principle of horizontal equity. As its name implies, this principle requires that people in similar circumstances face similar tax burdens. For illustrative purposes, suppose that capital income is exempt from tax. Two otherwise identical people would bear very different tax burdens if one received all of his income from capital and the other received an equivalent income exclusively from wages. This violates the principal of horizontal equity.

The personal income tax in many countries is being used to pursue so many different and perhaps contradictory goals that it is nearly impossible to understand the true nature of the incentives being provided. As a result, there are frequent calls for tax simplification that often include recommendations to adopt a flat rate income tax, such as the one enacted in

Russia. Proponents of flat rate income taxes often point out that a progressive income tax actually achieves very little meaningful redistribution of income; consequently it may be best to pursue this goal on the expenditure side of the budget.

In terms of the political economy of taxation, some maintain that a single low income tax rate reduces the incentive to expend effort seeking tax concessions. Even with a single rate personal income tax, however, governments may still attempt to use exemptions, deductions, credits and concessionary rates to promote non-revenue goals through the tax system, as the behavior of the Russian Federation aptly illustrates.

In the remainder of this section, we will analyze the personal income tax of the Russian Federation by providing a detailed account of the current tax as well as changes that have occurred to the tax over the last decade.

Tax Rates and Brackets

Under the Soviet system, the personal income tax was a tax on wages and withheld at a rate of 12 percent on incomes up to 99 rubles and a maximum rate of 13 percent for incomes over 100 rubles of monthly income. There was virtually no capital income tax at the individual level during that period. The Russia Federation had the option of imposing tax on income or consumption. And, like many countries, Russia chose a hybrid system in which the personal income tax was an important component of the tax structure.[2]

Since 1991, and especially after 1993, the personal income tax has been reshaped as a schedular tax, with different tax rates applying to wage income from primary employment. Certain types of capital income only became taxable in 1997; prior to that capital income had been excluded from the tax base. During the nineties, the number of tax slabs varied from three to six and were frequently changed. The result was a personal income tax with a conventional progressive marginal tax rate structure for combined employment income, with separate taxes imposed on dividends and certain types of interest income.[3] Throughout the nineties and until this writing, capital income has been treated differently from wage income in the Russian Federation.

In legislation which was enacted in 2000 and became effective on January 1, 2001, the personal income tax was revolutionized into a flat rate tax on income, with separate rates of tax on some sources of income. The tax now has a single tax rate of 13 percent on all income above a certain threshold, with exceptions listed in Table 5.1. Taxable income consists of all income of 'tax residents of the Russian Federation from sources in the Russian Federation and (or) from sources outside the Russian Federation

Tax Reform in Russia

and physical persons who receive income from sources in the territory of the Russian Federation but are not tax residents of the Russian Federation'. The tax base is determined as all income received by a taxpayer 'in cash, or in-kind, or for which he has acquired the right to dispose of, and of income in the form or material gain'.[4]

It is somewhat curious that in the summer of 2000, the Duma passed a package of tax reform bills that included a flat rate personal income tax. Prior to its adoption, there was considerable political support for a progressive marginal tax rate structure. The State Duma repeatedly declined to take up proposals for flat tax rates or a reduction in the general progressivity of the tax schedule. Acceptance of the flat rate tax was not easy. There were fierce discussions of this issue both within the Government and State Duma. The reform measure was adopted as part of a larger package of reform initiatives.

Table 5.1   Personal Income Tax Structure Effective January 1, 2001 with amendments through 2005

Type of taxable income	Rate (%)
All types of income except for those listed below:	13
Lottery winnings Value on any winnings and prizes Interest income above the Central Bank refinancing rate for deposits in rubles, and above 9% for deposits in foreign currency Interest income generated from borrowed sources where the rate is less than 9%	35[a]
Illustrative examples of excluded income: payment of damages, state benefits, some state-provided pensions, alimony, one-time material assistance for certain disasters, student stipends, rewards for 'treasures' handed over to the State, interest on government bonds	0
Income of non-residents	30
Dividends	9

Deductions	Rubles/Month
Individuals suffering from radiation, Chernobyl catastrophe, WW2 invalids or other categories	3,000
Heroes of the USSR, Russian Federation, participants of the WW2, disabled and other categories	500
Low-income families, those with income less than 20,000 rubles	400

Table 5.1   Personal Income Tax Structure Effective January 1, 2001 with amendments through 2005 (continued)

Deductions	Rubles/Month
Child support for children up to 18 years of age or full-time students to age 24 and income 20,000 or less (doubled for widows, single parents or guardians)	600
Charitable contributions	Up to 25% of income allowed as deduction
Educational expenditures	Up to 38,000 rubles
Medical expenses	Up to 38,000 rubles
Capital gains on housing	Up to 1 million rubles (held 3 or more years); up to 125,000 rubles (held less than 3 years)

Note: [a] In May 2002 the lower chamber of the Russian Federation parliament – State Duma passed the amendment to reduce tax rate on lottery winnings to 13 percent. To become effective the amendment has to be approved by the Federation Council and signed by the Russian Federation President.

Source: Tax Code of the Russian Federation (Ministry of Finance of the Russian Federation, 2005).

The arguments advanced by proponents of the flat rate were motivated by the overly burdensome and little complied with system of personal income taxation. The specific arguments were as follows:

- A flat rate tax would simplify the filing process and exempt a significant portion of the population from filing. This would reduce the administrative costs in a system for which tax filing was often not complied with under existing law.
- A flat rate tax could increase tax compliance because of the perceived fairness of a 13 percent tax rate versus the higher existing rates. This applied to both individuals working for employers as well as entrepreneurs.
- The reality of the existing system was that the personal income tax was largely a flat tax under the existing structure. In 2000, Ministry of Finance figures showed that about 97 percent of taxpayers paid income tax at a rate of 12.9 percent, and only 0.1 percent of the taxpaying population paid tax at the maximum rate of 30 percent. Opponents of the flat rate tax were ultimately persuaded to support the reform

package by the decision to allow a variety of deductions and
exemptions for individuals and families with special circumstances,
such as low income and war veterans.

The new personal income tax also brought with it a new set of
intergovernmental sharing arrangements. Personal income taxes are
generally believed to be 'good' local taxes. In most cases, the base of the
personal income tax is not very mobile and the tax handles associated with
it are relatively easy to define and observe.[5] Throughout the 1990s, the
Russian Federation did not assign the income tax to regional governments,
but it did share large portions of the tax with the oblasts. This proved to be a
relatively stable and consistent source of revenue for regional governments,
which in turn shared revenues with local governments within the oblasts. In
fact, prior to 1999, the personal income tax was shared nearly 100 percent
with regional governments.

In April 1999, a new sharing arrangement was installed, whereby the
federal government would tax income at a flat rate of 3 percent, and the
regional governments would receive the revenue from the higher tax rates
according to the federally set progressive tax rates. The effect was to
increase the federal share of the personal income tax relative to historic
levels. The regions had no discretion in setting these tax rates, unlike the
situation for the piggyback arrangement of the enterprise profit tax, as
discussed in greater detail in the following section. However, in 2000 the
tax rates were reduced and lowered, and the flat 3 percent rate payable to
the federal government was abolished. The budget legislation of 2000
provided that 16 percent of personal income tax liability was to accrue to
the federal budget and 74 percent to the regional budgets. With the
introduction of the flat 13 percent rate in 2001, the federal budget received 1
percent of the personal income tax liability. In 2002, the situation reverted
to a sharing arrangement where regional governments receive 100 percent
of the personal income tax revenue. Box 5.1 describes the evolution of the
rates and sharing rules.

The flat rate tax imposed in the Russian Federation may be seen as a
move in the direction of tax simplification. By sharing 100 percent of the
tax with the regional governments, the federal government also restored
some of the revenue stability that was lost in the late 1990s. Given the
relatively flat nature of the previous structure, the equity of the system is not
expected to be dramatically affected by the rate change.

While the tax was cleaned up in the 2000 legislation, a number of
deductions still apply, though these are generally conventional ones (family,
income and social issue based), property-related and professional. However,
the flat tax still maintains many of the previous exemptions, deductions

Box 5.1   *Evolution of Personal Income Tax Rates and Sharing Rules*

RATES

1999 Rate Structure

Taxable income rubles/annual	Federal budget rate	Regional budgets rate
Up to 30,000 rubles	3%	9%
from 30001 to 60,000 rubles	3%	2,700 rubles +12% on income over 30,000
from 60001 to 90,000 rubles	3%	6,300 rubles +17% on income over 60,000
from 90001 to 150,000 rubles	3%	11,400 rubles+22% on income over 90,000
Over 150,001	3%	24,600 rubles +32% on income over 150,000[a]

2000 Rate Structure

Taxable income rubles/annual	Regional budgets rate
Up to 50,000 rubles	12%
From 50,000 to 150,0000 rubles	6,000 +20% on income over 50,000
Over 150,000 rubles	26,000 + 30% on income over 150,000

2001 and beyond Rate Structure

Taxable income/rubles annual	Tax rate
All taxable income	13%

INTERGOVERNMENTAL SHARING

Distribution of personal income tax between federal and regional governments, by year:

Under 1999 legislation
Example:
Taxable income = 25,000 rubles
Overall tax liability = (25,000*0.12) = 3,000
Federal tax liability = (25,000*0.03) = 750
Regional tax liability = (25,000*0.09) = 2,250

Under 2000 legislation
Example:
Taxable income = 25,000 rubles
Total tax liability of taxpayer = (25,000*0.12) = 3,000
Federal share of tax = (3,000*0.16) = 480
Regional share of the tax = (3,000*0.74) = 2,220

Box 5.1   Evolution of Personal Income Tax Rates and Sharing Rules (continued)

Under 2001 legislation
Example:
Taxable income = 25,000 rubles
Tax liability = (25,000*0.13) = 3,250
Federal share of tax = (3,250*0.01) = 32.5
Regional share of tax = (3,250*0.99) = 3,217.5

After 2001 100 percent 'shared' to regional government

Note: [a] The 45 percent rate for incomes over 300,000 rubles was adopted as part of the amendments to 1999 personal income tax legislation but suspended and ceased in 2000 upon introduction of the new personal income tax scale.

and special treatments of earlier personal income taxes in Russia, which could continue to diminish the equity, efficiency and administrability of the tax system. Exemptions and deductions often create opportunities for tax evasion activity and thus burden the tax administration which has to monitor the use of these features of the tax system. We discuss these issues in greater detail below.

Tax Base

Under both the old progressive marginal tax rate structure and the new flat rate tax, the base of the personal income tax has been worldwide income but with separate tax rate schedules applied to capital and labor income. Prior to 2001, the tax base was narrowed considerably by a substantial number of exemptions and deductions. In the 2001 reform and subsequent changes through 2005, the tax base has been broadened by the elimination of a variety of deductions and exemptions.

More specifically, the tax code stipulates that residents should include income earned from sources in the Russian Federation as well as foreign sources, and foreigners should include income received from activities in the Russian Federation. The types of income included in the personal income tax base are typical of such taxes around the world. The following are the specific items that are subject to the personal income tax (Tax Code 2005, Chapter 23, Article 1):

- Dividends and interest received from a Russian organization and interest received from Russian private entrepreneurs and (or) a foreign organization in connection with the activities of its permanent establishment in the Russian Federation;

- Insurance payments in connection with the occurrence of an insured accident which are received from a Russian organization and (or) from a foreign organization in connection with the activities of its permanent establishment in the Russian Federation;
- Income received from the use in the Russian Federation of copyrights or other related rights;
- Income received from the renting of property in Russia;
- Income from the sale of immovable property which is situated in the Russian Federation, or sale in the Russian Federation of shares or securities and of share interests, in the charter capital of organizations;
- Remuneration for the performance of employment duties or other duties, work performed, a service rendered or the performance of an act in the Russian Federation;
- Pensions, benefits, stipends and other similar payments;
- Income received from the use of any means of transport, in connection with transport to and (or) from or within the Russian Federation;
- Income received from the use of pipelines, power supply lines, fiber-optic and (or) wireless communication lines and other communications facilities;
- Income received as a result of carrying out activities in the Russian Federation.

The list of exemptions for the personal income tax is long and includes some common and some less common ones. For example, many countries exempt certain government benefits, such as pension, unemployment and maternity benefit payments, and these are not taxable in the Russian Federation. The exemptions fall into four general categories:

- Exemptions for certain types of activities, for example, income of taxpayers received from the sale of certain livestock and agricultural products, or the exemption of grants and stipends for students;
- Catastrophic circumstances, such as the exclusion of payment for damage caused by personal injury or other damage to health;
- Exemptions for interest income from State treasury bills; bonds and other State securities of the former USSR; the Russian Federation and constituent entities of the Russian Federation; and on bonds and securities issued by decision of representative local government bodies;
- Other exemptions such as inheritances and gifts.

The list of exemptions is rather generous to certain individuals, including academics and those in the agricultural sector. In addition, the long list of exemptions adds to the complexity of tax administration.

Individuals who do not receive special tax treatments believe the tax system is unfair, especially as many of the exemptions are not means tested. Due to the lack of information from individual tax returns, it is difficult to determine how many Russian citizens are eligible for the various exemptions.

Capital Income

The taxation of capital income is treated as a special case under the personal income tax. The income tax in the Russian Federation follows a hybrid model where declared income is generally taxed at 13 percent, but capital income is treated separately. Under a progressive tax rate structure, schedular taxation of capital versus wage income reduces the complexity of income tax withholding and taxpayer calculations of liability since employer withholding could be calculated without regard to the level of capital income earned by an individual. Under a flat rate tax structure, there is less administrative benefit to schedular taxation. However, under a flat rate tax, a schedular system is one way to introduce greater progressivity into the system, assuming of course that capital income is disproportionately received by higher income individuals and therefore taxed at higher rates than wage and salary income. On the other hand, lower tax rates on the income from capital could be used as a mechanism to encourage investment and economic growth.

The tax treatment of capital income under the personal income tax is different from the conventional treatment. For ruble deposits, interest income earned in excess of the Central Bank refinancing rate is taxable at a rate of 35 percent; interest income earned at a lower rate is exempt from tax. This treatment creates a large differential in the net-of-tax returns based on the interest rate that is applied to savings. In addition, interest paid by Russian governments, including federal, regional and local, to an individual is also exempt. Finally, dividends are taxed at a flat rate of 9 percent, regardless of source.

It is difficult to detect a policy rational for these different tax treatments of capital income. In some cases, it is taxed at preferential rates (that is, dividends, interest on certain ruble deposits and interest from government), and in other cases it is taxed at discriminatory rates (that is, certain ruble deposits).

Policy Issues of the Personal Income Tax

The problems with the personal income tax in the Russian Federation are quite obvious. The large number of exemptions and deductions for certain types of income overly complicate the system and give rise to opportunities to evade tax. Even with the flat rate income tax, the differential rates for capital income coupled with the exemptions and deductions can cause problems with administration. While theoretically it may be better to eliminate all special deductions and exemptions and handle such specialized treatment through the expenditure side of the budget, this is ultimately a political and social decision for Russia. However, it is prudent to re-examine such deductions and exemptions over time to make sure that they still fit the country's social needs, possibly in the form of a tax expenditure budget (TEB).

A tax expenditure budget would calculate the revenue loss associated with exemptions, deductions, credits and concessionary rates. Just like explicit budgetary expenditures on education, transportation and the like, these tax expenditures are costly to government in the form of foregone revenue and deserve regular public scrutiny. A tax expenditure budget would provide policymakers with a source of information with which to analyze the relevance and equity of these tax expenditures as well as their cost in terms of foregone revenue over time.

Another problem with the current personal income tax system is the failure to index certain parameters of the tax, such as the standard deduction for inflation. If deductions are justifiable and supported by the political system, the failure to index these features of the tax erodes their real value over time, and thus reduces the fairness of the tax system.[6] For example, over time, individuals who were not paying income tax because their wages were less than the tax threshold, eventually become liable for tax as inflation causes their nominal wages to exceed the tax threshold, that is unless exemptions are regularly adjusted for inflation. There are also very large marginal effects since the standard deduction for low income individuals is eliminated when income reaches 20,000 rubles per month. While the value of these deductions and exemptions can change regularly, there is no provision in the law for regular indexing of them.

The switch to a flat rate income tax significantly lowered the statutory marginal tax rate on wages from over 83 percent in 1999 to 48.6 percent in 2002, including social taxes. The expectation is that this reduction in statutory tax rates on labor income will reduce the shadow economy in the Russian Federation. Martinez-Vazquez et al. (2006) and Ivanova et al. (2005) analyze the impact of the flat rate tax reform on personal income tax revenues. While they both find that revenues increased, they attribute the increase to different factors. Ivanova et al. (2005) contend that the growth in tax revenues largely comes from increased tax enforcement effort and the resulting increases in voluntary compliance. In contrast, Martinez-Vazquez et al. do not find evidence of increased tax enforcement, at least according to publicly available information on the number of tax returns filed, audits and so on. They tentatively conclude that the growth in revenues is the result of an increase in voluntary compliance as a result of the marginal tax rate cuts resulting from the flat rate personal income tax reform. This conjecture is supported by a more recent paper by Gorodnichenko et al. (2007) which looks at the difference between reported consumption and reported income as an indication of the level of tax evasion. With the goal of separating the tax evasion effect of flat rate income tax reform from other factors, these authors use the difference-in-difference approach and regression discontinuity analysis and find that, other things the same, the consumption-income gap decreased by about 9 to 12 percent more for households that experienced a reduction in marginal tax rates; this means that the most significant reduction in tax evasion was for taxpayers that experienced the largest decrease in tax rates after the flat rate income tax was introduced. Gorodnichenko et al. (2007) also find that the decline in tax evasion was likely due to changes in voluntary compliance as opposed to greater enforcement effort by the tax administration authorities. These authors also analyzed the productivity effect of the flat tax reform and found it to be relatively small by comparison to the tax evasion effect.

Finally, the treatment of capital income has been significantly improved relative to the treatment provided for in the 1999 law, when a taxpayer could face one of six tax rates on capital income, depending on the its source. Still, the preferential treatment of low-interest bearing capital income could distort investment decisions and creates opportunities for tax evasion.

ENTERPRISE PROFIT TAX (EPT)

The enterprise profit tax is levied on the profits of corporations (legal entities). Since interest, dividends and capital gains are often included in the base of the personal income tax, one may reasonably ask why there is a need for a separate tax on corporate profits. There are several justifications for this tax. Since the owners of corporations enjoy limited liability, the enterprise profit tax can be justified as a type of user fee for the benefits of limited liability. Another justification that one often hears is that the enterprise profit tax is a progressive tax on income. The popular belief may be that taxes on corporate profits are paid by the owners of such firms. If this is indeed true, then the enterprise profit tax may be a progressive tax on income because high income individuals tend to get a greater share of their income from capital than low and middle income individuals. However, matters are not quite so simple.

The burden of the enterprise profit tax may fall on the owners of capital, but they will try to shift the tax forward onto consumers by increasing the prices of the goods that they produce or shift it backward on to the suppliers of factors of production by reducing the prices that they pay for inputs, such as wages. Since the incidence of an enterprise profit tax is potentially dispersed among consumers, suppliers of inputs, owners of capital and so on, the distributional justification for imposing an enterprise profit tax may be called into question.

Another justification for an enterprise profit tax is that it provides a backup to the personal income tax, and this seems to be the consensus view of the rational for an enterprise profit tax. In the absence of an enterprise profit tax, corporate profits are not taxed unless and until they are distributed as dividends or as realized capital gains. Thus, in the absence of an enterprise profit tax, corporate profits enjoy the benefit of deferral, or as the saying goes 'a tax deferred is a tax foregone'. Goode (1984) points out that even distributed profits may escape taxation if an enterprise profit tax is not used as a means to impose and collect taxes. So, from the point of view of horizontal equity, the enterprise profit tax may be justified as a means of ensuring that taxes are paid by individuals who earn income from particular forms of capital.

As discussed below, taxes such as Russia's enterprise profit tax are not the best taxes to use in terms of economic efficiency, equity or administrative costs. Theoretically, an enterprise profit tax or corporate tax can be designed to minimize administrative burdens and other economic distortions. As with many taxes, the implementation of an enterprise profit tax or tax on corporate profits tends to afford special treatments to certain industries or sectors, which violates horizontal equity and distorts investment decisions. In many countries, dividend payments are not deductible from taxable corporate profits so profits are double taxed, once at the corporate level and then again when they are distributed at the individual level. In addition, differences in individual and corporate tax rates give rise to income shifting to avoid tax. Depreciation rules are often complicated and may bear little relation to economic depreciation, which further affects the equity and efficiency of the enterprise profit tax.

Despite these problems, corporate income taxes are widely used. In the member countries of the Europe Union (EU), it is not a heavily used source of revenue. Luxembourg, for example, relies most heavily on the enterprise profit tax for revenue purposes. There is somewhat greater reliance on enterprise income taxes in East Asian countries, especially China, Japan, Taiwan and Korea (Woller, 1999). In transition countries, the use of the enterprise profit tax is widespread and reliance of central governments on this revenue source has been higher than in EU member countries.

General Description of the Russian Federation's Enterprise Profit Tax

At its inception, the enterprise profit tax did a poor job of providing deductions for normal business expenses, such as expenditures on advertising, and the system was riddled with special tax treatments for certain types of businesses. Limitations on such basic business expenses as wages, depreciation and interest increased the cost of operating an enterprise vis-à-vis other countries. Some of these shortcomings have been eliminated or at least reduced; depreciation allowances are now more generous as are the treatment of some business expenses; and the rate structure has been rationalized.

Reforms through 2005 have improved the structure of this tax. The enterprise profit tax is now governed by Chapter 25 of the Russian Federation Tax Code, Part 2, which became effective on January 1, 2002. The tax rate structure reflects the intergovernmental fiscal structure, as there are three rates: 7.5 percent to the federal budget, 14.5 percent to regional budgets and 2 percent to local budgets through 2004. As of January 1, 2005, local governments no longer receive a portion of enterprise profit tax revenues. The current intergovernmental rates are 6.5 percent to the federal budget and up to 17.5 percent to regional governments. The federal government establishes the minimum and maximum tax rates and the tax base of the enterprise profit tax. As such, regional governments have limited rate setting authority in that they can reduce the regional tax rate by up to 4 percentage points. The minimum combined rate of tax on business income is therefore 20 percent and the maximum rate is 24 percent.

The Russian Federation's enterprise profit tax is complicated by a variety of statutes regarding the tax treatment of foreign companies, and companies engaged in certain types of industrial activities. If a foreign company is not registered as a permanent corporation in the Russian Federation, the federal tax rate on capital gains is 20 percent in most cases. Like the personal income tax, the enterprise profit tax is a schedular system in that interest and dividend income paid to enterprises is taxed at different rates than ordinary income. As previously noted, dividend income paid by Russian enterprises to a Russian resident, entity or individual is taxed at a rate of 9 percent. Dividends paid by foreign organizations to a Russian one is taxed at a rate of 15 percent or received by a foreign company from a Russian one. Interest received from certain government bonds by enterprises is taxed at a rate of 15 percent, and other interest income is taxed at a 20 percent rate.

It should come as no surprise that this tax has proven to be as difficult to administer in Russia as in many other countries. Furthermore, a number of important issues remain for the enterprise profit tax in Russia, which are similar to issues facing other countries.

Tax Structure

As noted, the tax is shared between the federal and regional governments via a piggyback scheme. Regional governments can reduce the tax by up to four percentage points, so that regions may levy a rate between 13.5 and 17.5 percent. Losses can be carried forward for a period of ten years, but not carried back. The amount of losses carried forward may not exceed 30 percent of the tax base in 2005, but this is expanded to 50 percent in 2006, and the limitation is removed as of January 1, 2007 (Ernst and Young, 2005).

By international standards, the basic enterprise profit tax rate in Russia is not high, although the piggyback arrangement among the two levels of government is unique, especially given the relatively high rate for the regional portion of the tax. However, there are a number of important issues regarding the tax base which influence the effectiveness of the tax. In Russia, the number and type of allowed exemptions and tax holidays, as well as the type of depreciation imposed, are important issues in establishing the effective tax rate for business. There are also severe problems with tax administration, some of which are mentioned in this section, but most of which are discussed in a subsequent chapter.

Tax Base

In theory, the enterprise profit tax should not interfere with business decisions, but is designed to tax the profits of incorporated businesses. By the effective Russian Federation law, profit is defined for Russian organizations as 'income received, reduced by the amount of expenses incurred as determined in accordance with the law'; and for foreign organizations which carry out activities in the Russian Federation through permanent establishments as 'income received through those permanent establishments, reduced by the amount of expenses incurred by those permanent establishments as determined in accordance with the law'. Foreign entities without permanent establishments in Russia are to apportion their income and expenses based on activities within the country.

In the Russian Federation, as in most countries, there are a number of exclusions and exemptions under the enterprise profit tax. The nature of some of the exclusions is broad and may be interpreted to cover a number of organizations. In this case, they create opportunities for tax evasion. Some of these exclusions and exemptions are as follows:

- Resources received under credit and loan agreements (other similar resources, irrespective of the form in which borrowings are arranged, including debt securities);
- Assets received by a Russian organization from another organization where no less than 50 percent of the charter capital of the transferring party consists of a contribution of the receiving organization; and
- Special-purpose receipts including those allocated from the budget to budget recipients.

The law provides that a taxpayer shall reduce income received by the amount of expenses incurred and defines those as 'justified and documented' expenditures which are made or incurred by a taxpayer. Prior to 2002, many deductions were limited. Currently, the limitations are much less common, and instead the list of allowable expenses is an open list subject to satisfying a test of a business related expenses. A few important limitations are still included in the law:

- Representation costs (limited to 4 percent of labor-related expenses);
- Contributions for voluntary personal insurance; and
- Interest expense is subject to an arm's length transaction and is also subject to a thin capitalization test.

There is also a list of non-deductible expenses; some of which include legitimate business expenses. These include the following:

- Penalties, fines and other sanctions that are paid to the budget;
- Costs of acquisition and (or) creation of amortizable assets;
- Resources transferred to trade union organizations;
- Remunerations provided to management or workers in addition to remunerations which are payable on the basis of labor agreements (contracts);
- Bonuses paid out of special purpose resources; and
- Payment for supplementary leave (over and above leave envisaged by current legislation) which is granted under a collective agreement to employees.

The combination of these excluded and non-excluded income and expense items results in a tax that is better in 2005 than in the 1990s, but there are restrictions and regulations in the system that make it difficult to administer. The changes brought into effect in 2002 and 2003 also reduced the number of industry-specific exemptions.

Depreciation

Depreciation allowances for tax purposes represent deductions from revenue for the cost of using up capital equipment.[7] When an enterprise purchases new capital equipment, it has not incurred a cost because it has simply exchanged one asset, cash, for another, the equipment. Presumably, the enterprise could sell the equipment the following day and get its cash back. In contrast, when an enterprise purchases an hour of labor services from a worker that hour is immediately used up. The enterprise and the worker cannot get the hour back, so a true cost is incurred. Accordingly, the full cost of labor should be immediately deductible from enterprise income. Since an enterprise that purchases new capital equipment does not incur a cost until it is used in production, it should not be allowed to deduct the full purchase price of the capital equipment or expense in the year that that equipment is purchased. It should only be allowed to deduct the share of the purchase price of the capital equipment that has been used up during the year. The economic reason behind depreciation allowances is to allow deductions for the cost of using up capital and thereby levy tax on true economic profit; the residual value of the equipment remains an asset of the enterprise

In reality, depreciation allowances provided for in tax laws often do not equal economic depreciation or the true rate at which capital equipment is being used up. There are two reasons for this. First, it is impossible for depreciation allowances to exactly match the rate at which many different kinds of enterprises use up many different kinds of capital equipment. The best that can be done is to come up with simplified depreciation rules that are considered close enough and acceptable to both enterprises and the government.

The second reason is that many countries provide accelerated depreciation rules as a way of promoting the purchase of capital equipment and foster economic growth. With accelerated depreciation rules, enterprises can deduct the cost of using up capital equipment long before that equipment is actually used up. Of course, an example of accelerated depreciation is to allow enterprises to expense purchases of capital equipment or fully deduct the purchase price of the capital equipment in the year in which it is purchased. This is as if the equipment is entirely used up in the first year.

Although some form of accelerated depreciation allowances exists in most industrialized countries, no industrialized country universally allows expensing. Such generous depreciation allowances would push the tax treatment of enterprise profit far from the ideal of taxing true economic

---

Box 5.2   Depreciation Rules Worldwide

Austria – Generally requires a fixed percentage of the value of capital assets to be deducted each year. General categories of capital assets include transport vehicles, machinery, office equipment and buildings, which are typically depreciated at a rate of 4 percent per year (bank buildings are depreciated a 2.5 percent per year.

China – A fixed percent of the value of capital assets must be deducted each year. Assets subject to depreciation include buildings, machinery, transport vehicles. Buildings are typically depreciated over 20 years; large transport vehicles and machinery over 10 years; and electronic equipment, furniture and some other assets over 5 years.

Czech Republic – Typically a fixed percent of the value of capital assets must be deducted each year. Some accelerated depreciation methods are allowed. The estimated life of general categories of capital assets for depreciation are as follows: Buildings – 30–45 years; Machinery and trucks – 8–15 years; office Equipment – 4 years; Passenger Vehicles – 4 years

England – Typically, the value of buildings and structures are deducted as a depreciation expense at a rate of 4 percent per year. Some plant and machinery is allowed a 25 percent depreciation rate. Passenger vehicles are allowed a 25 percent depreciation rate. Capital expenditure for scientific research (specifically defined) is allowed to be 100 percent deducted in the year of purchase. England also allows 100 percent of capital purchases to be deducted if the capital is installed in certain predefined zones identified by the government as hardship areas.

Italy – Capital assets must be depreciated over the life of the asset according to a fixed percent per year. Some accelerated depreciation rules exist for certain assets. Assets costing over 100 million lira (about $30,000) can be deducted in the year of purchase.

Japan – The convention is to require a fixed percentage of the value of the asset to be deducted each year during the estimated life of the asset. The rates are: Buildings – 1.6 percent per year; Factory Equipment – 7.1–10 percent per year; Office Equipment – 16.6 percent per year; Computers 12.5 percent per year; Transport Vehicles – 16.6 percent per year. Accelerated depreciation is allowed in certain cases approved by the government.

United States – Depreciation of tangible business in assets for tax purposes in the US: In the US, taxpayers may deduct a reasonable allowance for the exhaustion, wear and tear of property used in a trade or business, or of property held for the production of income. Depreciation is not allowable for property used for personal purposes, such as a residence or a car used solely for pleasure. There are also limitations on depreciation for luxury automobiles and for certain property for which business use does not exceed 50 percent.

Source: USGTA (1999d)

---

profit, and it would imply a severe intervention and manipulation of market forces. It would also significantly reduce the revenue from a profits tax.

The reason is that new enterprises often have losses in the early years, and profit is not realized until some years after starting up. Thus, many start-up enterprises would not benefit from taking a full deduction of the purchase price of new capital equipment. Requiring firms to expense capital purchases would only increase the size of the loss in early years. Although the Russian tax code allows the carry forward of losses, these provisions are somewhat restrictive, although they are getting more generous over time. Thus, new firms can reduce the present value of their future tax liabilities by depreciating capital equipment over time rather than expensing the equipment and exercising the loss carry forward provisions.

Under current law in the Russian Federation, all depreciable assets are grouped into ten groups depending on the useful life periods. The government sets forth classification of assets for each group; for those assets not included, the taxpayer chooses the classification. The law provides that the straight-line method is applied to buildings, installations and transmitters, with useful lives over 20 years. For other types of assets, taxpayers may apply either straight-line or accelerated depreciation.[8]

While depreciation is based on historic costs with annual inflation adjustments for most assets, properties are classified according to a very detailed list of types of assets, and each category has a different recovery period. In general, the recovery periods are quite generous. For example, equipment and machinery may be fully depreciated over two years, although this can be longer for certain types of equipment and machinery; structures over three years, again this can be longer depending on the type of structure; and vehicles over three to ten years depending on type and engine capacity.

In the past, depreciation allowances for tax purposes were less that the rate of economic depreciation and thus may have discouraged private investment. However, the transition to new depreciation schemes may have resulted in a loss of revenue due to the generous depreciation schemes for new and, in some cases, old assets. In some cases, taxpayers have been able to categorize assets into inappropriate categories, in part because there are so many potential classifications. The recovery periods encourage turnover of capital, which may not be a bad thing in Russia, given the need to support new investment. However, this can be costly to the government because depreciation expenses reduce taxable profits and in turn revenues from the enterprise profit tax.

Capital Income

Capital income is again a special case of the enterprise profit tax. Dividends paid by Russian organizations and received by Russian organizations and physical persons who are tax residents of the Russian Federation are taxed at rate of 9 percent. In contrast, dividends received by foreign organizations from Russian organizations or received by Russian organizations from foreign organizations are taxed at 15 percent. Interest income from a Russian government entity is taxable at 15 percent, except for interest on certain government securities, defined in the law, which is exempt. Other forms of interest are taxed at 20 percent. Capital gains are taxed at 20 percent.

Taxation of Foreign Entities

Foreign entities acting on the territory of the Russian Federation are taxable depending on the status of the entity. Those registered as permanent representative offices in Russia are taxed on par with domestic businesses. Foreign legal entities do pay a higher capital gains tax rate of 24 percent.

Policy Issues of the Enterprise Profit Tax

As with the personal income tax, the exemptions and deductions afforded enterprises under the enterprise profit tax are many and varied. In this context, it is difficult to compare the experience of these preferences in Russia to those in other countries. Nearly every country uses such preferences at the cost of reduced revenue yield and added costs of tax administration. Over the long-run, the effect on voluntary compliance is the most important aspect of the current enterprise profit tax. The attitude of firms without preferences toward firms with special treatments could well affect compliance with the tax law. The paradoxical disallowance of some legitimate business expenses also serves to increase the price of doing business in Russia and encourages firms to hide such expenditures under alternative headings.

As previously noted, the treatment of depreciation is quite generous, and while this is a policy decision, it may be useful to examine the costs and benefits of such treatment. The lack of indexing for interest deductions increases the cost of such debt over time. In situations of high inflation, the lack of indexation of such expenses significantly increases the cost of doing business in Russia, especially for start-up and expanding firms. The asymmetric treatment of capital income is also problematic. The double taxation of dividend income provides an incentive to seek out other forms of financing.

Despite the issues identified above, the enactment of recent enterprise profit tax legislation can be viewed as a significant step forward, as this piece of legislation has reduced some preferences and modernized depreciation. The level of revenue from the enterprise profit tax has grown, although it is not possible at this point to attribute it directly to increases in voluntary compliance.

THE VALUE ADDED TAX (VAT)

The arguments for consumption taxes have been well developed over time. Consumption taxes, appropriately administered, can be more efficient than income taxes in terms of their impact on the savings decisions of individuals, although both consumption and income taxes distort the labor-leisure choice. The equity of consumption taxes has been a subject of much debate. Poterba (1989) makes the case for viewing taxation in a life-cycle framework, in which case, consumption taxes in the developed world are not necessarily regressive, or progressive for that matter. Ebrill et al. (2001) pursue this logic in the context of developing countries and suggest that if we include the concept of tax burdens across generations, current consumption is in part supported by wealth accumulation of previous generations. To the extent that is true, consumption taxes themselves may in part be taxes on wealth.

There is no doubt that consumption taxes are major sources of revenue in many countries. Since consumption is income less savings, a consumption tax could be fashioned in a variety of ways. A single stage sales tax and multi-stage sales tax are two common ways of taxing consumption, commonly called a final retail sales tax and value added tax, respectively. Another form of consumption tax is a personal consumption tax, levied on the difference between personal income and savings. The most commonly used method of taxing consumption is the value added tax.

The value added tax in Russia replaced a set of turnover taxes that were used during the Soviet period. The value added tax was introduced in 1992 and quickly became one of the leading sources of revenue for the Russian Federation. The original value added tax was introduced with a rate of 28 percent, which was subsequently lowered to 20 percent for most goods and 10 percent for basic foods, certain children's items, medicines and periodic printed publications. The value added tax has a number of exemptions, but by many standards the list is not overly large. The value added tax has undergone a number of improvements since its inception; nevertheless, some policy issues still remain.

The value added tax is a federal tax, and at times has been shared with regional governments on a destination basis. Sharing on a destination basis has long been recognized as problematic, and this was recently addressed by 100 percent of the tax now being allocated to the federal budget. In the mid- to late 1990s, the Russian Federation allowed regional governments to impose a retail sales tax. The imposition of the tax was the subject of much debate. The tax was levied at a rate of up to 5 percent. The introduction of the sales tax was a government compromise aimed at appeasing regional governments when the federal government reduced the sharing of the value added tax. The federal government also planned to further reduce the tax rate of the value added tax while increasing the sales tax rate for goods subject to excises up to 10 percent. This latter proposal was ultimately rejected within the government. The sales tax eventually disappeared under legislation in 2004.

The value added tax or sales tax debate centered around two main issues: revenue adequacy for subnational governments and the advisability in terms of economic efficiency and equity of having two different consumption taxes operating in the country concurrently. We briefly summarize this debate below.

Structure of the Value Added Tax

The value added tax base is defined by law as the turnover on sales of goods, implemented works and rendered services in the Russian Federation. For most industries, taxable turnover is defined as the cost of goods sold including excise duties when applicable. The base also includes the value of imports, with relatively minor exclusions, such as items for diplomatic missions.[9]

The basic rate of the value added tax in Russia is 18 percent. A lower 10 percent tax rate is applied to a number of goods, with an emphasis on equity. These goods include basic food items which are specified by law, commodities for children, periodic printed publications, educational and scientific books, and medicines, including medicinal substances, whether or not pharmacy prepared and medical products. Many countries apply reduced rates to a very similar list of goods and services.

In the Russian Federation, there are a number of goods that are either exempt or zero-rated. Exempting a good or service from value added tax differs from zero-rating. Exempt goods are not subject to value added tax at the stage of production that is exempt. This does not remove the value added tax paid on raw materials and intermediate goods at previous stages of production. In contrast, zero-rating provides for a credit mechanism for value added tax withheld at previous stages of production and does not impose further value added tax at subsequent stages of production. For exempt goods, value added tax on inputs becomes part of the price of the goods; while for zero-rated goods, there is no tax to be passed on in terms of price differentials.

Exports and the services arising thereof, namely loading, surveillance and transportation, are zero-rated, including exports destined for member countries of the Commonwealth of Independent States (CIS), with appropriate documentation proving the exportation of goods. This treatment of exports is universally accepted as the correct way to treat exports, as zero rating reduces the tax burden on exports on international markets and thus increasing their competitiveness. A few other items are zero-rated, including foreign aid and goods and services used in the context of foreign aid.

The following goods and services are exempt from value added tax: certain medical goods, eye-glasses, medical services, student meals, certain transportation services, services of housing accommodation, educational services, repair services for historical buildings, sales of religious items, certain banking services and the sale of goods produced by entities where at least 80 percent of the members are disabled.

The list of exemptions may seem long, but since 1996, there has been a significant decrease in the list of exempt goods. The tax code was amended in 1996 to clarify the exemptions and other parts of the value added tax law. The types of exemptions allowed in the Russian Federation are similar to those used in many countries. Except for hard to tax services, the exemptions could be viewed as part of the social tax policy used in the Russian Federation. Like all exemptions, these give rise to tax evasion opportunities as it creates the opportunity to misclassify goods in order to be exempt from value added tax.

Deadlines for Paying the Tax

The administration of the tax is consistent with international experiences. Generally, the tax is paid monthly, based on the actual volume of sales of goods, but not later than the 20th of the following month. The date of sale is based on the accounting policy utilized by the enterprise.

Policy Issues of the Value Added Tax

There have been significant changes to the value added tax over the last decade.[10] The number of exempt goods and services has been reduced; the law has been clarified; and the maximum rate has been reduced. However, there are still some problematic policy issues with the Russian value added tax, but most of these are a function of tax administration. The list of zero-rated and exempt goods falls within the standards of international practice, though it is not optimal. Originally, the tax was levied on the basis of cash flow which gave rise to opportunities to defer and evade the tax. The tax is now levied on an accrual basis, and this has alleviated issues arising from non-payment and payment arrears. Differential treatment for the construction industry has been eliminated, which also reduces the complexity of the system.

Applying value added tax to very small businesses is costly to the business entities as well as the tax administration. Many countries provide for a threshold based on annual turnover; if turnover of a business is below that threshold, they are not required to become part of the value added tax system. Russia's policy is based more on the form of incorporation than on the small business ideal for value added tax thresholds. From 1992 to 1994, individual entrepreneurs with sales less than 100 thousand rubles (1992) or 500 thousand rubles (1993–94) were not subject to value added tax. In 1996, the tax code was amended so that entrepreneurs with sales less than 1 million rubles were not subject to value added tax. As from 2001, no organization, including corporations and private entrepreneurs, is subject to value added tax if sales are less than 1 million rubles. This marks a significant change and a value added tax policy that is more in line with international best practice.[11]

Finally, the value added tax is now allocated 100 percent to the federal budget.   While sharing with the regions on a destination basis was problematic, the regions had to be compensated for the significant loss of revenue as the sharing rate was phased-out over the last five years. As explained in the Appendix to this chapter, the use of a regional sales tax was one measure used to compensate the regions for their loss of value added tax revenues, although the sales tax was ultimately repealed. The sales tax 'experiment' does present some interesting policy implications that are also highlighted in Appendix 5.1.

EXCISE TAXES

Excise taxes or selective taxes on specific goods have always made an important contribution to the budgets of the Russian Federation. In the Tsarist era, excise taxes accounted for 61 percent of state revenue (Romanovskii and Ivanova, 1999). In the Soviet era, excises were also very important, but they were classified as turnover taxes. The rates differed by product. For example, the highest rate was applied to beverage alcohol at 70 percent of the wholesale cost. For other goods, the tax was levied as a unit tax. In many cases, the tax was withheld from state enterprises by the government.

Beginning in January 1992, excises were first introduced as a system of taxes to replace turnover taxes on certain types of goods. The first list of excisable goods included the sale of liquor, beer, caviar, luxury seafood and fish products, chocolate, tobacco, tires, cars, jewelry, diamonds, furs, high-quality porcelain and cut glass, rugs and carpets and natural leather garments. These traditional luxury and 'sin' taxes have been the mainstay of the excise tax system. Over time, the list of excisable goods has changed to reflect needed increases in revenue and in response to pressures from interest-group lobbies.

In the early nineties, the excise rates were determined on an ad valorem basis to account for the high rate of inflation prevailing at that time. The excise rates applied to wholesale cost of excisable products on an excise tax inclusive basis. This approach to excise computation was of great advantage to imported products, as the tax base for imports was determined as their customs value excluding excise tax. Despite high customs duties and a higher wholesale cost, imported tobacco and alcohol became more competitive and flooded the Russian market, thus reducing legal domestic production of alcohol and, as a result, reduced excise tax revenues, too.

In early 1997, ad valorem excise rates were replaced by specific ones, which reduced the disparate treatment of imports versus domestic excisable goods. From January 2001, ad valorem excise rates apply only to jewelry and natural gas. The traditional base of excisable commodities has remained stable and includes cars, beverage alcohol, tobacco products, crude oil and gasoline. In 2001, diesel fuel and oils for diesel and (or) carburetor (fuel injection) engines became taxable, and the excise rate on gasoline was indexed by three to four times, depending on the octane number of the fuel. The above steps were taken to make up for the budget losses from abolished taxes on sales of fuels and lubricants. The excise tax on crude oil was abolished from January 1, 2002. The excise tax is deductible from income in calculating the enterprise profit tax.

In 2001, a special provision was introduced for alcohol wholesalers. A tax of 50 percent of the total excise tax is now levied on wholesalers, and stamps are issued after payment by the wholesaler. The stamped products are then sent to retail markets, and the remainder of the excise is collected from the retailer. Products from countries in the Commonwealth of Independent States are exempt from excise tax, but other imports are not. Differences in tax rates among countries in the Commonwealth of Independent States and other countries has resulted in a certain amount of arbitrage on transporting goods, which is a revenue drain for Russia.

Excise revenues accrue to federal and regional budgets. The federal government receives the excise tax revenues from natural gas, fuel, cars, diesel fuels, motor oils and imports; the rest are regional, except for vodkas and liquors, which are equally divided between the federal and the regional governments.

In general, the excise tax rates are relatively low (see Table 5.2). By international standards, the list of excisable goods is reasonable, but a lack of indexation over the 1990s resulted in very low effective rates. Current law provides for indexation on an annual or semiannual basis, but this indexation is not automatic. In the past, attempts to increase the excise rates are nearly always met with opposition from the State Duma; however, a compromise with slightly lower figures is always reached.

OIL TAXATION

The oil and gas sector has represented an important part of the Russian economy since independence, comprising between 20 and 25 percent of GDP. However, despite the fact that Russia has one of the richest natural resource endowments in the world, the direct contributions of the sector to public revenues have not been commensurate with its importance in the economy. To a large extent this has been due until more recently to the fact that there has been no effective special oil tax regime capable of capturing the pure economic rents associated with the exploitation of these natural resources.[12]

Up to the introduction of the Tax Code the taxation of the oil sector in Russia had not changed much from what it had been during the Soviet Union. During the 1990s, there were three particular taxes on oil products. The first was an excise tax set in rubles per ton and with no indexation to world market prices. The second levy was a royalty for gas and oil extraction, and the third levy a mineral replacement tax for gas and oil. The two latter levies were charged on an ad valorem basis but the valuation rules to be applied were unclear and generally poorly implemented. There was also an export tariff on oil products, but it was abolished in 1996 in the rush of trade reform and elimination of all export taxes. Thus during the 1900s, prior to the introduction of the Tax Code, the most important form of taxation in the oil sector were the general taxes including the corporate income tax, value added tax and excises; these general taxes in the sector had larger revenue significance than that of the natural resource taxes.[13]

Right after the 1998 financial crisis, several revenue-increasing measures were introduced affecting the oil sector. The most important one was to reintroduce the export tariff on oil products in 1999. Later in 2000 the export tariff was linked to world oil prices through a formula. Part II of the Tax Code incorporated the formula-adjusted export tariff and also introduced a new oil extraction tax. Effective in 2002, this new tax replaced the specific taxes falling on oil products in force during the 1990s: the oil excise tax, the royalty charge, and the mineral replacement tax. The new oil

Table 5.2   Excise Tax Rates, 2005

Types of excisable goods	Tax rate (as a percentage or in rubles per unit of measurement)
Ethyl alcohol obtained from all types of raw materials (including crude ethyl spirit obtained from all types of raw materials)	19 rubles 50 kop per 1 liter of anhydrous ethyl alcohol
Alcoholic products with an ethyl alcohol content by volume exceeding 25% (with the exception of wines) and alcohol-containing products	146 rubles per 1 liter of anhydrous ethyl alcohol contained in excisable goods
Alcoholic products with an ethyl alcohol content by volume exceeding 9% and up to 25% inclusively (with the exception of wines)	108 rubles per 1 liter of anhydrous ethyl alcohol contained in excisable goods
Alcoholic products with an ethyl alcohol content by volume of up to 9% inclusively (with the exception of wines)	76 rubles per 1 liter of anhydrous ethyl alcohol contained in excisable goods
Wines (with the exception of natural wines)	95 rubles per 1 liter of anhydrous ethyl alcohol contained in excisable goods
Champagne wines and sparkling wines	10 rubles 50 kop per 1 liter
Natural wines (with the exception of champagne wines and sparkling wines)	20 rubles 20 kop per 1 liter
Beer with a normative (standardized) ethyl alcohol content of up to 0.5% inclusively	0 rubles per 1 liter
Beer with a normative (standardized) ethyl alcohol content exceeding 0.5% and up to 8.6% inclusively	1 rubles 75 kop per 1 liter
Beer with a normative (standardized) ethyl alcohol content exceeding 8.6%	6 rubles 28 kop per 1 liter
Pipe tobacco	620 rubles per 1 kg
Smoking tobacco, with the exception of tobacco which is used as raw material for the production of tobacco products	254 rubles per 1 kg
Cigars	15 rubles each
Cigarillos and filter cigarettes of a length exceeding 85 mm	170 rubles per 1,000
Filter cigarettes, with the exception of cigarettes of a length exceeding 85 mm and cigarettes of classes 1, 2, 3 and 4 according to GOST 3935-81	65 rubles 60 kop. per 1,000

Table 5.2   Excise Tax Rates (continued)

Types of excisable goods	Tax rate (as a percentage or in rubles per unit of measurement)
Non-filter cigarettes, papirosy	28 rubles per 1,000
Jewelry	5%
Motor cars with an engine capacity of up to 67.5 kW (90 h.p.) inclusively	0 rubles per 0.75 kW (1 h.p.)
Motor cars with an engine capacity exceeding 67.5 kW and up to 112.5 kW (150 h.p.) inclusively	15 rubles 20 kop. per 0.75 kW (1 h.p.)
Motor cars with an engine capacity exceeding 112.5 kW (150 h.p.), motorcycles with an engine capacity exceeding 112.5 kW (150 h.p.)	153 rubles per 0.75 kW (1 h.p.)
Petrol with an octane number of up to '80' inclusively	2,657 rubles per 1 ton
Petrol with other octane numbers	3,629 rubles per 1 ton
Diesel fuel	1,050 rubles per 1 ton
Oils for diesel and (or) carburetor (injection) engines	2,951 rubles per 1 ton

Source: Tax Code of the Russian Federation (Ministry of Finance of the Russian Federation, 2005).

extraction tax and the export tariff were much more elastic to world oil prices and so they made a significant difference in the revenues actually collected from the sector, especially given the sharp and sustained increases in oil prices over the last several years. Kwon (2003) estimated that around 80 percent of the total gain in fiscal revenues after the 1998 crisis, representing 5 percentage points of GDP, came from the oil sector. In addition, within the oil sector, it is high oil prices, as opposed to changes in the tax laws that accounted for most of the revenue changes. However, the tax reforms made oil sector taxes more elastic vis-à-vis oil prices. The biggest contributions to revenues according to Kwon (2003) came from the export tariff on crude oils, followed by the profit tax (corporate income tax), the export tariffs on oil product exports, and dividends from state oil companies. Minor revenue gains were associated with the value added tax, excises on domestic gas sales, and excises on oil products, all of which are more moderately affected by world oil prices because of price regulations or the nature of the tax bases.

An important aspect of oil sector taxation and revenues has been the establishment of the Oil Stabilization Fund in 2004. The Fund is generally credited with being quite instrumental in preserving macroeconomic stability in Russia by absorbing the large windfalls in revenues associated with the sustained high oil prices in international markets. In particular, the Fund has been effective in preventing a more rapid appreciation of the real exchange rate for the ruble and thus avoiding the results of the Dutch disease which has afflicted many oil-rich countries in the past. The Stabilization Fund had accumulated up to 1.5 trillion rubles by early 2006.[14]

Besides the dangers of Dutch disease, the vast natural endowments of natural resources have created some other problems for Russia. The most important one is the division of revenues in the context of fiscal federalism. The ownership of natural resources continues to be controversial and in practice revenues from natural resource taxes have been shared between the federal government and the two subnational tiers of government. The revenue-sharing arrangements, as discussed in Chapter 7, have changed over time and have kept some of the stakeholders unsatisfied. One complicating factor is the high level of concentration of natural resources in a very small number of subnational jurisdictions; for example, most of the oil and gas production are located in two autonomous regions (Khanty-Mansi and Yamalo-Nenets). Whether the benefits of natural resource taxes accrued to the regions or the federal government has changed over time. It would be fair to say that while regional and local interests tended to prevail during the Yeltsin years, federal interests have prevailed in the Putin years.

PROPERTY TAXATION

The gamut of taxation in Russia includes other wealth taxes, namely the property tax. In many transition and developing countries, the property tax is looked at as a potentially stable and adequate source of revenue for subnational governments. As it is consistent with both the ability to pay and the benefits received principles of taxation, the property tax is well regarded as a means to support local public services. The problem in Russia, as well as in a number of other transition countries, is that the basis of property taxation is not well established. The market for land and structures is still developing, so that valuation of property is subject to wide-ranging errors and disparities among regions. The property rights that are needed to assess taxes are not well-defined. Those facing significant property taxes in the future are not supportive of this 'new' form of taxation. These difficulties set the stage for a long development horizon for the property tax in the Russian Federation.

There are a number of property taxes in use in the Russian Federation, none of which are a Western form of real property tax.[15] There are a number of taxes based on the assets of individuals and enterprises which increase the cost of capital in the Russian Federation. The property tax on enterprises is imposed on fixed capital, non-material assets and inventory on an enterprise's balance sheet. The tax does not apply to budget institutions, agricultural producers, enterprises producing prosthetic and orthopedic devises, educational and cultural enterprises, religious associations, enterprises producing handicrafts, housing and gardening societies, enterprises with more than 50 percent disabled workforce, enterprises for rest and recreation of children under 18 and others. The tax base itself does not include the value of housing, telecommunications satellites and certain land and property received in the first two years. The maximum tax rate is 2 percent of the taxable base as established by federal legislation. The regional governments may set specific tax rates, but in case they fail to enact specific rates, the federal maximum rate applies.

The tax on property of individuals is somewhat more limited. The tax base is the value of residential property and motor vehicles. The value for structures is based on the inventory value of property, which is almost never a reflection of market value. The tax rates are set by local governments, based on maximum and minimum rates established in federal law. The rates range from 0.1 percent to 2 percent of the inventory value of the asset. For motor vehicles, the tax rate is set as a percentage of the minimum wage and varies from 3 percent of minimum wage for small boats to 30 percent of minimum wage for each passenger seat of motor-launches, motor boats and other transport vehicles. Certain individuals are completely exempt from this tax, namely veterans, heroes, the disabled and others. Other categories do not pay tax on residential property, namely retired persons; those discharged from the Army, if serving in certain places; parents and members of family of deceased, on-duty military and government servicemen; and other categories.

The land tax is based on land use and applies to owners and renters of land. The tax rate is established by law as a unit tax per hectare of land. The federal law sets average tax rates for each region, and regional authorities establish specific rates. Tax rates are indexed annually. The base of the tax is developed according to a system of norms that are not necessarily reflective of the market value of land. The rates of tax are relatively low, but the payment procedure and administration of the tax are cumbersome. Reforms of this tax have been slow in coming.

This system of property taxation adds up to an important but still relatively small amount of revenue. The real property taxes proposed in Tver and Novgorod would be market-based taxes on structures and would seek to replace the personal property and land taxes in these cities. The development of the real property tax in these regions has been difficult due to a number of issues as discussed in Chapter 2. There we saw that the development of a fiscal cadastre, establishing property rights, and intergovernmental issues and issues surrounding which level of government owns the property tax, have all hindered the development of this tax in these two pilot cities. The Ministry of Finance still has plans to roll work in Tver and Novgorod to other regions in Russia.

OTHER TAXES

Imputed or presumptive taxes are based on notional income. Imputed systems tend to calculate taxable income based on key factors which are associated with income generation, such as sales, turnover and number of employees. Applying coefficients to these factors result in the imputed tax base. Presumptive taxes tend to be calculated based on aggregate indicators, such as industry and region, or external indicators of income, with less specific calculations for particular taxpayers. More recently, countries have introduced an imputed minimum tax, which is based on a presumptive measure of taxable income, typically gross sales, turnover or assets. Such minimum taxes are usually creditable against corporate income taxes.

The objectives of imputed or presumptive tax schemes are quite straightforward. One objective is to bring small, 'hard-to-tax' enterprises and individuals into the tax net at relatively low administrative and compliance costs. The tax rate under the imputed or presumptive tax may be set at a relatively high level to encourage firms and individuals to move from the simplified system to the normal tax system. The presumptive minimum tax is aimed at reducing tax evasion and avoidance in general. This scheme imposes a relatively simple tax on assets, with the tax creditable against corporate tax liability. Such a tax can serve to ensure that all taxpayers, large and small, pay some tax, and the relative ease of administration gets these taxpayers into the tax net as well.

Russia's current tax laws include a simplified tax and an imputed tax. The simplified tax is aimed at reducing the complexity of the tax system for small businesses by replacing many taxes with one tax and also reducing accounting and reporting costs. Small businesses qualify for the simplified tax based on thresholds of gross receipts (11 million rubles in 2005 which is a relatively high standard) and the number of employees (up to 100). Certain entities are not eligible, such as banks and insurance companies.

The system is optional for small businesses and is largely regulated by regional authorities. Legal entities electing the simplified system pay customs duties, state license duties, a single social tax and value added tax. Legal entities are taxed based on gross receipts or an alternative income calculation, at the discretion of the regional authorities, at a rate of 6 percent. The alternative income tax base allows deductions for some inputs but not all, and the tax rate is 15 percent.

The regulations of the imputed income tax are specified in the tax code, but regional authorities hold powers to enact their own list of activities subject to the tax, based on the federal list, the amount of tax and other components of the computation formula, exemptions, payment and deadlines procedures and other features. The tax applies to a variety of industries, as specified in the law. A tax rate of 15 percent is applied to imputed income, which is calculated via a complex formula. The formula is based on, among other things, the following factors: location, type of services, quality of premises, distance from highway, inflation and seasonality. The actual calculation is at the discretion of regional authorities. The tax takes the place of most taxes, with the exception of state duty and customs duty, license and registration duties, tax on vehicles, land tax, tax on purchase of foreign currency, withheld income tax, value added tax and social tax.

Russia's current law on imputed and simplified taxes is quite different from those of many other countries employing an imputed or presumptive tax. Russia's two imputed tax systems are relatively unique in the following ways:

- The imputed system extends to many types of businesses regardless of size.
- The number of taxes which are subsumed under the imputed (uniform) tax is more expansive than that found in most countries.
- The imputed tax law requires full accounting by taxpayers, which does not simplify the system for small taxpayers.

With regard to international practice, Russia's imputed income tax is more typical of a presumptive minimum tax rather than an imputed tax. Russia's simplified tax could be adapted to bring the small, hard-to-tax enterprises into the tax net by adjusting the threshold and the accounting requirements. The regional government experience with these taxes suggests that the lack of clarity in federal law is causing problems with the administration of this tax. In some regions, there have been claims that the complications of the tax far outweigh any of the benefits. Ironically, neither government nor business generally finds these taxes to be simplifications of the system.[16]

While there are numerous other taxes, an important change is related to the social taxes. Chapter 24 of the Tax Code defines the unified social tax: a tax that eliminated myriad payroll taxes in favor of a simplified system. The base of the tax is effectively payroll, and the tax is paid statutorily by the employer only. The tax rate is regressive with three tiers: 26 percent for annual income up to 260,000 rubles; 10 percent for income from 260,000 to 600,000 rubles per year; and 2 percent for income above 600,000 rubles per year. The revenue from this tax is distributed to three accounts: the federal budget, medical insurance fund and social insurance fund of the Russian Federation.

CONCLUSIONS

This chapter has focused on the details of the major taxes currently in effect in the Russia Federation and has provided the context of their evolution over time. The system has come very far since the early days of transition. Most of the major taxes have been rationalized in a way that conforms to international norms: tax bases have been broadened, and the number of exemptions has been pared down. While one could quibble with the structure of taxation in the Russian Federation in terms of certain tax rates and various exemptions, many of the remaining weaknesses in the system are a function of the tax administration and intergovernmental fiscal relations. The next two chapters are devoted to these two issues.

NOTES

1. The terms personal income tax and personal income tax are used interchangeably although, as pointed out by Goode (1984), as corporations and other legal entities are 'persons' under the law.
2. See McLure (1992) and McLure and Zodrow (1996) for a discussion of the differences between consumption and income tax bases.
3. In 1999, the progressive rate structure applied rates of 12, 15, 20, 25 and 35 percent. The rate of 45 percent for incomes over 300,000 rubles was adopted in 1999 but was never enforced. In 2000, the rates were flattened to 12, 20, and 30 percent.
4. Under Chapter 23, Part II of the Russian Federation Tax Code, enforced from January 2001.
5. The larger the share of capital income in the personal income tax base, the less fitting the tax is as a local tax. This is due to the great mobility of capital and the difficulty with administering such an income source.
6. While wages may be quite 'sticky' the effect of inflation is still to push individuals into the tax net whether or not they have an increase in real income.
7. USGTA (1999d).
8. The straight-line method of computing the depreciation deduction assumes that the depreciation sustained is uniform during the useful life of the property. The cost or basis, less estimated salvage value, is deductible in equal amounts over the estimated useful life. An asset may not be depreciated below its salvage value.

9.   Peculiar to the original Soviet model value added tax was the fact that imports were not covered by tax. This feature was reformed early in the transition.
10. For example, from July 2001 the value added tax applies the destination method for trade among the countries of the Commonwealth of Independent States. Previously, exports within the Commonwealth of the Independent States were treated as domestic sales so they were subject to value added tax.
11. The history of the value added tax treatment of small businesses is a prime example of the difficulty in imposing any tax policy in Russia. In 1994, President Yeltsin ruled (Presidential Ruling 2270) that all individual entrepreneurs would not be subject to the value added tax (no thresholds implied). But, the Tax Code was not amended to reflect the ruling, which subsequently was imposed (or not) based on the discretion of the tax administrators.
12. See Bosquet (2002).
13. In other oil-producing countries the bulk of oil revenues come from special tax regimes including the Production Sharing Agreement or similar deals such as cost-sharing arrangements or licensing agreements. Russia had passed a Law on Production Sharing Agreement in 1995, but it did not apply practically to any major oil producers, in part because of the uncertainty about the fiscal rules that would apply (Kwon, 2003).
14. So far the resources in the Fund have been managed conservatively and held as a ruble account at the Central Bank and the current law only permits investment in safe and highly liquid foreign government bonds. See Spilimbergo (2005).
15. From 1997 the cities of Novgorod and Tver were engaged in an ongoing experiment to implement a new market-based real property tax. The experiment was extended to 2003.
16. In late December 2001 Russian President Vladimir Putin expressed his concern about small businesses environment in Russia. Through the first half of 2002 all parties concerned developed proposals for reform. The efforts resulted in adopting Chapter 26 'Simplified System of Taxation', effective January 1, 2003.

APPENDIX 5.1: THE REGIONAL SALES TAX

In 1998, a regional sales tax was added to the list of allowable revenue items for regional governments of the Russian Federation. A previous experiment allowed for a regional sales tax until 1996. The reintroduction of the sales tax in 1998 was a government compromise aimed at appeasing regional governments when the federal government reduced the sharing of the value added tax. The federal government also planned to further reduce the tax rate of the value added tax while increasing the sales tax rate for goods subject to excises up to 10 percent. This latter proposal was ultimately rejected within the government. The sales tax itself was ultimately eliminated. In 2001, the tax raised over 45 billion rubles for subnational governments. This is equivalent to 8.5 percent of total subnational tax revenues for 2001. The tax revenue from the sales tax grew by over 133 percent from 1999 to 2001, due to increased usage and increased administration of the tax.

The 1998 introduced federal legislation guiding the sales tax gave significant authority to the regional governments to impose the tax, determine the tax base, and set the rate (up to 5 percent). The law (Federal Law No. 150-FZ) was somewhat vague and ambiguous regarding the base of the tax. In many regions, this opening was seized, resulting in significant differences in the sales tax base among regions imposing the tax (in 1999, over two-thirds of the 89 regions imposed the tax as a result of the 1998 legislation).

The ambiguity of the law as well as poor legal drafting provoked numerous claims by businessmen. Those claims, in particular the ones from Chelyabinks and Kirovks regions, Chuvash Republic, and the Arbitration Counrt of Chelyabinsk province, were considered by the Russian Federation Constitutional Court in January 2001. The Constitutional Court supported the majority of the claims and supported the sales tax as a regional tax, but ruled that the legislation had to be rewritten so as to remove ambiguities about the object of taxation and the actual tax base. The new sales tax legislation was adopted as a separate Chapter 27 of the Tax Code. The chapter was effective from January 1, 2002 until December 31, 2003. The revised law presents an interesting case study of the evolution of tax law in the Russian Federation and it eliminated the shortcomings of the previous version, namely:

• Chapter 27 provided that legal entities and individual entrepreneurs pay sales tax if they sell goods (works, services) in the Russian Federation region where the sales tax was introduced, that is if a sale takes place in a region where no sales tax is established, then no tax liability arises;
• Sales tax applied to sales of goods (works, services) paid by cash or credit card. As opposed to the old rules, no tax was assessed on sales paid from individuals' bank accounts. The transfer of goods (works, services) in exchange for other goods (works, services) would be excluded from sales tax;
• The maximum sale tax rate was set to 5 percent. The regions could reduce their rates;
• The regions lost their right to establish supplementary lists of exempt transactions. The list, set by the new sales tax legislation, (Chapter 27) was exhaustive.

The tax object was defined as sales to individuals of goods (works, services) on the territory of the region. Sales of goods (works, services) were deemed taxable providing they were for cash and credit/debit cards. A list of exempt goods included basic necessities and hard to tax items (bread, milk and dairy products, medicines, children's clothing and footwear, immovable property, educational goods and services, periodicals, child care services, financial services, public services). This list is quite similar to the value added tax exempt list.

Policy Issues of the Sales Tax

While the sales tax base as interpreted in 2001 was reasonable, certain policy and administrative provisions of the tax proved problematic for the regional governments. First, the previous ambiguous law gave rise to very different types of sales taxes across the federation. While the newer law changed that, there were many differences across the country. For example, many of the regions exempt bread and other basic foodstuffs, but in some cases, these are exempted if they are produced within the region.

Second, regions had to give up a number of local taxes to impose the sales tax. In more than one region, the estimated revenue effect of the sales tax would be negative due to the loss of important local taxes. Thirdly, the definition of nexus did not allow the imposition of use taxes. If one oblast had a sales tax and a neighboring oblast did not have a sales tax, purchases made in the non-taxing region were never subject to tax. This of course encouraged 'border bleeding' or shopping across regional lines and may be significant for certain oblasts. In the US, a use tax is coupled with the retail sales tax to allow states to impose a tax on the 'use' of an item in the taxing state. Use taxes are administratively feasible only when the tax administrations can work together, when the goods purchased are relatively expensive and when some secondary procedure (such as automobile registration) can be used to increase compliance.

Also, while there was a provision exempting business purchases from tax, it was incomplete, creating obvious incentive problems. Business purchases by entrepreneurs were taxable as the exemption is for 'legal entities'. One of the last policy issues associated with the sales tax was the requirement that the tax not be reported separately to the consumer. Prices had to be listed as sales-tax inclusive, thus reducing the transparency of the system. In some regions, this policy was not fully adhered to as a number of businesses gave receipts with pre-tax prices reported and the sales tax reported separately.

Value Added Tax and Sales Tax Together [1]

The value added tax (VAT) and the retail sales tax (RST) are, at least in theory, alternative ways of taxing sales to consumers. By comparison, a turnover tax applies to all (non-exempt) sales, including those to business. A tax on consumption must be applied only to sales to households; it cannot be applied to sales to business, including sales of capital goods. The reason for this objective is explained below. The value added tax and retail sales tax use different mechanisms to achieve this objective.

- *Retail sales tax.* An ideal retail sales tax achieves the objective of exempting sales to business directly; it is applied only to sales to households and exempts all sales to businesses. In practice all extant retail sales taxes are imposed on many sales to business, which increases the price of inputs in the production process. Note that this is a matter of administration and structure, not of the economics of the tax.
- *Value added tax.* The value added tax achieves taxation of consumption in a different manner. A value added tax is collected on virtually all sales. Taxation of business purchases is eliminated by allowing registered traders to deduct (take 'input credit' for) taxes paid on purchases from tax due on sales. Thus the only tax that is not eliminated by input credits is that paid by consumers.

The problem of eliminating tax on business purchases

The retail sales tax suffers from a basic administrative problem: how to achieve the objective of exempting sales to business (by suspending taxation of business purchases), without opening the door to evasion by households claiming to make business purchases. (In addition, there is the political problem that there is often pressure not to exempt all sales to business, thus converting the retail sales tax into a turnover tax.) Attempting to exempt all purchases by business places the vendor in the unenviable position of determining whether each sale is taxable or legally exempt and creates an incentive for the vendor to 'look the other way' when a household purchase masquerades as a business purchase. This problem can be ameliorated by the issuing of 'suspension certificates' by the tax authorities. Such a certificate identifies: (i) the purchaser as a registered business eligible to make exempt purchases, and (ii) the business use of the item which makes it exempt. In this case vendors do not have to make the decisions themselves regarding what purchases ought to be exempt. However, auditors still must trace exempt sales to the purchaser to determine whether they are for legitimate business expenses.

By comparison, under the value added tax, since all sales are taxable, the vendor does not need to make the distinction between taxable and exempt sales, but must account for tax paid on purchases, in order to claim input credits. Although it operates indirectly to remove tax on business inputs, for both administrative and political reasons, the value added tax achieves the objective of avoiding taxation of sales to business much more thoroughly than does the retail sales tax.

Exemptions and zero-rating

The concept of exemption is straightforward under either the retail sales tax or the turnover tax; the sale of a particular good or service is simply not taxed. The situation is not so clear under the credit-invoice value added tax. One must distinguish between exemption and zero-rating and according to the stage of the production-distribution process (retail or pre-retail). If a sale is exempt, there is no tax, and no credit is allowed for tax paid at prior stages of the production-distribution process. By comparison, if a sale is zero-rated, there is no tax but credit is allowed for tax paid at prior stages.

If a retail sale is exempt, it nonetheless bears value added tax from prior stages. Moreover, if a pre-retail sale is exempt, the aggregate tax on the retail sale is greater than in the absence of exemption, not less. By comparison, zero-rating of retail sales eliminates all tax and zero-rating of pre-retail sales has no effect on the aggregate amount of tax on retail sales; in either case the aggregate tax is determined by the tax rate imposed at the retail stage.

Administration and compliance costs of dual central value added tax/subnational retail sales tax systems.

Both the retail sales tax and the value added tax involve considerable administrative and compliance costs, especially for small businesses. Clearly, imposing both systems on business does increase significantly their compliance costs. Because the two systems operate quite differently, implementing both also increases tax administration costs significantly.

How much compliance and administration costs are increased by a dual value added tax/ retail sales tax system depends crucially on how different the bases of the two taxes are. These costs are substantially higher if the exemptions provided by the retail sales tax and the value added tax are not substantially identical. In this case, vendors would need to distinguish between four possible combinations of tax treatments: taxable under taxes, exempt under both and taxable under one, but not the other. To minimize this type of complexity, the bases of the two bases should be coordinated, so that a given sale to households is either taxed or exempt under both taxes.

Economic Effects of Value Added Tax and Retail Sales Tax

Value added tax

Because the value added tax is, in effect, levied only on sales to consumers, it is essentially neutral with regard to most economic decisions. That is, it does not affect the cost of capital and thus does not distort the choice between saving and consuming, the capital-labor ratio or other production decisions. It does, of course, raise the price of consumer goods. This is an important point to understand because of the widespread perception in

Russia that the value added tax is paid by businesses and that this type of tax distorts business decisions.

Retail sales tax

A pure retail sales tax (one that is applied only to consumer goods) would have the same effects as a value added tax. In fact, in the real world retail sales taxes are far less pure than value added taxes. It has been estimated that about 40 percent of the retail sales taxes levied by the states of the United States and some of the provinces of Canada fall on sales to business, including many capital goods. Thus they distort many choices: the saving/consumption choice, the capital-labor ratio and production decisions. (See also the discussion of the effects of turnover taxes, which an impure retail sales tax resembles.) Moreover, unlike the typical value added tax, retail sales taxes typically exempt many services provided to consumers, thereby distorting consumer choices.

Value Added Tax/Retail Sales Tax in the Intergovernmental Context

Two general principles for the proper design of a system of intergovernmental fiscal relations have a significant bearing on the choice between the value added tax and the retail sales tax. The first is the principle of revenue sufficiency or vertical balance between the federal and subnational governments. According to this principle, subnational governments should have revenue sources that are proportionate to their expenditure responsibilities. This revenue sufficiency for subnational governments can be achieved through the exclusive assignment of taxes to subnational governments and also through revenue sharing in federal taxes or transfers from the federal government.

The second principle of intergovernmental fiscal relations is that of revenue autonomy. This means that subnational governments should have a significant degree of discretion in raising their own revenues. Without this discretion a decentralized system of intergovernmental finances foregoes the efficiency gains associated with responsibility and accountability to local taxpayers and the ability to match local residents' preferences for the level of subnational public services.

The value added tax is about the poorest choice to fulfill either of those two principles. The introduction of regional value added taxes to provide regional tax autonomy can easily lead to chaotic situations, as the experience of Brazil has shown in recent years. In pure technical terms, the value added tax may also be a poor tax to be shared with subnational governments on a derivation basis. The crediting and debiting of value added tax in different regions make the value added tax absolutely unsuited for direct revenue sharing on a derivation basis. Russia's federal government has shared value added tax revenues with the regions since the beginning of the transition. Besides the arbitrariness of crediting and debiting of value added tax across regions, the value added tax has not truly been shared on a derivation basis (that is according to where the tax is generated) but rather it has been paid according to the place of registration of business firms.

In the past few years, the potential for a subnational value added tax has attracted more positive attention than in the previous decades in the international arena. New legislation in India has mandated the development of a subnational value added tax, although the few specific plans have yet been made to institute a subnational value added tax. The advent of the European Union has led to unique opportunities to develop a value added tax that crosses international borders. Canada's system of Harmonized Sales Tax and Quebec's sales tax are two examples of the coexistence of sales and value added taxes. In these cases the federal government plays an important role in assisting or carrying out the tax administration. In the case of Quebec, there is no attempt to tax inter-provincial purchases made by final consumers (Bird and Gendron, 2001). While Canada, Brazil and Argentina offer some examples of the potential to impose regional value added taxes, in most respects a value added tax at the subnational level would entail high administrative requirements and high administrative costs.

Because of these problems, there is a very strong case to be made in favor of the full assignment of value added tax revenues to the federal government, as is currently done. This was not an easy political decision, but now that value added tax is fully assigned to the federal government, the issue of revenue sufficiency becomes even more important for subnational governments.

A subnational retail sales tax, on the other hand, is in theory an adequate instrument to fulfill the two principles of revenue sufficiency and revenue autonomy for subnational governments. A retail sales tax can be a reliable source of revenue for subnational governments and it does not require a high degree of coordination among those governments. In theory, a retail sales tax could also be more easily shared among different levels of government. The problem with this solution lies in the costs of administering and complying with a regional retail sales tax when a value added tax already exists at the federal level. In addition, there are many other reasonable alternatives besides a retail sales tax for providing revenue autonomy to subnational governments. One such alternative used in many countries, and often recommended in Russia, is a subnational government personal income tax with some degree of rate discretion that piggybacks on the federal personal income tax. This option appears less attractive than the retail sales tax option because in Russia subnational governments have historically been assigned almost the entirety of revenues collected from the personal income tax, although there have been changes to this intergovernmental arrangement in many years.

The introduction of an intergovernmental fiscal relations perspective in the choice between the value added tax and the retail sales tax reveals the existence of worthwhile but also conflicting objectives and the possible need for a compromise. While the value added tax may be superior to the retail sales tax from economic efficiency and tax administration viewpoints, the goals of revenue sufficiency and revenue autonomy for subnational governments cannot be fulfilled with the value added tax choice under the current tax administration in the Russian Federation. These issues offer food for thought for the future discussions of consumption-based taxation in the Russian Federation.

Appendix Note

1.   Much of this discussion is taken from USGTA (1998b).

6. The Evolution of Tax Administration and Tax Morale

Few today would question the idea that the principal determinant of a country's economic success is the quality of its institutions and policies. This is especially true in the area of taxation, where the distinction between policy and administration is not as clear as in other areas of economic policy. Good tax administration is good tax policy. The best tax policy which cannot be enforced by the tax administration cannot be regarded as good policy. These principles have taken special importance in the Russian Federation over the transition years and not only for the success of federal tax policy but also for the success of intergovernmental fiscal relations reform. The federal tax administration from the start has been in charge of assessing and collecting most of the taxes assigned to regional and local governments.

The first goal of the chapter is to present an overview of the structure and evolution of tax administration in the Russian Federation from its rocky start in the early years of the transition to the most recent accomplishments following extensive efforts to modernize tax administration institutions. The second goal of the chapter is to document the effectiveness of tax administration on taxpayer compliance as measured by tax arrears and tax evasion and also by the evolution of tax morale, that is, the general attitude of taxpayers toward paying taxes.

The chapter is organized as follows. In the first part we review the changes in tax administration institutions before and after the approval of Part I of the Tax Code, which is the part of the code that dealt with tax administration and compliance issues. In the second part of the chapter we review the performance of the tax system, including the tax arrears, tax evasion and the evolution of tax morale.

THE EARLY YEARS IN TAX ADMINISTRATION

The transformation from a planned socialist system to a market economy left Russia with an enormous handicap in the area of tax collection and enforcement. Before its independence from the Soviet Union, Russia never had a tradition of voluntary tax compliance. However, this does not mean that tax enforcement may have been inadequate in Soviet times. Although the tax administration had a small capacity prior to 1992, the relatively small number of taxpayers meant that the state could conduct a reportedly 100 percent audit each year to ensure compliance. Restrictions on payment methods and the monopolistic role of the state banks facilitated administration and enforcement. In addition, the state could, and often did, retroactively adjust the structure of taxes and administrative procedures to meet its perceived revenue needs. There was little opposition to otherwise controversial tax measures because the state served the dual role of owner of enterprises and tax collector. On the other hand, tax administration in the previous regime was quite fragmented. Collections and enforcement were performed by local offices which then passed a share of the collections up to the next higher level of government. At any rate, despite these problems, the other tools and powers that socialist planning provided to tax administrators were sufficient to ensure that the tax administration system was functional and quite adequate for the previous economic regime.

Several features of the past regime left a problematic legacy for Russia's incipient tax system which started in 1992. Under the Soviet tax system, very few individuals actually filed tax returns, paid taxes during transactions or were aware of the existence of turnover taxes or profit taxes. In addition, personal income taxes were practically nonexistent. Taxes were mainly paid through opaque retention systems in the course of financial transactions and they were difficult to identify from other discretionary actions of the government, such as fixing prices for most commodities and production inputs. This initial condition or legacy presented the new tax administration authorities with a very significant challenge. In the transition to a market economy, the tax administration system would have to rapidly adopt a system based on voluntary compliance and self-filing, concepts that had been entirely foreign to the Soviet tax system. .

The enormity and difficulty of transforming the previous system of tax administration to the demands of a market-based economy hampered the ability of the Russian government to generate sufficient amounts of revenues for the budget during practically the first decade of the transition. However, the process of modernization was slow in coming and traditional approaches persisted for many years. The organization of the tax administration in Russia continued to preserve for much of the 1990s the structure it had inherited from the Soviet Union. The administration apparatus was highly deconcentrated across the territory. At the bottom of the organization there were the 'territorial tax inspectorates' (TTIs) which employed most of the personnel, followed by intermediate-level organizations, the 'regional tax inspectorates' or RTIs, which function to coordinate information flows from the territorial tax inspectorates and at the center in Moscow there was State Tax Service (STS) which was extremely thinly staffed.[1] The entire tax administration from the territorial tax inspectorates to the headquarters of the State Tax Service in Moscow was organized along traditional lines by type of tax or type of taxpayers.[2]

At the territorial tax inspectorate level, taxpayers were assigned to deal only with specific tax inspectors, who were supposed to provide advice and assistance with the filing of tax returns; actually, taxpayers were expected to have their declaration validated in face-to-face meetings with their designated inspectors. In turn, those tax inspectors undertook a cameral audit of the returns, but often a significant amount of negotiations ensued, giving rise to different opportunities for corrupt practices. The advantages of a self-assessment system, in which taxpayers fully complete their tax declarations without intervention by tax inspectors, became very soon obvious but many years would pass before this would be achieved. Modern technology was very slowly introduced. Even in the late 1990s when many offices had been computerized, most often computers were used mostly for producing reports and information for the upper-level management while the basic information was still processed manually.

Progress was also slow in other areas of tax administration. For example, audit selection and practices advanced little during the 1990s; field audit rates had always been quite high by international standards but with limited effectiveness because of the lack of depth and prior preparation for the audit. Audit selection criteria lacked sophistication and were based on a combination of local knowledge and referrals from other agencies (primarily from customs and Tax Police); later on some selection criteria transmitted by the regional and central headquarters were introduced.

Taxpayer services were an extremely deficient area of tax administration for many years. Russia's tax administration authorities were slow in internalizing the lesson learned by many western tax administrations in the 1980s and 1990s. This lesson is that taxpayer services can be as effective as or more effective in increasing taxpayers' voluntary compliance than the threat of enforcement actions. In a way taxpayer services of some sort did exist. As indicated above, taxpayers actually met in person with their designated inspectors to fill out and review the tax return together. However this truly only added to taxpayer compliance costs.

The high taxpayer compliance costs came from several other sources, for example, taxpayers having to wait for hours in line outside with sub-zero temperatures to pay their taxes, taxpayers having to pay for forms and instructions which were routinely not available, or confronting filing procedures that were complex and vague and continuously changing.

The other side of the coin of these labor-intensive processes was high administration costs. The traditional practices allow little time for tax administrators to facilitate taxpayer compliance and to carry out audits to detect non-compliance and fraud. The traditional practices also meant an inefficient distribution of personnel, with overstaffed local offices and understaffed and weak central headquarters.

From the time of its creation, the State Tax Service had been in need of radical reform to transform itself from a passive, declaration- and collections-oriented organization to a pro-active, customer- and enforcement-oriented tax administration. In order to accomplish this transformation the tax agency needed to undertake several major steps. First, to evolve from an organization structured around different types of taxes and taxpayers to an organization structured around the basic functions of tax administration. Second, to completely overhaul standards and procedures in the most important functional areas of tax administration, including taxpayer services, audit, registration, collections and information systems. Third, to carry out the massive training of tax officials at all levels in modern administration techniques.

In the following paragraphs we provide a more detailed description of the problems facing the federal tax administration during the 1990s:

Organizational Issues: By the late 1990s the structure of tax administration in Russia continued to have the organizational and territorial structure it had received from the Soviet Union. Most collection and enforcement activities were still carried out by territorial tax inspectorates. The role of regional offices, the regional tax inspectorates, continued to be limited to supervising and somewhat coordinating the effort of local offices and to report aggregate data on collections to the federal authorities in Moscow. Although de jure the federal authorities had significant control over the operations and standards of regional and local inspectorates, de facto, however, this was very often not the case.

The organizational structure of territorial tax inspectorates by type of taxpayer (for example individuals, enterprises and foreigners) and by type of tax often led to duplication of tasks. Organizationally, tax inspectors were accountable to several as opposed to a single managerial or organizational authority. This reduced the level of personnel specialization and the integration of activities to realize economies of scale. The waste of available resources was apparent in many ways; for example, highly trained tax inspectors continued to perform menial, low-revenue yield tasks, such as data entry and the numerical verification of tax declarations. These quite visible inefficiencies called into question the repeated complaint from the federal tax administration authorities to the government about the lack of adequate resources for tax administration. The complaints were justified because indeed budget allocations for tax administration were small; however, the administration's own behavior and lack of efficiency took credibility from those complaints. The fact was that the tax authorities could have done much more with the available resources. This was made apparent by the fact that in regional inspectorates where functional reorganization had taken place on a pilot basis in the later half of the 1990s (Volograd and Nizhny Novgorod), administrative efficiency and revenue collections had increased visibly.

There were during this period other important organizational issues that were not adequately addressed. One of them was the role played by the so-called Tax Police and its relationship with the tax administration (the State Tax Service). The Federal Tax Police Service (*Federal'naja sluzhba nalogovoi politsii*) was established in 1993 to intensify the fight against tax evasion and under pressure to increase overall tax revenue.[3] But, as Nerre (2001) points out, the Russian tax police and especially its methods of enforcement with armed raids on firms and private homes created a negative image for the tax authorities and could have backfired. Over time, the range of activities for the tax police has been reduced toward criminal investigations and the like. Discussions ensued for many years as to whether the Tax Police should be integrated into the tax administration as is the case in many other countries, or whether it should function separately.[4] Another issue was whether the State Tax Service should be put in charge of collecting and enforcing social security contributions to the federal extra-budgetary funds.

Registration Issues: Two issues in the taxpayer registration area continued to plague the tax administration: (1) the detection of non-filers and stop-filers, and (2) the registration of new taxpayers. Few resources were made available for these tasks and practically no innovative methodology or systematic methods were used for detecting non-filers or stop-filers. For non-filers, there was no systematic canvassing and little use was made of inter-agency cooperation. The problem of stop-filers was made more difficult because of the lack of effective use of Taxpayer Identification Numbers. Taxpayers could choose to 'drop out' of the tax net with relative impunity. The lack of Taxpayer Identification Numbers for individuals made it impossible to use third-party information to detect evaders. The problem was often aggravated by the lack of cross-comparability of information systems in tax offices vertically and horizontally. For example, stop-filers that moved to different locations under another territorial tax inspectorate could be assured that in the vast majority of cases their tax records would not be electronically transferred to their new territorial tax inspectorate.

Collections Issues: The effectiveness of collections was also quite low. For many years, tax arrears represented a substantial problem for tax collections in Russia. As we discuss further below in this chapter, there were multiple causes for these arrears, not the least of which was the existence of, at times, considerable governmental arrears with some taxpayers. From the perspective of tax administration, the problem was compounded because the monitoring of collections was, in many cases, unproductive. The focus of collections was on the current revenue stream (what was owed) as opposed to the potential revenue stream (what could be effectively collected). In addition, the reporting of arrears routinely contained only aggregate information with little detail on the profiles of arrears cases (how old they were, and so on). This made it more difficult to impart rationality and greater effectiveness to collection efforts.

Another practice that affected collections negatively was the tradition – carried over from Soviet times – of setting revenue targets for each tax office. It seems that once revenue targets were fulfilled, there was much less motivation to vigorously pursue the collections of delinquent accounts. Regional and local tax administration offices were also known to adopt an array of techniques to satisfy the official quotas in some artificial ways; for example, local inspectorates put pressure on taxpayers for increased advanced payment of taxes. Of course, these practices led to substantial revenue declines in the next period. One main reason for the lasting practice of setting revenue targets is that the federal tax administration authorities and the Ministry of Finance were remiss in adopting modern statistical techniques to analyze revenue trends and for forecasting. The lack of forecasting models in some cases led to unrealistic revenue targets, with demoralizing effects on tax officials.

Increasing collections required from the State Tax Service a series of measures to reorient resources from simply processing taxpayer declarations and payments to pro-active collection programs in the areas of

- Non-Registration
- Taxpayer Identification Numbers
- Non-Filing or Stop-Filing
- Delayed Filing
- Non-Payment/Delayed Payment of Declared Tax Liability

In addition, the problem of collections required continued political will by the federal authorities to enforce rules with all big delinquent taxpayers in arrears. The monitoring and enforcement of collections with small taxpayers (stop-filers, non-filers and those in arrears) required foremost computerized procedures. One of the main technical issues that needed to be solved was obtaining taxpayer information from the taxpayers themselves and from third parties regarding taxable transactions. The development of protocols for accessing third party information from Goskomstat, regional statistical committees and other governmental agencies (Customs, Extra-budgetary funds) was slow in coming.

Audit Issues: There are some historical reasons for this area being the slowest to reform. In Soviet times, taxpayers were restricted to a single account and state banks were used to monitor compliance. Those instruments, of course, disappeared with the transition to a market economy. For many years of the transition most audit work was mainly limited to conducting 'cameral' or numerical audits of taxpayer declarations. This was reflected not only in the organizational structure of local tax inspectorates (which contained a Cameral Audit Department) but also in the audit policy of the federal authorities (for example, establishing that every taxpayer must be 'audited' within a two-year time period). Office audits were often perfunctory and did not generate significant amounts of revenues.

A different problem was created by the weak control exercised by Moscow authorities over the regional and local tax administration offices. For example, various attempts by the federal tax administration authorities to ensure standards for the conduct of cameral and field audits were routinely ignored by regional and local tax inspectorates and deemed to be unrealistic and unaware of local conditions. This situation had complex roots. On the one hand, the federal headquarters did not have the sufficient qualified staff to adequately plan and monitor a modern audit program. Also, there was a near complete dearth of taxpayer information at the national and regional levels. Practically all data on individual taxpayers was in the hands of the local inspectorates. The lack of a common information system even within regional inspectorates practically eliminated any ability to obtain concrete information on large numbers of taxpayers and, therefore, to use this information to formulate local and regional audit plans, and much less a National Audit Plan, determining *ex ante* what groups of taxpayers are more likely to evade. The inability to tailor audit programs to local conditions resulted in the use of a 'shotgun' approach to auditing: auditing specific sectors in the forlorn hope of detecting evasion.

Taxpayer Services: This area of tax administration was virtually nonexistent for many years during the transition. To be fair, taxpayer service was an unknown concept under the previous system of the Soviet Union. In general, taxpayer familiarity with the tax system remained low. In fact, taxpayers often did not even have access to elementary regulations, tax forms or filing instructions without having to pay for them first.[5] Nevertheless, the interest of federal officials in creating a taxpayer services section in local tax inspectorates had been high and actually, some local inspectorates took their own measures to promote taxpayer education. There was awareness of the potential of good customer service and taxpayer education to lead to increased compliance. However, while well intentioned, at times these measures were a reversion to the previous system in which, for example, local inspectorates required taxpayers to submit their business plans for approval. In the few instances where taxpayer services did exist, tax administration officials had to combat the confusion created by rapid changes in the tax laws and the deep-rooted mistrust by taxpayers of government institutions.

Information Issues: Although the authorities from early on injected resources for the development of information systems in tax administration, the application of these resources was often haphazard. The result was a multitude of tax administration information systems in use throughout the Russian Federation, the majority of which were incompatible in terms of data exchange. This incompatibility meant that information exchange between elements of the tax service did not occur, that third-party information could not be incorporated into information audits and that, in many cases, basic taxpayer information was not contained in the computer files.

The development of an adequate information system became a challenge for the State Tax Service, much like it had been in western countries several decades before. It became clear that the tax administration needed to design a unified information system, with all offices of the State Tax Service (at all levels) being able to operate using the *same* system and covering all functions including registration, audit, assessment and collections. The information system also would enable the authorities to carry out evaluations of different programs. The implementation of this program would have to wait.

PROBLEMATIC PERFORMANCE

The rough start of the tax administration was reflected in a problematic performance in different areas. In this section we review the main issues that arose during that period.

The Accumulation of Tax Arrears and Reversion to Barter

Tax arrears accumulated fast during the early years of the transition (see Box 6.1). There were multiple causes for this. For example, Berkowitz and Li (2000) argue that arrears were the result of the struggle for revenues and

---

Box 6.1   The Tangled Web of Arrears in the Russian Federation

Tax arrears, the non-payment of tax liabilities to the government, were just one
part of the system of non-payment in Russia during the 1990s. The problem of
non-payment was so pervasive that government and private enterprises
included special accounts for non-payment items in their books. Tax arrears
rose quickly, in part because firms were not paid by the government for their
services. Also, individuals did not receive wages and pensions, so both the
government and private sector firms developed wage arrears. This, in turn,
reduced the ability of individuals to comply with the tax system.

The accumulation of arrears had reached its peak in the late 1990s. Still the
types and levels of arrears as of December 2000 were significant:

Total overdue payables of enterprises (billion rubles)	1,571.5
Of which:	
To suppliers	712.5
To budget and non-budgetary funds	668.5
Total overdue receivables of enterprises	916.3
Total wage arrears	31.7
Of which:	
Budget wage arrears	4.9

---

competences among different levels of government; in many cases, regional
and local authorities intervened for the deferral of firms' tax payments to
the federal authorities. Often, they were successful in doing so because of
the *de facto* dual subordination of tax administrators. Although tax
administrators were federal employees, they received housing and other
benefits from the local authorities. A system drenched in arrears also
provided better opportunities for hiding information from the tax
administration.

Non-payment of tax liabilities to the government (tax arrears) were
mirrored by arrears from the government to private firms, state-owned
enterprises, state employees and pensioners (payment, wage and pension
arrears). Enterprise arrears include non-payments to the government (tax
arrears) as well as non-payments to suppliers (inter-enterprise arrears). In
December, 2000, the level of overall arrears had reached 1,571.5 billion
rubles, with over 42 percent accruing as tax arrears to the government.

But prior to the passage of the tax code, arrears already had started to
fall. Wage arrears, non-payment of wages by both enterprises and
government, fell faster than any other type of arrears. By December, 2000,
total wage arrears were 72 percent of the 1999 level and government wage
arrears in December 2000 were only 48 percent of their 1999 level.

The other half of the arrears story is the overdue receivables of enterprises. This category represents non-payments to enterprises for goods and services delivered – both from other enterprises as well as from the government. Large firms were principal actors in the accumulation of arrears. One of the most complete studies of this problem at the time was carried out by the Interdepartmental Balance Commission (IDBC) of the Russian government. This commission reviewed 210 enterprises with the largest tax arrears and found that as of December 1, 1997, each had tax arrears in excess of 1 billion rubles. However, surprisingly, these were generally successful enterprises in sectors such as oil and gas, utilities, nuclear power, railways, automobile manufacturing or coal mining. One of the most revealing findings of the commission was the extraordinary use of tax offsets – mutual cancellation of debts between the taxpayer and the government – by nearly every enterprise in that group. On average, these companies paid only 8 percent of accrued tax liabilities in real cash ('live money'). The rest of the taxes were paid through different tax offset schemes.

Another interesting fact was that over a long period of time, the share of tax arrears to the federal budget grew faster than the share of tax arrears to subnational governments. Frequently, this was explained by the closer allegiance of regional and local tax officials with subnational authorities than with federal authorities, despite the fact that the tax administration is nominally a federal agency. In this view, regional and local tax officials would give preference to subnational budgets when delinquent taxpayers had limited resources to pay all existing arrears. In 1998, the federal share of arrears represented 60 percent of total arrears. In the 1990s regional authorities had been suspected of manipulating tax audits and enforcement in their favor. With the advent of Putin's administration things seem to have changed around. For example, Libman and Feld (2007) argue that in the 2000s increasing bargaining power of the federal government seems to have induced tax administration in the regions to manipulate tax audit and enforcement in favor of the federal government.

The imbalance in the distribution of arrears between the federal and subnational governments also received an alternative explanation. Delinquent payments of corporate income tax liabilities, and to a lesser extent of value added tax liabilities, were the main source for the increase in arrears starting 1997. According to this view, the different rate in the accumulation of arrears can be explained by the fact that the federal government increasingly demanded the payment of taxes in cash ('live money') while regional and local governments had been more willing to accept payments in-kind and in the form of tax offsets. The higher sharing rate of the federal government in value added tax collection, 75 percent through 1998 and 89 percent for 1999, affected the accounting of arrears for different levels of government.

It is difficult to determine how or why the arrears problem began, but for many observers the high level of arrears for many years during the 1990s was just another testimony to the depth of the tax non-payment culture that existed in the Russian Federation. The persistence of these arrears and attempts of the government to 'clear the decks' through mutual offsets and tax amnesties helped to maintain a culture of tax non-compliance in the Russian Federation. It would appear that, from the start, the government was not forceful enough to stem the arrears practice. In retrospect, the most effective way to control tax arrears would have been to implement bankruptcy proceedings for delinquent taxpayers. But there were reasons why the tax authorities decided not to enforcement payments this way. Under the bankruptcy laws, tax authorities did not have first claim to proceeds. In addition, closing enterprises may have caused high unemployment rates, stopped the provision of social services that otherwise local government could not afford, or involved the worst offenders, who were politically well connected (Alexeev, 1998).

One main cause of tax arrears was government budget arrears to the rest of the economy. Poor and unrealistic budget formulation and weak budgetary controls in budget executions were the main culprits behind budgetary arrears. During 1992–96, the high inflation rates allowed actual collections to exceed easily planned expenditures and revenues in the budget. However, after inflation came under control, planned budget expenditures continued to routinely exceed any realistic expectation of tax collections. This practice was only sustainable by allowing spending units to accumulate budget arrears to suppliers and employees (Kurlyandskaya, 2001). The ability of budget organizations to run up arrears varied. A large share of the budget arrears were with public utilities. Monopolies, such as Unified Energy System (UES) or Gazprom, were prominent examples of how the government actually forced enterprises that were partially or wholly owned by the state to subsidize the government budget.

Inter-enterprise arrears also played a role in the growth of tax arrears. This interplay between inter-enterprise arrears and tax arrears was actually complex. The lack of financial intermediation, the poor enforcement of contracts and the overall lack of rule of law all contributed to the increase in inter-enterprise arrears in the economy. Enterprises that were not being paid by their clients were less likely to make timely payment of their tax liabilities. But inter-enterprise arrears also grew as a means of tax avoidance. Because enterprises are allowed to use cash accounting for their tax obligations as opposed to accrual accounting, any two enterprises could hold mutual arrears and defer tax payments on their operations without any penalty.

There is additional support for the theory that economic pressure on enterprises at least in part helped to begin the arrears run-up. Ivanova and Wyplosz (1999) find empirical support for the hypothesis that as enterprises become strapped, they run arrears to the budget and then to other enterprises and finally to their own employees. They view this impact as a long-term phenomenon, where enterprises under long-term duress were more likely to add to the arrears problem. The large barter system still in use in Russia during the 1990s also quite likely contributed to the growth in arrears.[6]

Federal government policies also contributed to the growth of tax arrears. Ironically, a set of policies designed by the federal government to combat arrears, periodic tax amnesties, seems to have worked to make the problem worse. The evidence does seem to show that arrears got decisively worse with every tax amnesty announcement by the federal authorities (Ivanova and Wyplosz, 1999). Each amnesty seems to have built up expectations that new arrears would be at least partially forgiven in the future.

The Russian tax system also responded to the arrears problem by developing tools for crediting and debiting arrears through offsets and mutual settlements. The rapid growth in tax arrears starting in 1996 was enhanced by the government practice of tax offsets. Under budgetary pressure, a resolution of the Ministry of Finance of December 1994 allowed explicitly for the first time the settlement of federal budget arrears with tax arrears owed by enterprises. Enterprises were also allowed to settle their overdue tax liabilities using different forms of securities issued by the Ministry of Finance. Starting also in 1994, the Ministry of Finance encouraged regional governments to make use of mutual offsets to settle tax arrears. Tax offsets actually took a variety of forms, including bilateral or direct offset, but also complex offsets involving a chain of taxpayers for settlement, cash and non-cash substitutes were used.

Tax offsets rapidly became regular behavior in federal and subnational budgetary practices. Despite the many problems tax offsets created, they offered many attractions. First, they allowed federal and subnational governments to maintain the fiction of higher levels of expenditures and better balanced budget execution. A key feature of tax offsets was that budget officials could overstate actual revenues by manipulating declared values. Second, offsets allowed budget officials to bypass legislative oversight of the budget. Because the budget formulation was incrementalist, relying on past expenditures to allocate resources in the new budget period, each budget agency has an incentive to protect or expand its budget through offsets. Third, the arrangement of tax offsets also allowed agencies to lighten the effects of budget sequestering. Fourth, the use of offsets, more importantly, allowed regional but also the federal governments to customize tax burdens for selected enterprises, in effect subsidizing many of them and allowing negative value added activities to survive. Fifth, the use of tax offsets also created opportunities for graft and corruption. On the side of taxpayers, tax offsets were attractive because they could lower actual taxes through the exaggeration of prices used in offset and because they facilitated the sale of otherwise unsellable goods, all leading to personal profit (Kurlyandskaya, 1999).

The main impacts of mutual offsets were a loss in real revenues since prices were exaggerated and goods were purchased that otherwise would not be, and they created incentives for taxpayers, those that can pay their taxes on time and those that cannot, to accumulate more tax arrears. With these problems becoming more obvious, and under pressure from international lending institutions, the federal government started a series of half-hearted measures to control or get rid of tax offsets. A resolution of the federal government of April 1996 prohibited the use of non-monetary forms of payment (including securities) to the federal budget. In March 1997, the Duma passed the Law on Drafts and Notes which prohibited all levels of government from practicing offsets, although the federal government could still use 'monetary offsets'. The latter were given up in February 1998, under heavy pressure from the IMF. The federal government got back to using tax offsets after the financial crisis of 1998. At the subnational level things evolved more slowly. After the Duma prohibited the use of promissory notes in offsets, the regions continued the practice of offsets using alternative tools, such as regional clearing centers for arrears.

The upturn in economic activity in 1999 driven by import substitution and improving international prices for oil finally slowed down the growth of arrears and tax offsets. In 1999-2000, about 26,000 enterprises were allowed to restructure their arrears with the federal government for a total of 90 billion rubles, with approximately half represented by accumulated interest and penalties. In this operation about 74 percent of the enterprises that requested restructuring were actually allowed to do so. This was a controversial move with some observers arguing that federal policy had gotten unduly soft. In actuality, Government Ruling #410 of 2001 on the restructuring of tax arrears contained softer provisions than any time before. The goal of the government was to send a clear message that this was the last chance for those in tax arrears to get regularized and function in the market system or otherwise they would need to close up their business.

At the same time that tax arrears and other arrears in the economy were developing, a large sector of the economy reverted to barter in their transactions. Rather than paying in cash, companies paid each other with commodities they had produced or that they had acquired from a third party. Not long afterwards, taxpayers were fulfilling their tax obligation in kind, especially at the local and regional levels. Actually, there had been a long tradition of this in Russia. Well after the 1918 Revolution peasants in Russia had been fulfilling their tax obligation exclusively by transfers in kind. Even in Soviet times, they had to deliver agricultural goods to the state at a price below producer costs as one part of their tax duties. Accordingly, settling tax obligation and especially tax arrears 'in kind' was a familiar method of payment to the Russian people.[7] But barter seem to have caught particular impetus during the earlier years of the transition; the better ability to evade taxes was no doubt a reason for the popularity of barter, but other reasons may have been at work. For example, Woodruff (1999) argues that one main reason for barter was the legal prohibition early in the transition for companies selling commodities 'below market prices', where that meant prices that always yielded a profit for the seller. To get around the possible fine and taxes on the 'potential profits' firms cut their prices by overvaluing the commodities they received in the payment from the bartered exchange. The process started a slippery slope that led to major companies, such as public utilities, to accept barter and eventually subnational governments and the federal authorities followed suit.

The practice of barter led to the inefficient allocation of resources and set the Russian economy in an inferior economic dynamic path which contributed to dismal performance of the real economy in the 1990s. Some observers had argued at the time that arrears provided low-cost financing for enterprises and government. The fact is that in any economy, including the Russian economy, economic agents learn and develop forward expectations on payments from transactions. Eventually, the cost of the arrears gets internalized in contracts and those advantages disappear. For example, local governments ended up paying considerable price premiums for gas or electricity services. An intriguing question is why the practice of arrears endured and grew over a considerable period of time. In a normal economy, arrears from one client are a one-time phenomenon or they lead to significant increases in the cost of provision to any government or enterprise. Obviously, there were strong built-in incentives for their repeated use among economic agents. Arrears helped enterprises that were at the short end of the arrears to evade taxes or it gave budget officials an indirect way to expand their own budgets.

Corruption in Tax Administration

During the early 1990s, the operation of tax administration in many ways facilitated and, at times, encouraged corrupt practices by tax officials.

Wages for tax administrators were extremely low, tax penalties excessively high, the tax laws were particularly obscure and the contacts between taxpayers and tax officials mandated and very frequent.[8] In this environment, corruption easily grew and it was quite common for tax officials to accept bribes from taxpayers to lower their tax liabilities. It would have seemed to have been common practice that '[i]n return for bribes, regional governments offered to protect enterprises against central tax collectors'.[9] On the other hand, the job of tax inspector was not only poorly paid but it also was very dangerous. For example, in 1996 it was reported that 26 Russian tax inspectors were killed and 74 injured, while 6 were kidnapped and 41 saw their houses burn down.

Levin and Satarov (2000) calculate that the level of corruption in the early years of the Russian transition exceeded the total expenditures on science, education, health care, culture, and art, and that, in some industrial branches, criminal groups spent up to 50 percent of their revenues to bribe officials. They also report that in 1995 there were 270 cases of illegal tax inspector activities that were exposed.

Corruption was rampant in other areas of the public sector too. Administrative corruption was deeply entrenched in Russia reflecting the fact that under the Soviet Union bribery was ingrained even in the most ordinary bureaucratic processes.[10] The available data still show high levels of administrative corruption in more recent years (Hellman et al. 2000) while petty corruption appears to be quite common in basic social services, such as health and education.

The combination of permissive societal morals regarding corruption and the complex process of transition from planned socialism to a market economy, involving the massive privatization of state assets, created particularly favorable dynamics for political corruption in Russia. During this period of reforms, enormous gains could be easily obtained by the manipulation of public decision making at high levels of government. In Russia these activities gained significant heights with the rise of the Russian oligarchs. Survey data show that at the end of the 1990s, Russia was among the countries with the highest levels of political corruption and state capture even among other transitional countries (Hellman et al., 2000).

The process of privatization of state assets in Russia, of unprecedented scale in transition countries, was characterized by an extended number of financial scandals and allegations of corruption. What made the case of corruption in the privatization of state assets in transitional economies unique was the fact that it took place in the face of the recent design of new legal frameworks, which were to prevent corruption in the first place. What seems to have failed where there was adequate legislation was an unprepared judicial system, with the courts unable to settle cases, and many court officials corrupt themselves, favoring the interest of organized crime through bribery and extortion. The most prominent example may have been the privatization process in the Russian Federation, where a public official estimated that as much as 30 percent of the public assets privatized from 1992 until the summer of 1993 were in control of the Russian mafia.[11] The privatization of state assets in the Russian Federation also led to the concentration of immense fortunes in the hands of few individuals, who became known during the 1990s as the Russian oligarchs. There have been multiple allegations of political corruption whereby Russian federal government officials favored some of these oligarchs in the further privatization of state assets either in a hidden way or sometimes in rather open ways, as was the case in the 'loans-for-shares deals' that some oligarchs were able to close with President Yeltsin from 1995 to 1996 (Salacuse, 1998). Allegedly, the Yeltsin administration, in need of cash to prop up the troublesome presidential campaign, sold at bargain-basement prices highly profitable companies and assets to the oligarchs (Glinkina, 1999).[12] This episode may be one of those cases where it is difficult to draw the line between dubious political behavior and political corruption. Corruption was just part of the problem with firms disappearing and hiding from the formal sector. Johnson et al. (2000) document how firms in Russia (and Ukraine) faced not only worse corruption among public officials but also higher effective tax rates, greater incidence of mafia protection, and less faith in the court systems in comparison to a number of Central European countries.

During Putin's mandate there has been a high profile fight against corruption in tax administration and the rest of the public sector. For example in 2006, Russia ratified the United Nations and the Council of Europe Conventions on corruption. However, progress against corruption remains uneven.[13]

The Severity of Tax Evasion

By all accounts tax evasion in Russia was very high during the earlier years of the transition and it appears to have remained at a high level during the 1990s. High levels of tax evasion were common in transitional countries.[14] However, the evidence on the level of tax evasion in Russia at the time is still fragmented. There has been no comprehensive study of the problem.

Perhaps the most basic form of tax evasion is the failure to file the required tax forms. In the Russia Federation, there is evidence that for many years, corporations failed to file required annual and/or quarterly tax returns. In 1999, according to the Ministry of Finance, a little less than 50 percent of registered firms filed tax returns. Some of this non-compliance was due to a lack of understanding, some due to a lack of trust in the government regarding proprietary information and tax-related abuse, and some certainly due to outright fraud. For example, in 1999, the Ministry of Taxes reported a rise in the existence of 'one-day companies', which were 'paper companies', used to pass cash through the system. The Ministry of Taxes in 2002 reported that as many as 52 percent of registered companies were of the one-day variety (1.6 million companies).

At the individual level, compliance was not better. For example, Easter (2003) reports that in 1994 less than 6 percent of citizens in the labor market filed income tax statements; in 1996 only 16 percent of the taxpayers paid their taxes fully and on time, and 34 percent did not pay at all.

The record on tax reporting was also poor. For example, Martinez-Vazquez and Wallace (1999) report a personal income compliance rate of approximately 50 percent and a value added tax compliance rate in the range of 38 and 55 percent.

In the latter half of 1999, the Ministry of Taxes reported that one out of six enterprises and more than half of all individual tax filers that were audited violated the tax code in some way. As a result of non-compliance with Tax Year 1999 liabilities, criminal sanctions were levied on 4,700 people and administrative sanctions were imposed on 213,000 people. See Box 6.2 for a discussion of estimates of tax evasion for specific taxes.

An alternative approach to measuring tax evasion is to estimate the size of the 'shadow economy', with the expectation that this measure would be highly correlated with overall tax evasion. For example, Schneider and Enste (2000, 2002), utilizing a variety of methods to measure the underground economy found that its size for Russia is around 46 percent of GDP.[15] Other estimates of the underground economy range from 20 to 40 percent of GDP (Yakovlev and Vorontsova, 1997).[16]

The prevalent mechanics or venues for tax evasion varied depending on the type of tax and taxpayer but a frequent approach was to conduct transactions in cash. Yakovlev (2001) analyzed survey data regarding forms of payment by wholesalers, and found that cash transactions (off the books) were about 30 percent of all reported wholesale transactions. But tax evasion in Russia took some innovative forms not commonly seen in other countries. For example, Yakovlev (2001) describes the 'obnalichivanie' tax evasion scheme as an operation in which legal firms make payments for fake work to the bank account of a sham firm. The sham firm returns a report of services rendered and transfers cash back to the legal firm and this cash does not enter the books of the legal firm. Another scheme introduced right after the 1998 financial crisis consisted of taxpayers with tax arrears going to bankrupt banks which still were registered banks and paying only part of their taxes; then, the bank and the taxpayers would claim that the

Box 6.2   Empirical Estimates of Evasion in Particular Taxes

Personal income tax

The Bureau of Economic Analysis of the Russian Federation and the Higher School of Economics (1998) estimated personal income tax evasion for 1997 to be about 57.3 percent. Their estimate was based on aggregate Goskomstat data, by income group of cash income, and other income, of the population. Another study by USGTA (1998c) estimated an evasion rate of 45 percent for the personal income tax using micro-level survey data from the Russian Longitudinal Monitoring Survey (RLMS).

Value added tax

Estimates of the level of value added tax evasion have been made by comparing the ratio of value added tax revenues to GDP for Russia and other countries. This approach is attractive for value added tax because Russia's rate and base structure were more similar to those of other countries than, say, for the personal income tax or other taxes. For example for 1995, the average ratio of tax revenues from taxes on goods and services to GDP in OECD countries was 11.9 percent according to GFS data from the IMF, while the average value added tax rates in OECD countries ranged from 19 to 22 percent, which were similar to that of Russia at the time (20 percent for most goods). In contrast, Russia's value added tax to GDP ratio was approximately 6 percent of GDP in the post-1994 period, meaning the existence of a tax gap in Russia of almost 50 percent. The estimate of evasion was lower when Russia's performance was compared to that of a small group of transitional countries (Czech Republic, Poland, Hungary). For these countries the value added tax to GDP ratios were in the range of 7 to 7.8 percent for 1995. This means that with similar tax rates, tax evasion in Russia was about 25 percent relative to this group of peers.

An alternative estimate of value added tax evasion was developed by USGTA (1998d) using data from a regional Input-Output Model of the Russian Federation. This model produced an estimate of the value added tax compliance rate by comparing the simulated tax liability based on production information in the economy and flow-through to output by 25 sectors of the economy with actual payments made in those sectors. From this model, the average weighted value added tax compliance rate of all sectors was approximately 55 percent. Similar procedures used in a Computable General Equilibrium Model of the Russian Economy produced weighted compliance estimates of 38 percent.

Enterprise profit tax

The Ministry of Finance conducted in 1998 an analysis of aggregate tax return data for the enterprise profit tax by industry. Comparing these data side-by-side with GDP estimates by sector, the study concluded that the overall compliance rate for enterprise profit tax was approximately 64 percent, or equivalently that the evasion rate for the enterprise profit tax was around 36 percent. However, the actual evasion was probably higher because of the

---

Box 6.2   Empirical Estimates of Evasion in Particular Taxes (continued)

underestimates of GDP by sector due to the underground economy (USGTA 1998e).

Excises
Some data exist indicating that compliance may also have been a significant problem for excises. For alcoholic beverages, the Ministry of Finance reported that illegal sales of alcohol were about 50 percent of the total alcohol sales in 1997 (USGTA, 1999e). However, data from the RLMS suggests that in 1996, consumption was about 70 percent of the volume of alcohol sold as reported by official Goskomstat figures. This could be due to the misreporting of either the consumption or sales figure, or it may simply mean that all sales did not result in domestic consumption.

---

taxes were paid in full and finally the bank would run tax arrears with the government.

The final part of the tax cycle regarding the collection of taxes was another area that showed substantial abuse in Russia. This is an issue very much related to the problem of tax arrears discussed above. The outright underpayment or non-payment of tax would seem to have been effectively sanctioned by the tax administration because of the lack of persistence in collecting overdue liabilities.

More generally, federal tax policy has been thought to have contributed to the high levels of evasion in Russia, prior to the enactment of Part I of the Tax Code in 1999. In the previous regime official penalties for tax evasion arising from simple mistakes to outright fraud were very severe. Under the pre-1999 legislation, upon audit, tax authorities could collect the amount of underreported tax as well as a sanction that often was equal to the amount of underreported tax. The sanctions were to be doubled in cases where violations were repeated; moreover, if the court found intent in income underreporting, the penalty increased fivefold. High interest rates also applied to overdue liabilities. These statutory penalties and interest rates were extremely high by international standards, even among transitional and developing countries. However, there is little hard evidence on the extent to which these penalties were actually imposed over the 1990s.

Anecdotal evidence from press reports and discussions with business people showed different reactions to the potential for tax sanctions. Some perceived that the audit and penalty system were so ad hoc that they underreported as much as they could and just waited for the negotiations with the tax inspectorate to ensue. Other taxpayers viewed audit and penalties as serious threats and therefore complied with their full tax obligations. These sentiments permeate the hierarchy of the government.

One Deputy Minister of Finance described the tax system to a group of international experts as a system whereby taxpayers report the same tax liability from quarter to quarter, whatever their true circumstances or tax liabilities. His explanation of this phenomenon was that taxpayers pay a set amount of tax to avoid detailed audits. If a taxpayer paid significantly different amounts of tax from quarter to quarter, this would trigger an audit as an inspector would assume that previous taxable income had been concealed. According to this account, the tax laws themselves had little to do with taxes paid.

The level of tax compliance during the 1990s was no doubt affected by the level of non-monetary transactions in the country. Traditional barter, arrears (wage, tax, other budget and enterprise), tax offsets and mutual settlements, and other non-monetary transactions (debt swaps, promissory notes) all affected the effectiveness of the tax administration. Barter is often thought of as the exchange of in-kind goods as payment for goods and services. In Russia, barter could actually refer to this type of in-kind transaction, or the transfer of other non-monetary instruments such as promissory notices and debt-swaps, or offsets. Barter did not necessarily imply tax evasion. However, the value of barter transactions was generally subjective and the true value was larger or smaller than the stated value of the bartered transaction depending on what was desired for tax evasion purposes. This increased the complexity and cost of audit due to the need to evaluate barter transactions with limited knowledge. On some occasions, in-kind payments were even accepted as payment in lieu of taxes. Negotiation would determine the value of the bartered goods to serve as a payment against tax liability. So, two levels of negotiation were present: first the negotiation over the taxes owed and then negotiation over the value of the bartered goods leaving additional room for evasion.

Illegally exported capital in violation of tax and currency legislation appears to have been quite common during the 1990s. A commonly cited figure is that up to the late 1990s as much as $15 billion fled Russia annually and in the process both large legal companies as well as criminal organizations were involved. With the return of macroeconomic and political stability, it would appear that a good share of the exported capital has made it back to Russia as foreign direct investment.[17] Several forms of amnesties were discussed in the early 2000s to make it more attractive for capital return.

The Negative Impact of Tax Amnesties

During the 1990s, the Russian government made frequent use of tax amnesties. In the international practice, amnesties have been typically used for bringing non-registered taxpayers into the tax net and to increase tax collections. Advocates of amnesties emphasize a potential immediate and short-run revenue impact, as individuals pay unpaid taxes. Advocates also argue that future tax compliance may increase if the amnesty induces individuals to become registered taxpayers. These benefits are most likely to come to fruition if the amnesty is accompanied by better taxpayer services, better education on taxpayer responsibilities, stricter post-amnesty penalties for evaders, and greater expenditures on enforcement. On the other hand, critics contend that the impact of amnesties on revenues is almost always small. They also question the long-run impact of a tax amnesty. Amnesties may in fact reduce compliance among honest taxpayers who resent the special treatment provided in the amnesty to tax evaders. In addition, if individuals come to believe that the amnesty is not truly a one-time opportunity to pay back taxes, then taxpayers may reduce their current compliance in anticipation of future amnesties.[18]

The tax amnesties offered by the Russian government are described in Box 6.3. The tax amnesty of 1993 was relatively generous. About two years later it was followed by a more far-reaching amnesty. The amnesty of 1996 helped to solidify the use of tax arrears as a regular way of doing business for organizations that applied for the amnesty before April 30, 1996. De facto, a number of enterprises were taken into the program after April 30, 1996. While no full-scale amnesty program has been introduced since 1996, the government issued rulings in the case of payment of overdue arrears.

For example, on April 5, 2000, the government announced a new program of arrears repayment that allowed arrears restructuring through zero-coupon bonds. On October 24, 2000, the government announced a ruling that established an arrears restructuring for one company, the Gorky Automobile Factory. On September 1, 2001, the government reported that it had made rulings on the requests for arrears restructuring of 5,352 enterprises. These enterprises requested restructuring of 108.3 billion rubles of taxes and penalties. The government restructured tax and penalty arrears for 2,640 of the enterprises for a total of 47.1 billion rubles. No data on the amount of requested restructuring per enterprise were available, but the authorities reported that in most cases in which restructuring was allowed, it was for a 'major portion' of the tax and penalty arrears.

An important element of the culture of amnesties in Russia was the very public tax payment negotiations with big enterprises. For example, Gazprom has been one company that has often been singled out by the government for 'individualized treatment' as it is one of the single largest taxpayers. The agreements with Gazprom were often reported in the press and therefore contributed to the perception of special treatment and favoritism for certain taxpayers.

Box 6.3   Tax Amnesties in the Russian Federation

The first amnesty was introduced on October 27, 1993 as Presidential Decree No. 1773 ('On Tax Amnesty in 1993'). This Decree established an amnesty from October 27, to November 30, 1993, and stipulated that all enterprises, organizations, and private entrepreneurs who disclosed their unpaid taxes for 1993 and all preceding years would not be liable for any sanctions on these unpaid liabilities. The Decree also specified that any concealed incomes discovered after November 30 would be penalized by the State Tax Service (STS) at three times the unpaid tax liability. As part of the amnesty, banks were required to provide the State Tax Service with account information.

The design of the amnesty was flawed by the short period within which a taxpayer was allowed to disclose unpaid tax obligations, by the requirement that the liability be repaid within one month, and by a failure to allow for inadvertent or unintended mistakes. Actually, the 1993 amnesty was repealed by Presidential Decree 746 of July 21, 1995.

The next amnesty was introduced by Presidential Decree No. 65 of January 19, 1996 (with amendments of April 22, 1996). Under this Decree, enterprises and organizations with tax arrears were allowed to defer payments on the arrears, provided that all current payments were made in time and in full. Those wishing to apply for a deferment were required to submit a request before April 30, with a decision given by the State Tax Service within 15 days. Enterprises and organizations that were granted deferments were required to pay 50 percent of the total amount due by October 1998, with payment made via quarterly payments of 5 percent of the liability; interest penalties were imposed at an annual rate of 30 percent on unpaid amounts. Deferment of the remaining 50 percent liability was granted over the following five years in equal payments, with no interest penalty.

This Decree was widely seen by taxpayers as too burdensome, due largely to the requirement that 50 percent of arrears be repaid and the high interest penalties that were applied. In any event, this amnesty was continued in somewhat modified form by Presidential Decree No. 685 of May 8, 1996. This decree also contained provisions requesting Duma passage of a draft law on a tax amnesty. Provisions of the new Decree that were immediately effective included such things as reduced interest penalties on late payments and on tax arrears, and an allowance for 'technical errors' (or simple arithmetic mistakes) in the preparation of tax returns, all of which were intended to reduce the burden of tax payment. At the same time the State Tax Service was expected to increase the frequency of tax audits.

Presidential Decree No. 65 was followed roughly a year later by Budget Law 29-FZ of February 26, 1997, which established guidelines for newly granted deferments on taxes and other mandatory payments. Under Article 20 of the Law, an interest rate of 50 percent was charged for newly granted deferments (or payment by installments) on taxes and other mandatory payments to the federal budget. More significantly, the Law requested that the government specify the procedures by which tax arrears were to be handled. Given the growing importance of tax arrears, these general procedures were closely

Box 6.3   Tax Amnesties in the Russian Federation (continued)

watched. Eventually, these procedures emerged in Budget Law No. 42-FZ of 26 March 1998, which established various grounds for deferment of taxes, and reduction in interest penalties.

Source: Alm, Martinez-Vazquez and Wallace (2006)

An additional element influencing evasion permissiveness and a mentality of amnesty was the very public way in which large amounts of taxable income were moved offshore. The well publicized Bank of New York scandal in 1999 reminded Russians and the international community of the severity of this problem. This problem was not unique to Russia at the time, since other countries in transition were experiencing similar problems. However, the magnitude of this activity in Russia seems to have been larger in relative terms. One estimate put this problem at one- to two-thirds of projected total government revenues for 2000 (Loungani and Mauro, 2001). Another study by Garibaldi et al. (1999) found that Russia had been the only transition economy that was a net exporter of capital during the 1990s. This money was funneled to many different countries, but a taxpayer-friendly treaty agreement with Cyprus made it one of the more popular destinations for Russian offshore funds. Several factors accounted for higher incidence of capital flight in Russia. First, individuals with large private fortunes exclusively in Russian assets, especially the new oligarchs, would naturally seek to reduce country-specific risk by investing some of their portfolio offshore. Second, the tax administration authorities have not been willing or able to track down those funds; thus, capital flight to a large extent reflected efforts to evade taxes. Third, macroeconomic instability and political risk within Russia also contributed to capital flight. Loungani and Mauro (2001) cite five specific problems causing capital flight: macroeconomic instability; high and unevenly enforced tax rates; lack of confidence in the banking system; widespread corruption and weakness in property rights; and corruption in the process of privatization.

THE NEW TAX CODE AND TAX ADMINISTRATION REFORM

The main answer of the Russian government to the poor performance of the tax system during the first eight years of the transition was comprehensive reform of the tax administration system. The reform strategy was based on two pillars. First, the introduction of a comprehensive tax code which among other things would restructure the operations and rights and obligations of the tax administration and taxpayers. Second, the adoption of an ambitious modernization program of the tax administration apparatus, known as the Tax Administration Modernization Program (TAMP).

The New Tax Code brought Solutions but also Problems

Following the financial crisis of 1998, the Government managed to pass Part I of the Tax Code in Parliament; this came into force on January 1, 1999. Part I of the tax code addressed taxpayer and tax administration issues; passage of Part II of the tax code, dealing with the structure of particular taxes, would have to wait several years. There were many reasons and pressures for the immediate reform of tax administration, such as confusing norms, tax compliance disincentives to investors and so on. But clearly the strongest pressure came from the need to raise revenues in the aftermath of the 1998 crisis and the budget imbalances of the previous years. The crisis provided a political window of opportunity for reform.

Over this period of reform things were made more difficult by the rapid succession of heads of the top federal tax agency, now known as the Ministry of Taxes and Fees (former State Tax Service). For a number of years, the responsibility for the direction of tax policy was disputed and went back and forth between the Ministry of Finance and the Ministry of Taxes. This issue was finally settled in 2004 when the Ministry of Taxes became the Federal Tax Service and a dependency of the Ministry of Finance.

The introduction of Part I of the Tax Code was a significant step forward but it also created some new problems. Many criticized Part I of the new code on the grounds that it gave taxpayers too much leverage against the administration, in some cases going a bit overboard on the side of the taxpayer rights. For example, it was feared the new code would cause a reduction of revenue since taxpayers could easily put off payments of principle and penalty until a court heard their case.

However, on the other side of the equation, important progress was made with Part I of the Tax Code. Among other things, the new code did make the penalty structure much more reasonable,[19] it clarified important concepts such as place of business, provided a legal basis for the use of a taxpayer identification number, and it set up a mechanism for developing tax regulations, which until then had been controversial.

Soon it became clear what needed to be fixed; for example, containing the ability of taxpayers to use the court system so freely to decide disputes or the need to issue regulations for the interpretation of the code. We address these in the next subsection.

In addition, the fear that tax collections would drop dramatically with the passage of Part I of the new code did not materialize.

Some of the problems from the 1990s continued to linger and were slow in disappearing. Although more of a local government issue, in-kind payments continued to be practiced for several years at all levels of government, distorting actual tax burden and reducing tax collections. The practice of tax offsets also continued. Third-party information from bank records, automobile registration and so on was still not allowed, significantly hampering the effectiveness of the administration.

Some Issues with the First Version of Part I of the Tax Code

Many observers coincided in pointing out several important shortcomings with the first version of Part I of the Tax Code. Highfield and Baer (2000), identified the following problems:

First, Part I shifted the statutes heavily in favor of taxpayers and against tax administrators. Now the burden of proof lay with tax administrators even though most taxes had become self-assessed taxes. There were also a variety of provisions offering the deferral of tax payments.

Second, significant limitations were introduced to the audit and enforcement powers of the tax authorities. These included restrictions on the duration and frequency of audits and limitations on the impositions of penalties for late payments.

Third, the new Tax Code limited flexibility for tax authorities in the specification of audit, collection and taxpayer registration procedures in the law. For example, there was a continued reliance on the settlement accounts and no provisions were added granting the tax authorities access to bank records for the purpose of gathering information to combat tax evasion and avoidance.

Fourth, little advancement took place in organizational structure. Part I of the Tax Code left the status quo untouched with still three agencies responsible for government revenue collections and enforcement actions: Ministry of Taxes and Fees, the Tax Police, and the Customs Committee. In addition the social funds (Pension, Medical, Social and Employment Funds) were still left to collect contributions separately from each other.

Regarding the tax administration itself, Part I of the Tax Code left untouched the highly fragmented territorial organization of the Ministry of Taxes and Fees. With still over 2,600 local tax inspectorates for the collection of taxes, administration costs were significantly high; meanwhile, the headquarters of the Ministry of Taxes in Moscow continued to be poorly organized and thinly staffed.[20]

In short, many of the problems with tax administration that had been identified in the early 1990s continue after the approval of Part I of the Tax Code. Some progress had been made with the creation of a directorate to supervise large taxpayer operations and plans to create ten large data processing centers, but by 2000 not enough resources and attention had been given to these initiatives. It took several years for those initiatives to get going.

Another problem that persisted was the lack of standardization and centralization of taxpayer data. The problem of de facto dual subordination of tax administrators to the local authorities and their federal employers, also continued unabated for several additional years.

Committing to the Further Reform of Tax Administration

Upon taking office, President Putin set out an official long-term work plan for the Russian Federation Government (2001), in which there was a prominent chapter on the 'Reform of tax and customs systems', and citing tax administration improvement among the key tasks of the tax reform plans.[21] The emphasis in that plan was put on reducing opportunities for the arbitrary actions of tax authorities and on improving overall taxpayer compliance. Several of the specific measures put forward in that strategy included organizational measure such as

- Setting up inter-territorial tax inspectorates able to serve several regions of the Russian Federation, with the objective, among others, of ensuring independence of tax bodies from regional authorities.
- Designing and developing integrated information systems of taxpayers.
- Setting up a Federal Tax District for the registration and management of large taxpayers.
- Giving priority to the development of IT in tax administration, in particular setting up data processing centers to serve many parts of the national territory.

Other proposed measures to improve tax enforcement included:

- Fighting tax evasion by 'one-day enterprises', that render fake services (return cash reduced by the amount of commissions to the 'client' instead of supplying services due under the contract); also introducing special registration for service providers whose services can be used for tax evasion purposes (marketing, consulting, advertising, research and development) with tax authorities.

- Enhancing control over taxpayers by means of mandatory assignment of a taxpayer identification number to entities and individuals, with registration of taxpayers' actual place of business, and the mandatory registration of all taxpayers' bank accounts with tax authorities.
- Enhancing control over the cash flows of registered business and closing loopholes for transferring the flow to the shadow economy.
- Improving the banking system legislation to disallow the opening and closing of bank accounts without notification of the tax authorities, and preventing operations with fake bank deposits.
- Fighting illegal capital flight by revising double taxation treaties with the states with low taxation zones; actively participating in the global regulation of offshore activities; disallowing contract prices distortion for export-import operations; including the use of world market prices for reference, and other similar measures.
- Changing the system of sanctions enforcement, allowing the resort to the court system only if the taxpayer had appealed the tax administration decision.
- Introducing a system of automatic indexing for all parameters of the tax system;
- Simplifying the system of accounting, adopting international standards, and transferring to accrual accounting for the purposes of the enterprise profit tax, value added tax and excises.
- Narrowing the list of circumstances for tax deferral and payment by installment, plus banning regional and local authorities from modifying the above list, and increasing interest payable on any deferred liabilities to the level of market rates.
- Securing fulfillment of tax liabilities by allowing taxpayers to issue bank guarantee during the period of appeal for a tax liability. Abolishing limits for holding and using property under lien; and by allowing unrestricted access to ready goods, and fixed assets with prosecutor's sanction.
- Abolishing the qualification of tax violations as intentional and careless and establishing a relatively low sanction benchmark as a percentage of sales, increasing it, if there are grounds pointing to the intent, and allowing courts to reduce the amount of the sanction only in those cases where a taxpayer presents sufficient grounds.
- Isolating departments for tax disputes within the tax authorities and with disputes handed over to arbitration courts.

Many of these measures were echoed in a number of publications from about the same time, for example Ivaneev (2000) and Zolotareva and Shishkov (2000). A major emphasis for the review and proposals for the reform of Part I of the Tax Code followed the principle of a better balance between taxpayer rights and the tax administration's ability to enforce taxes. Some of the measures proposed by experts went beyond those in the Governemnt strategy. For example, Zolotareva and Shishkov (2000) recommended using information on taxpayers' large expenses for the alternative assessment of their income tax base. These authors also recommended reducing the number of bodies responsible for tax control by making Tax Police and divisions of off-state Budget Funds report to the Ministry of Taxes with the goal of reducing administration and taxpayers' compliance costs.

As early as 2001, the Ministry of Taxes had created an ambitious and focused reform program of the tax administration containing 107 measures ranging from the improvement of tax audits to data processing. The major thrusts in the reform package included the following:

First, the Tax Code would allow the central government to clarify and explain the articles in the Tax Code via interpretative regulations and instructions. As pointed out above, this had been a controversial issue in the final rounds of preparation of Part I of the Tax Code, when supporters (mainly in the executive branch) of providing government with this ability lost to opponents, (mostly in Parliament), who argued for the supremacy of the law and for granting 'the benefit of the doubt' to taxpayers.[22] This had been a thorny issue since the early stages of preparation of the Tax Code. After the Duma approved Part I of the Tax Code, the actual interpretation of the law has been carried out through 'Rulings' of the Assembly of the Highest Arbitration Court. What the tax authorities wanted was an amendment of Article 31 making clear that the Ministry of Taxes had the authority to write instructions and regulations that apply to taxpayers, but with the provision that if taxpayers felt that the ruling contradicted the intent of the law, the ruling could be challenged in the courts.[23]

Second, the Tax Code would repeal all 'benefit of the doubt' provisions indicating that taxpayers should benefit from any ambiguity in the tax laws. This also had been a contentious issue for some time. The intention was to change Article 31 to state that all doubts should be resolved by making a determination about the intent of the legislator.

Third, and this was even more controversial, the Tax Code would establish that taxpayers' obligation to pay taxes is only fully discharged when the funds are received in the government accounts. This was to address the problem that some banks were late in transferring, or actually did not transfer, to the government accounts the funds that had been paid by taxpayers through the banking system. This also became another thorny issue. At the time there were numerous newspaper reports of banks receiving payment orders from taxpayers and then failing to turn the money over to the Ministry of Taxation. While Article 45.2 of the new code stated that a taxpayer fulfills his tax obligation when he submits a payment order to the bank, the tax authorities tried unsuccessfully to amend it so that the taxpayer would fulfill his tax obligation only when the bank debited the taxpayer's account.

Fourth, Part I of the Tax Code was interpreted to say that a court order may be necessary to demand payment from taxpayers for their tax liabilities due. This would not be a problem if a court order had been required to confiscate property or get payment from bank accounts. But clearly it would become a real problem if a court order were to be needed to send a notice of additional assessment or a demand for payment.

In 2001 the Government issued a ruling to develop the Tax Authorities Development Program for 2002–04. This ruling included provisions to revise the structure of the tax administration with a uniform tax inspectorate structure at the federal district and inter-rayon level, uniform regional management structure, and uniform data processing systems.

In more practical terms, the Ministry of Taxes developed a large taxpayer program based in Moscow which facilitated the jump in collections from 1999 to 2000 by a factor of 1.8. Actually large taxpayers, including companies like RAO, UES, MPS, GazProm and 18 oil companies, represented more than a third of all federal tax collections in that year. The development of the large taxpayer units was part of the first Tax Administration Modernization Project (TAMP) with support of the World Bank. Besides the work on the large taxpayer units, TAMP developed pilot operations for the collection and enforcement of business taxes in the Volvograd and Nizhny Novgorod regions and for the personal income tax in Moscow. During 2001 the Ministry of Taxes continued to prepare for the second part of the World Bank Tax Administration Reform loan or TAMP II. Although the Ministry of Taxes was genuinely interested in getting the funds, there was significant indecision on the best way to proceed. The plans for TAMP II were to roll out the institutional developments achieved in several regions under TAMP I to another 13 regions but also to go further in strengthening the entire tax administration system, with a focus on organization, management and operation weaknesses at the federal, regional, and local levels. TAMP II built on the Ministry of Taxes strategic framework for 2000–06. Particular reform items in TAMP II included the adoption of a functional organization of the tax offices, introducing modern information systems, improving analytical capabilities for revenue and compliance analysis and so on (World Bank,

2002). The eventual implementation of TAMP II has significantly contributed to the modernization of Russia's tax administration.[24]

Besides the technical assistance offered by the World Bank, institutional development for tax administration continued with the support of other foreign technical assistance and funding projects. In 2000, Tacis (the European Union's technical assistance program to the Commonwealth of Independent States) earmarked $3 million for the training of tax officials by creating training centers outside Moscow and St Petersburg, to support the training of approximately 30,000 tax officers ever year. Another example was the United States Treasury pilot program for modernizing the regional tax office at Volvograd; this modernization was based on an Internal Revenue Service model in the US. The experiment was considered to be quite successful in reducing taxpayer compliance costs (eliminating long waiting lines at the tax inspectorates) and it yielded considerable differential increases in tax collections for that regional inspectorate. Its success prompted the Ministry of Taxes to seek ways to roll out similar programs in all other regional inspectorates around the country.

Meanwhile, Part I of the Tax Code has been amended several times, especially to curb perceived abuses by the tax enforcement authorities. But for many years the spirited debate between the advocates of taxpayer rights, mostly in the Duma, and advocates of the powers of tax administrators, mostly in the Ministry of Finance, has continued. In 2006 the reforms established new rules for tax audits, making them less cumbersome for taxpayers, and tax violations now do not always result in taxpayers' bank accounts being immediately frozen, although penalties for tax violations can be levied by automatically debiting bank accounts no matter the amount involved.[25] In addition, the powers of the Ministry of Interior to initiate tax-related criminal charges have been curbed by requiring a court order for those proceedings. Other recent amendments to Part I of the Tax Code have been measures related to transfer pricing.

THE TERRITORIAL ORGANIZATION OF TAX ADMINISTRATION

Russia, like other countries during the last decade experiencing a rapid process of decentralization, has continued to confront the question of what is the most appropriate approach to organizing the vertical structure of tax administration. Should there be separate tax administrations at the central, regional and local government levels? And how should the territorial officers of the federal administration be organized?

The international experience shows a variety of approaches to the organization and degree of decentralization in tax administration.[26] For example, where there is a high level of decentralization, like in the Scandinavian countries, tax administration is highly centralized; in other rarer cases, like in Germany, tax administration is highly decentralized.

The argument for separate tax administrations by level of government is that the economies of scale obtained by more centralized models of tax administration may be lost with differences in the definition of tax bases across local governments. More significantly, the political accountability of local government officials to residents provided by tax autonomy may be enhanced when local taxes are also collected by local authorities (as opposed to central administration authorities). However those arguments are not airtight; for example, economies of scale may be quite considerable in the case of centralized administration of piggyback local personal income taxes or excise taxes.

In the context of deciding upon the appropriate level of tax decentralization, two fundamental objectives may be considered. The first is the maximization of revenues subject to two constraints: a budget or administration cost constraint and a compliance cost (for taxpayers) constraint. The second objective is the accountability of government elected officials to taxpayers, which may depend not only on the degree of normative autonomy provided to local governments but also on how taxes are actually collected. We will call this second objective the accountability objective.

What the best approach to the organization of tax administration may be depends on the objectives of tax administration and the constraints faced in the pursuit of those objectives. The final choice of a model of tax administration organization eventually may depend on how these objectives are weighted and the nature of the tradeoffs among them. Clearly a central government perspective on these objectives (that is, the relative weights assigned to them) may be quite different from a decentralized government perspective. Thus, disagreement between different levels of government on a particular country arrangement or the observation of quite different international practices can be explained to some extent by how those objectives are defined and weighted.

The choice of approach to the territorial organization of the tax administration in Russia is heavily weighted by recent history. To better understand the roots of the current approach to the territorial organization of tax administration, we make a detour in history going back to the last years in the Soviet Union. Under the Soviet regime, tax administration was very decentralized. All taxes were administered by the finance department of the local Soviet (the local government council), which was subordinated to the finance department of the higher level of the administrative hierarchy. The bulk of budget revenue came from taxes (mostly on turnover, payroll and profits) levied on and traditionally negotiated with state enterprises.[27] In fact taxes levied on state enterprises were substitutes for the remittance of their net profits to the state budget. As the owner of these enterprises, the state could ensure tax compliance in the course of annual audits covering all enterprises. Moreover, the state could routinely monitor bank accounts of enterprises through the state banking system. The transition to a market economy required modernization of the tax administration. In January 1990, the Soviet Government decreed the establishment of the Chief State Tax Inspectorate as a department of the Ministry of Finance as well as State Tax Inspectorates at lower levels of the administrative hierarchy under supervision of their respective regional and local level departments of finance.

Before the Perestroika era, each administrative unit was governed by two parallel bodies: the local committee of the Communist Party and the local Soviet (council). However, elections to the Soviets were not contested and a single candidate for each district was effectively nominated by the Party. Thus, all decision-making was made within the Party apparatus and local Soviets were only legitimizing these decisions and implementing them through the local executive branch. The subnational elections of March 1990 provided competition among several candidates for each seat in all subnational Soviets. This introduced some horizontal accountability (to the constituency) of the subnational tier in otherwise centralized administrative hierarchy. Political autonomy of local government effectively introduced dual subordination of local executives both to the elected local council and to the higher-level executive bodies.

Subnational authorities were created out of the local branches of the former state hierarchy. As a result implementation of many federal policies continued to rely on the now autonomous subnational authorities. However, the reliance on subnational implementation units made the center vulnerable to the actions of subnational authorities, especially when the legislation gave limited control to central authorities over subnational governments.

This was demonstrated with the demise of the Soviet Union. Boris Yeltsin set out to destroy Gorbachev's Soviet Union from within by pulling the financial rug from out under the center (McAuley, 1997). He ordered Russian banks to withhold tax payments made by enterprises to the Union budget. He also encouraged regional administrations to ignore revenue-sharing arrangements by not transferring their share of taxes to the Union budget. In order to turn Russian regions away from the Union he exempted them from paying taxes to the center. Regions were being given the opportunity to reduce their dependency on the center and to learn how to bargain with Yeltsin in order to benefit themselves. Yeltsin, in his fight for power, become involved in the business of granting tax concessions for political favors. The other tactic was to challenge the center for the ownership of enterprises and farms on the territory of the Russian Federation. In the chaotic days of 1991, these economic units could choose under whose auspices they wished to be. Ownership of Russian enterprises (Russia produced about 75 percent of the Soviet GDP) was absolutely crucial in the political struggle between Gorbachev and Yeltsin. The level of taxation and the amount of state social benefits which were distributed through the enterprises depended on whether the enterprise was Soviet or Russian. Yeltsin began to outbid the Union authorities, promising lower taxation and higher social benefits.

However, defeating Gorbachev was a two-edged sword. Yeltsin, without meaning to do so, was laying down the fiscal rules of the new Russia. Regional authorities soon learned to take advantage of the situation in Moscow. Fiscal advantages could be gained by smart bargaining. It would seem that Yeltsin had dug his own grave when it came to dealing with regional authorities in the new Russia. Starting from the very creation of independent Russia, a number of regions demanded greater autonomy, greater devolution of authority, and special tax regime. These regions were mostly comprised of areas inhabited by non-Russian ethnic groups, areas rich in natural resources and industrially well-endowed.

In the extreme case of Bashkortostan, a demand for a 'single channel system' was made so that all revenue would flow initially to the regional government and then a negotiated single payment be made to the federal government. This is exactly what Yeltsin tried to do under Gorbachev (Fowkes, 1997, p.174). Thus, for example, in 1991 Yeltsin said: 'We are prepared to take part in financing the army but only in proportion to our national revenue.' Other Russian regions, such as Tatarstan and reportedly 20 other oblasts and republics, proceeded to determine their own sharing rates unilaterally.

The federal government in Moscow in the early years of the transition remained reactive and tried to adapt to the agenda set by the maverick regions. In fact, the federal government in 1992-93 did not seem to have much of a choice but to accept the reality of an asymmetric system of intergovernmental relations, which was being fast shaped by the demands of a small number of ethnic republics. In fact, it was the regions which early on dictated the agenda of the federal contract: the shape and form the Russian Federation should assume. In stark contrast to the central control during the Soviet era, during the early transition, regions were able to take advantage of the fact that they had de facto control over key elements of government administration, including tax administration and the internal security forces. This left the federal government without tools to deal with noncompliant regions and enforce federal legislation. Thus, for the most part the asymmetric relations were implemented in a de facto and presumably illegal manner.

In November 1991 the State Tax Service was separated from the Ministry of Finance and directly subordinated to the Government and the President of Russia and given the rank of a federal ministry. Its organizational structure consisted of three levels: central, regional, and local. The regional offices coordinated and supervised local offices under their jurisdiction and provided the central level with tax revenue data, yet the vertical structure of Russia's federal tax administration remained extremely deconcentrated – even more deconcentrated than the federal public administration as a whole. For example, in 1995 the State Tax Service Headquarters employed 710 persons while the territorial branches employed 161,000 persons. Interestingly, while the deconcentrated employment in the territorial tax offices accounted for more than one-third of the total public administration employment of the federal government, the State Tax Service Headquarters staff accounted for less than 3 percent of the federal public administration core in Moscow. The highly deconcentrated structure of the federal Ministry of Taxes did not allow for taking advantage of, for example, economies of scale in designing procedures, processing returns, or conducting specialized audits. On the other hand, regional branches were allowed and often encouraged to experiment with their own innovations and approaches (Firestone, 1998). However, the lack of coordination and logistical support from the Moscow headquarters made federal tax agents in the field dependent on the support of local authorities through investing and fringe benefits.

Russia would have to wait until the election of Vladimir Putin as president to substantially bring all regions in compliance with federal laws including tax laws and administration regulations. However, best principles and international experience suggest that the vertical structure of tax administration should be related to the assignment of taxing powers among the different levels of government. In a fairly centralized system, with little or no tax autonomy at the subnational level, tax administration should remain centralized. In decentralized systems where subnational governments have been assigned their own taxes and with authority to modify rates or other aspects of the tax structure, and whose base is not shared with the central government, there is a strong case for multilevel decentralized tax administration. This is so because separate tax administrations can help to enhance the accountability and efficiency of decentralized governments. Thus, in all there is a strong case for multiple levels of tax administration where there is full separation of tax bases

among different levels of government. The way fiscal decentralization has
evolved in Russia, especially after President Putin took office with less and
less tax autonomy at the subnational level and toward recentralization in the
political arena , it would seem that there is little pressure to decentralize tax
administration. Technical reasons such as economies of scale and heavy
concentration of tax revenues for a relatively small number of taxpayers and
locations also argue for a more centralized tax administration system. [28]

THE EVOLUTION OF TAX MORALE[29]

The fundamental changes in the role and effectiveness of the public sector
that have taken place in the Russian federation since independence from the
Soviet Union in late 1991 are likely to have had an impact on citizens'
attitudes toward paying taxes – or what is known as their 'tax morale.' This
section reviews how changes in government policies and institutions have
affected tax morale in Russia. As we have seen all throughout this book,
the 1990s were a transforming decade for Russia. It spans the presidency of
Boris Yeltsin, who was elected President by popular vote in June 1991 and
who served until December 1999, when he resigned and Vladimir Putin
became acting President. Putin was elected president shortly after with
considerable popular support and authority to carry out a backlog of
reforms. The 1990s were a period during which major legislation was
enacted transforming the Russian Federation, and which together with other
events shaped the life and views of ordinary citizens. Some of these events
included   the political struggle and final victory of Yeltsin over the
communist-dominated parliament in the early 1990s, the centrifugal
separatist forces in ethnic regions, the massive privatization of state assets
and the rise of the Russian oligarchs, the questionable alliance of the
oligarchs with the Kremlin for Yeltsin's reelection, the financial crisis and
debt default of August 1998, and the beginning of the economic recovery
and the consolidation of power in Putin's hands the next year. In the 2000s
the country gained political stability and strong economic recovery driven to
a large extent by Russia's extensive oil and gas reserves and the sharp
increase in international prices for those commodities. One question we
may ask is this: how did all these changes affect citizens' attitudes toward
paying taxes in Russia?

Not surprisingly, Alm, Martinez-Vazquez and Torgler (2006), show a
reduction in tax morale in the first four years of the transition from 1991 to
1995 followed by a small recovery in 1999 (Figure 6.1).

This evolution of tax morale would appear to be consistent with the
relevance of social norms in taxpayer compliance. In the early years of the

transition there was widespread perception of tax evasion and that was a time when social expenditures took a dramatic dive. The increase in tax morale in 1999 also coincides with the restoration of a higher level of trust in the state and more solid progress toward a market economy.

The following paragraphs draw on Alm, Martinez-Vazquez and Torgler (2006) to describe the changes in tax morale in Russia. Isolating the determinants of tax morale in Russia is facilitated by the existence of two data sets, the World Values Survey (WVS) and the European Values Survey (EVS). These surveys provide information at the individual level on some of the factors that may affect citizens' attitudes toward paying taxes. The WVS data set for Russia is available for 1991 and 1995, while the EVS data set, a similar survey that focuses only on European counties, contains data for 1999. Both surveys ask a question that is used to develop a proxy for the intrinsic motivation to pay taxes: 'Please tell me for each of the following statements whether you think it can always be justified, never be justified, or something in between: ... Cheating on your taxes if you have the chance'.

There are, of course, some limitations that accompany the use of survey data including reporting errors, overstated willingness to pay taxes, reluctance to respond honestly to a survey question given the delicate nature of tax compliance, and so on. Nevertheless, one can expect greater honesty and accuracy than when asking individuals directly about tax evasion.

The distribution of aggregate tax morale scores in Russia for the years 1991, 1995, and 1999 from the World Values Survey (WVS) and the European Values Survey (EVS) are shown in Figure 6.1. The graph shows the mean score values in these three time periods, calculated as the simple average across all individuals in the data sets. The scores range from zero (tax evasion is justifiable) to three (tax evasion is never justifiable). These numbers show a significant decay of tax morale between 1991 and 1995, from 1.86 to 1.66 (where a lower number indicates lower tax morale). In the next four years tax morale recovered, with an increase from 1.66 to 1.73. Thus, we observe on average a decline in the willingness to pay taxes during the first four years of the transition and a less than full recovery in the following four years.

Figure 6.2 presents a histogram with the distribution of tax morale scores in each of the three different years. The results indicate large differences between the percentage of individuals with a high tax morale (a score of 3) and those with the lowest scores across these years; the distributions for score values 1 and 2 are quite stable. The deterioration in tax morale in Russia from 1991 to 1995 was strongly affected by a reduction in the share of those citizens who believe that tax evasion is never justifiable (the score of 3), and an increase in the share of individuals

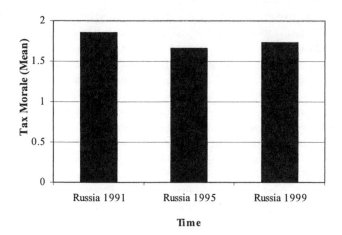

Source: Alm et al. (2006)

Figure 6.1   Aggregate Tax Morale in the Russian Federation – 1991, 1995, and 1999

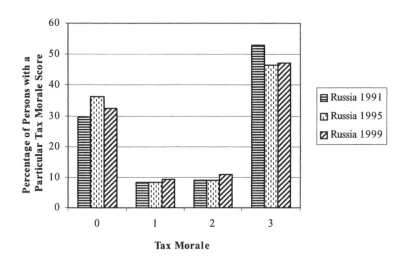

Source: Alm et al. (2006)

Figure 6.2   The Distribution of Aggregate Tax Morale in the Russian Federation – 1991, 1995, and 1999

who believe that tax evasion is justifiable (the score of 0). The tax morale improvement between 1995 and 1999 is based mainly on the reduction of the share represented by those who believe that tax evasion is justifiable (the score of 0) and also on steady but small increases in the share of individuals in the other three categories.

These broad swings in tax morale in the aggregate data reflect well what was happening to and around Russian citizens at those different periods during the transition. Although government was still providing many basic services just before the beginning of the transition process in 1991, the overall performance of the public sector was poor and corruption levels were high. From the very start of the transition at the end of 1991 and through the early months of 1992, the socio-economic conditions confronting Russian citizens suddenly deteriorated, on a massive scale, as the level and quality of public services declined even further. The rapid collapse of institutional structures produced a vacuum in the country, followed by worsening income inequality and poverty rates. Many taxpayers were likely to react adversely to many of the economic and tax policy changes that were necessary for the transition from a centrally planned to a market economy. Further, as we discussed above in this chapter, individuals were for the first time faced with the direct payment of taxes, including being asked to file different tax returns. However, voluntary compliance and self-filing, two important pillars in a modern tax system, were completely absent at the start of the transition (Martinez-Vazquez and McNab 2000). Following the early transition, tax evasion reached very high levels as the new tax administration was not prepared to enforce taxes in a market-based economy with large numbers of taxpayers. Further, the connection between the payment of taxes and the provision of public goods had been largely concealed under socialism, which might have reduced the identification with the state and thus the willingness to pay taxes. For example, Easter (2003) reports the findings of a poll conducted by the tax administration in the Tambov region in the early years of the transition, which indicates that only one-third of the respondents answered that paying taxes to the state would provide any benefit to themselves.

Thus, to the extent that in the first years of the transition Russia did not succeed in designing an adequate tax system, or other government structures and institutions (especially improved public service delivery), tax morale should have been expected to deteriorate. Further, as Kasper and Streit (1998) stress, law and order, never strongly upheld in the former Soviet Union, later deteriorated in the new Russia. A lack of the 'rule of law' tradition did not help with the institutional transformation process or the improvement of tax morale, at least in the first phases of the transition. Corruption also increased in the early years, which reduced citizens' trust in government authority (Levin and Satarov, 2000). Corruption was quite likely heightened by a privatization process that lacked effective legal regulation and impartial oversight.

The evolution of tax reform also likely played a role in the evolution of tax morale. Despite the declared objectives for decentralization of the public finances, the system remained highly centralized as regional shares and local revenues or expenditures were dictated by a higher level of government (Lavrov et al. 2000). The suspicious processes imbedded in the centralized structure of the tax system, where the taxes collected regionally had to go first to the central government before returning to the regions in the form of transfers, contributed little to local citizens' beliefs that their preferences counted at all (Levin and Satorov, 2000).

Even so, there was a trend toward an improvement in tax morale from 1995 to 1999, although most of this change likely took place in 1999. There are several factors that may explain this improvement. The increase may have been influenced by the drafting of a new Tax Code and Budget Code and some other significant legislative initiatives but most importantly the succession of President Yeltsin by President Putin. The latter had considerable popular support.

In summary, during a good share of the transition years, Russia did not succeeded in designing tax systems, tax administrations, or government structures that encouraged high tax morale. As policies and economic conditions changed for the better toward the end of the decade, tax morale improved although not very significantly. More recent data, not available at the time of the writing, will tell whether this trend has been sustained in more recent years. Our conjecture is that it has.

CONCLUSIONS

It has become increasingly clear during the transition that whether or not the tax reform effort would succeed in Russia would ultimately depend upon the modernization and strength of the tax administration system. Russia was able, at different stages and with varying degrees of success, to adopt Western-style tax structure. Yet the country struggled for many years, continuing with low rates of revenue mobilization and high rates of tax evasion. The modernization and structural reform of the tax administration system lagged behind. This delay was in part explainable by the lack of a tax administration tradition, but perhaps Russia continued to struggle with the modernization of its tax administration longer than expected.

In an assessment of Russia's experience with tax reform Shatalov (2006), who is widely recognized as the 'father' of Russia's tax reform, concludes that among the major accomplishments of the Russian tax reform have been a 'better tax administration' and a 'shrunk shadow economy sector'. It would be hard to dispute those conclusions in an absolute sense. However, the difference would need to be in the degree that those two results have been accomplished. For other observers, tax administration in Russia has improved too slowly and the shadow economy and tax evasion have not shrunk sufficiently. Actually, Shatalov ends his interesting assessment referring to the near-term priorities for reform and practically all of these priorities have to do with the improvement of tax administration. These priorities include:

- to drastically modify tax audit rules and administrative procedures to better protect legitimate rights and interests of taxpayers;
- to improve the quality of taxpayer services to be comparable with the best world practice;
- to determine criteria to differentiate between admissible and inadmissible tax optimization techniques;
- to legislate new rules and instruments for transfer pricing, foreign affiliate companies, and so on.

That being said, Russia's tax system continues to struggle with tax administration. The reform of the system remains a critical part for the long-term success of the tax reform effort. The difficulties that remain are of a technical nature, but also of a political nature. This is particularly true in those areas where the reform of the tax administration affects the relations between the federal and subnational government, including the reorganization, and even the closing, of regional and local offices. But the vast territory of the Russian Federation and regional peculiarities need to be taken into consideration in setting any reform strategy.

It is fair to end this chapter on a positive note, emphasizing how much has been accomplished in tax administration, tax compliance and enforcement over the last ten years. During this period there have been significant reforms associated with Part I of the Tax Code and the modernization of the tax administration system along the lines suggested in the expert literature.[30] By some standards, the Russian Federation is performing as well as, and sometimes better than, many other countries around the world, which have had longer times and less constraining initial conditions to overcome. As shown in Table 6A.1, for 2005-06, Russia scores better than the average country in most other regions of the world for 'time spent to prepare and pay taxes', or for 'average time spent in meetings with tax officials', although in the latter case, Russia does not perform as well as the average for OECD countries. It is quite encouraging also that the federal authorities have largely regained control over the tax administration and the tax police; it is no longer the case that subnational authorities can increase their own revenues at the cost of federal revenues or even use the tax authorities for political extortion against rivals. However, Russia still scores considerably worse than the average in other regions of the world in areas such as 'expected to pay bribes in meetings with tax inspectors', or 'the percent of firms that are expected to give gifts in meetings with tax inspectors'. In addition, the tax administration authorities are still being judged as applying in a somewhat arbitrary way the new much improved tax laws. However, taxpayers now have a much easier time appealing these decisions in the arbitration courts; Antel and Lozovskaya (2005) report that taxpayers win more that 70 percent of all cases brought to court.

NOTES

1. Over the years the federal authority in charge of administration has changed names and status. The State Tax Service became the Ministry of Taxes and Fees (often also called Ministry of Taxation) in 1998 with entirely separate Cabinet standing from the Ministry of Finance. In 2004 the Ministry was downgraded to Russian Tax Service and became a unit of the Ministry of Finance.
2. See Firestone (1998).
3. See Gregory and Brooke (2000).
4. For example, in Western Europe, countries like Belgium and Italy have separate tax police bodies. But see Highfield and Baer (2000) for a reasoned argument for the integration of the Tax Police in the Ministry of Taxation limiting the responsibilities of the Tax Police to tax fraud associated with illegal economic activities, and possibly with staff security functions.
5. Frequently, instructions, forms and regulations were issued without significant review for clarity or conflict with existing instructions, forms, and regulations resulting in the confusion and increased compliance costs for taxpayers. Services such as automated phone assistance or an internet web site were non-existent, despite the fact that the cost of providing and maintaining these service is negligible relative to one-on-one interactions with the taxpayer by a tax inspector.
6. In Ukraine, oblasts with relatively low levels of barter had relatively low levels of arrears (Thirsk, 2000).
7. See Nerre (2001).
8. See Korolenko (1998) for a description of Russian tax collection practices during the 1990s.
9. See Treisman (2000).
10. See, the Economist Intelligence Unit and the DRI/McGraw Hill Global Risk Service of as reported in EBRD (1997).
11. Celarier (1997).
12. Allegedly cash received from small cooperatives in exchange for state company assets exchanged at a 1:3 ratio, that is, 3 rubles-worth of assets for one ruble of cash.
13. See Schmidt (2006).
14. See, for example, Martinez-Vazquez and McNab (2000) and Alm and Martinez-Vazquez (2003).
15. See Alm, Martinez-Vazquez and Schneider (2006).
16. For some, the informal economy played the important role of partially offsetting the fall in income. In this view, informality also helped channel resources to more productive activities in the economy and generated entrepreneurship and employment. See Rutkowski (1999).

17. For example, in 1999, foreign direct investment from Cyprus into Russia was the third largest after the United States and Germany. Of course, Cyprus was reputed to be one of the most favored destinations for Russian capital flight during the 1990s,
18. See, for example, Alm, Martinez-Vazquez and Wallace (2006).
19. Previously, penalties were so high, that after a couple of months, a taxpayer could be wiped out by the penalties alone.
20. A continuous problem had been the weak headquarters operation with a staff under 1,000 vis-à-vis a total staff at its peak of 160,000.
21. The program had been developed initially by the Centre of Strategic Research Foundation headed by Minister of Economic Development and Trade, German Gref.
22. Actually, a provision allowing government agencies to issue rulings, regulations and methodological guidelines on the application of tax laws had been introduced in Article 4.2 of Part I of the Tax Code in July 9, 1999 (Fed Law 154FZ that came into effect on August 17, 1999.) However, the legal status of these regulations continued to be questionable, given the obviously superior legal standing of the Tax Code. The weak judiciary system in Russia did not help with these matters.
23. Gennady Bukaev, at the time (2000) Minister of Taxation, complained in an interview in the newspaper *Vedomosti* (February 2001) that today it is more difficult to close the loopholes in the legislation, as MinTax do not have the powers to issue regulations, only methodological guidelines mandatory for tax authorities.
24. The World Bank also implemented a modernization project for customs starting in 2003 (World Bank, 2003).
25. See Antel et al. (2006).
26. See Martinez-Vazquez and Timofeev (2006) for a discussion of the international experience. Some parts of this section draw on that study.
27. See Martinez-Vazquez and McNab (2000).
28. For example in 2001 the Ministry of Taxes reported that 50 percent of total collections were paid by 260 large taxpayers.
29. This section draws on Alm, Martinez-Vazquez and Torgler (2006)
30. See, for example, Silvani and Baer (1997) and Bird (2004).

APPENDIX

Table 6A.1 Summary Indicator on Bribery and Tax Administration, Enterprise Survey 2005–06

Indicators	Russia	East Asia & Pacific	Europe & Central Asia	Latin America & Caribbean	Middle East & North Africa	South Asia	Sub-Saharan Africa	OECD
Tax								
Average time firms spent in meetings with tax officials (days)	2.47	4.91	2.78	2.89	3.52	3.37	5.08	1.65
Time to prepare and pay taxes (hours)	256.00	270.06	437.92	548.80	281.36	197.19	331.71	394.00
Corruption								
Unofficial payments for typical firm to get things done (% of sales)	1.01	1.81	1.04	1.4	2.72	2.02	2.14	0.13
Firms expected to give gifts in meetings with tax inspectors (%)	58.04	33.59	44.79	6.29	40.09	46.94	20.78	28.26
Value of gift expected to secure government contract (% of contract)	1.59	1.82	1.57	2.55	1.3	3.32	4.09	0.55
Pays bribes to get things done (% firms)	59.89	56.2	33.9	32.7	46.1	55.0	37.7	16.5

Table 6A.1 Summary Indicator on Bribery and Tax Administration, Enterprise Survey 2005–06 (continued)

Indicators	Russia	East Asia & Pacific	Europe & Central Asia	Latin America & Caribbean	Middle East & North Africa	South Asia	Sub-Saharan Africa	OECD
Informality								
Sales amount reported by a typical firm for tax purposes (%)	85.25	69.3	89.35	76.51	73.55	93.55	93.7	78.39

Source: The World Bank, Enterprise Surveys 2005–06, http://www.enterprisesurveys.org/

7. Tax Policy Development and Intergovernmental Fiscal Relations

CONTEXT

One of the critical issues in designing a federal system is the role of the central government vis-à-vis subnational governments. The intergovernmental fiscal system must assign responsibility for expenditures to a particular level of government and assign revenues and taxing authority to a particular level of government as well. Thus, the choices that a country makes regarding the design of the intergovernmental system or expenditure and revenue assignments have important implications for general tax policy. For example, Tanzi (2000) argues that the status quo 'ownership' of certain types of taxes and the level of decentralization have been detrimental to tax reform in Brazil, India and Argentina.

Intergovernmental relations also impact tax administration, which, in turn, has important implications for tax reform. For example, systems of shared taxes are common in a number of countries, including Russia. In the case of shared taxes, the tax base and rate may be determined by the central government but the tax revenues are shared among levels of government according to an established formula. A centrally controlled tax administration may put emphasis on collection of revenues accruing in large part to the central government and may allocate less administrative resources to the collection of taxes accruing in large part to subnational governments.

Another challenge to tax policy, fiscal decentralization and tax administration is the dual-subordination of tax administration, which is found in some transition countries. In countries where the tax administration is centrally controlled but the regions have influence over local tax collectors, the tax collectors may feel torn in their loyalties. In Russia, regional and local governments have responsibility for part of the compensation package of tax officials in the form of housing, schools, health care, transportation, vacations and the like. There is evidence in Russia that local collectors would fill the coffers of the local governments first and then remit to the center. In other cases, revenue collections may 'stick' at the subnational level. Under such circumstances, it is difficult to achieve consensus on many elements of tax reform and even more difficult to implement reforms.

In the Russian Federation, the debate over the system of intergovernmental fiscal relations has played an important role in the evolution of comprehensive tax reform. Some observers argue that the intergovernmental system in Russia has plagued tax reform and economic growth on the national level to the extent of being a primary deterrent (Blanchard and Schleifer, 2000).[1] In the post-Soviet era, the combination of political instability at the central level and the well-oiled networks of regional governors resulted in de facto decentralization in some areas of the country, while other regions continued to rely on Moscow for economic support. Some regions such as Tartarstan and Bahskiria have pushed for and been granted semi-autonomous status, while Chechnya has lobbied for complete independence. Other regions in the Far East (Yakutya and Tyumen oblasts, for example) have lobbied for increased revenue autonomy in the form of control over oil revenues, while other, poorer regions, continue to look to Moscow for more and more generous grants. The governments subordinate to the regional governments (some cities, municipalities, towns and villages) have also played a role in demanding a codification of their status, rights and responsibilities. This intra-regional dimension of fiscal decentralization has received less attention in the Russian Federation. However, there is no doubt that this third tier of government has increased the pressure for policy reforms that may conflict with the goals of federal tax reform efforts.

The varied circumstances of the regions and other subnational governments have demanded reforms aimed at intergovernmental fiscal reform in the Russian Federation. The situation early on gave rise to what has been called 'asymmetric federalism' in which there is a policy of treating regional governments differently depending on various circumstances.[2]

The codification of intergovernmental relations in Russia not only diverted the time, energy and bargaining power of various players in the policy debate away from the general debate over tax reform at the central level, it directly affected the type of tax reforms available to the central government. The flavor of intergovernmental fiscal reforms was directly impacted by the changing political climate at various points in time. In the early years of economic liberalization, concerns over fractionalization of the country led to centralization of tax policy. The value added tax was a new tax for a new country and was instituted as a central government tax. During the Yeltsin period, strong regional governors were able to push for a share of value added tax revenues and such sharing continued throughout the Yelstin era. This arrangement complicated the system of invoice-crediting and refunding of the value added tax, thus compromising the performance of the value added tax since the local portion of the value added tax was determined based on collections net of any refunding. A region that was concentrated in export industries would have a relatively small net value added tax base as exported goods receive credits for value added tax on inputs. This normal working of the value added tax discouraged making refunds on a timely basis and put some regions at a disadvantage in terms of generating value added tax revenue. Various efforts to make the value added tax a central government only tax failed in large part due to opposition from regions with large value added tax collections, concerned for loss of their revenue base. Early in his mandate, Putin was able to recentralize the value added tax – one of many policies the President has undertaken to increase central authority in the country.

Another example of reforms being influenced by a changing political climate at various points in time concerns the personal income tax. This tax was changed from a 100 percent 'shared' tax to a piggyback system and then back again to a 100 percent 'shared' tax no less than three times between 1992 and 2003 as the central government weighed the benefits of a relatively stable tax base against the need for a significant source of subnational revenues.[3] The pressure to develop sources of subnational government revenue also led to experiments in market based property taxes and regional sales taxes.

In short, the pressure to develop sources of revenue at the central and subnational government levels has complicated the tax reform debate. Tax policy, tax administration and intergovernmental fiscal relations can not be dealt with as discrete and independent policy issues. In the Russian Federation, as in other transition countries, both shared central government taxes and grants are the major form of intergovernmental transfer so that tax policy changes at the central level affect the flow of resources to subnational governments. The revenue generation of the tax system depends crucially on the efficiency of tax administration and, in Russia, the tax administration is under the control of both the central and subnational governments. This complex interplay between tax policy, fiscal decentralization and tax administration means that central government tax policies and development of tax administration are key decisions that also affect the design of the intergovernmental fiscal system. For example, any change to a shared tax affects the budgets of all levels of government, thereby creating proponents and opponents of tax proposals affecting shared taxes. Proposals to recentralize taxes through the tax code increases opposition from the more autonomous and resource-rich regions, while poorer regions would likely support such proposals. In short, it is impossible to separate the tax reform debate from the intergovernmental fiscal system: changes to one will directly impact the other in important ways.

THE SYSTEM OF INTERGOVERNMENTAL RELATIONS: WHAT SHOULD IT DO?

The relationships among levels of government reflect a complex combination of economic efficiency and political power. From the perspective of economics, fiscal decentralization is aimed at enhancing the efficiency of the provision of public goods by closely matching the needs of local populations with goods and services produced by government. Economic theory maintains that lower levels of government are best used to provide for local public goods – those with benefits that exclusively accrue to citizens within the borders of a local jurisdiction (Oates, 1972). Public goods providing benefits to all the citizens of an entire country, such as national defense or income redistribution, are typically thought to be better handled by the central government.

The notion of assigning certain expenditure responsibilities to a certain level of government is referred to as expenditure assignment. A critical factor in the design of intergovernmental relations is the 'appropriate' allocation of those responsibilities among levels of government. Giving local governments the job of providing services whose benefits extend well beyond the borders of their jurisdiction makes it very difficult for local politicians to respond to the needs of 'their' population.

Giving local governments responsibilities which they can not afford is another way of undermining subnational governments' ability to respond to the needs of their constituents. Financing expenditure responsibilities is therefore the second piece of intergovernmental design. In other words, revenue assignments should be consistent with the expenditure assignments. There are many available revenue options: purely subnational taxes and fees, shared revenues with the central government and intergovernmental grants. Furthermore, purely subnational taxes may grant subnational governments the statutory authority to define the tax base, set the tax rate or administer the tax and any combination of these three functions. The greater the share of revenues from purely subnational taxes in total subnational revenues, the greater the autonomy of subnational governments. The greater the share of revenues from shared taxes and intergovernmental grants, the greater the influence that the central government will have over the decisions of subnational governments and, thus, weakening the autonomy of subnational government. There is an obvious link between tax reform and the development of subnational finances: the way in which the tax code defines the tax structure will directly affect available options for revenue assignments.

In the following sections, we briefly review the basic tenets of expenditure and revenue assignment in order to provide a context for evaluating the Russian Federation's revenue system of fiscal decentralization.

Expenditure Assignment

There are many ways that expenditures may be assigned to various levels of government, and there are many models among countries. Changes in assignment over time are natural as an economy develops and the needs of citizens' change. Still, there are good and not so good ways to do it. Musgrave (1959), Bird (1999) and Martinez-Vazquez (2007), among others, summarize some general principles of expenditure assignment: expenditures aimed at economic stabilization and income distribution are best assigned to the central government, while some of those related to allocative efficiency (the best way to use available resources to provide goods and services) may be assigned to local governments. For example, it is not thought to be efficient policy to give subnational governments a role in combating inflation: macroeconomic stabilization is a proper function of the central government. On the other hand, choosing between building an additional elementary school or a new local road are expenditure decisions that are best handled closer to the source of the users of these public goods.

The law should be clear on both the areas of exclusive responsibility that are assigned to each level of government as well as explicit about the respective roles or competences regarding shared functions. Failure to do so will result in incentives for various levels of government to shirk responsibilities and thereby remain unaccountable to the local population.

Revenue Assignment

Simply stated, revenue assignment should follow expenditure assignment. Once expenditure responsibilities have been determined, it is important to have a revenue system to support the various levels of government in the provision of publicly provided goods and services. In many countries including Russia and other transition countries, the revenue side of fiscal policy has not been developed in a way that supports subnational government. Not only is revenue adequacy important, but the type of revenues allowed at different levels of government should be in line with an overall strategy of macroeconomic stabilization and economic efficiency.

Musgrave and Musgrave's (1976) classification of the proper economic functions of government provides a useful guide to the assignment of revenue sources across different levels of government. Oates (1972) argues that macroeconomic stabilization and income redistribution should for the most part be the responsibility of the central government. Hence, tax instruments that can significantly affect macroeconomic stabilization and income redistribution should be assigned to the central government.

For example, progressive income taxes are redistributive by nature and most economists would argue that these taxes should generally be assigned to the central government. A flat rate subnational surcharge ('piggyback') on a central income tax is not as redistributive in nature and more appropriate as a subnational tax. As subnational governments are mostly prescribed to engage in activities to improve the allocation of resources in the case of local public goods, externalities and some merit goods, they should be assigned taxes for which it is easier to establish a link with the benefits received by residents from local government spending. There are many good examples of benefit type taxes including those levied on motor vehicles through licensing and registration, charges for local sewer use and sanitation. Property taxes are often hailed as 'good' local taxes as they are considered a benefit tax that can provide relatively stable revenue.

Public finance theory and practical policy experience provide three desirable characteristics for good local revenue sources:

- They generally link revenue collections to locally provided benefits.
- They generally have a tax base that is relatively evenly distributed across jurisdictions.
- They generally have an immobile base.

Conceptually, the benefit principle of taxation (Musgrave, 1959) should be the primary guidance for the assignment of local government taxes because redistributive taxes should be assigned to the central government since redistributive taxes will influence migration. At the national level, redistributive taxes will have less impact on migration, as the only movement to avoid taxes is either to another country or to the underground sector of the economy. The second factor upholds a principle of maintaining horizontal equity and reducing fiscal competition among jurisdictions. If some jurisdictions have larger tax bases due to the definition of local taxes, there arises a natural competition both for businesses as well as for constituents.

If, however, non-benefit taxes are applied to mobile tax bases, then inefficiencies can arise as taxpayers move to low tax jurisdictions to avoid paying the full price of locally provided goods and services. This is the classic free-rider problem or tragedy of the commons associated with public goods.

Local taxes that can be 'exported' to taxpayers in other jurisdictions are also highly distorting. Although clearly tempting and attractive to individual local governments, assigning taxes to local governments that can be exported lead to inefficient and irresponsible behavior by local governments. Many local governments will attempt to export taxes to non-residents, which will create a nasty form of tax competition. Furthermore, residents will not face the full price of providing locally provided goods and services, and, consequently, they will tend to overconsume them. Therefore, revenue assignment needs to consider not only revenue adequacy, which depends primarily on the expenditure assignments, it also needs to grapple with which taxes are going to be assigned to which levels of government.

For example, two quite similar taxes, a turnover tax and a retail sales tax, could both be supported as decent local tax instruments according to the benefits received principle. However, the turnover tax is just a bad tax and leads to multiple distortions in the market; therefore, it is not an appropriate source of subnational or, for that matter, central government revenue. The information in Table 7.1 provides a summary of reasonable assignments of various types of taxes.

The intergovernmental setting will determine which taxes are used by which level of government and, as illustrated in Table 7.2, the arrangements can vary significantly among countries. In the most decentralized countries, such as the US, the central government provides very few constraints on the subnational government's ability to tax. In those cases, subnational governments have the authority to define the tax bases, establish the tax rates, and, in many cases, administer the taxes. Attempts in the US by the central government to encroach on subnational tax instruments, such as proposals to impose a general consumption tax at the national level, are met with great resistance (Rosen, 2003).

The level of true subnational revenue autonomy in countries around the world is difficult to assess. It is difficult to determine 'purely' local taxes based on generally published data. In Table 7.3 below, we consider a purely local revenue source as a tax for which a subnational government has tax rate and tax base setting authority, though the central government may set a cap on the tax rate as well as restricting in some manner the authority of the subnational government to vary the definition of the tax base. Thus, shared taxes for which the central government exclusively sets the rate and defines the tax base are not considered purely subnational taxes. In fact, shared taxes have more in common with grants than purely subnational taxes.

Table 7.1   Revenue Assignment

Revenue source	Appropriate central or subnational?	Why
Progressive personal income tax	Yes central Piggyback subnational	Redistribution is best handled by central government to reduce incentives for migration; subnationals can effectively piggyback
Enterprise profit tax	Yes central No subnational	Compliance, stabilization factors and cost of administration make this a more useful central government tax
Value added tax	Yes central No subnational	'Exporting' across regional borders within a country lessen the effectiveness and viability as a subnational tax
Retail sales tax	Yes central Yes subnational	Subnational rates should be set relatively low to reduce regional competition
Excise taxes	Yes central Piggyback subnational	Can be relatively easy to administer and with relatively low local rates, less chance for purchases over borders
User fees and charges	Yes subnational	These benefit taxes are most appropriate at subnational level due to relatively simple structure and correspondence with benefits provided by subnational governments.

Sources: compiled by the authors

Table 7.2   Type of Revenue Assignment

Type of assignment	Description	Example
True subnational taxes	Rate and base setting authority controlled locally	State income tax in US
Piggybacked taxes	Rate setting (typically as a surcharge with a maximum rate) allowed on top of centrally controlled base	Piggyback local personal income tax in Scandinavian Countries
Shared taxes	Distribution is made by central to subnational governments based as a share of collections; central government controls rates and bases	Value added tax in Russia (until 2001)

Sources: compiled by the authors

Table 7.3   Cross-country Comparisons: Effective Revenue Decentralization

Country	Illustrative revenue sources	Total true own source revenue as a share of total revenue
Russia (as of 2002)	Regional: • Enterprise assets tax • Sales Tax (abolished in 2004) • Presumptive income tax (in 2003 became a federal tax but shared with subnational units) • Forestry tax(abolished in 2005, became non-tax revenue administered by the federal forestry service) • Transport tax • Fees	29.8 percent (2002)
	Local: • Land tax • Individual property tax • License fee for alcohol retailing (abolished in 2004)	14 percent (2001)

Table 7.3   Cross-country Comparisons: Effective Revenue Decentralization (continued)

Country	Illustrative revenue sources	Total true own source revenue as a share of total revenue
	• Resort tax (abolished in 2004) • Advertisement tax (abolished in 2005) • Charges	
India	• State:	38.1 percent (2001)
	• Local:	25 percent (2001)
Indonesia	Provincial: • Charges motor vehicle fees, registration and licensing • Motor fuels surcharge • Fees for provincial parks • Income tax • Severance fee	21.7 percent (North Sulawesi, 2000)
	Local: • Hotel • Restaurant • Street advertising • Street lighting • Entertainment • Land excavation • Water tax	6 percent (average of all local governments, 2001); 8.7 percent (average of municipalities in East Java, 2000)
China	Provincial: • No true provincial levels taxes	
	Local: • No true subnational taxes	< 5 percent (all subnational government)
US	State: • Income tax • Sales tax • Property tax • Fees	66.4 percent (2001-02)
	Local: • Sales tax • Property tax • Fees • Income Tax	55.1 percent (2001-02)

Table 7.3   Cross-country Comparisons: Effective Revenue Decentralization (continued)

Country	Illustrative revenue sources	Total true own source revenue as a share of total revenue
Canada	Provincial and Territorial:	83 percent (2002– 3)
	Local:	59 percent (2002)

Sources: Bahl (1999), Mahi (2002), US Census Bureau (2004), Rao (forthcoming), Statistics Canada (2008)

Piggyback taxes are a hybrid between purely local taxes and central government taxes because the central government retains exclusive authority to define the tax base though the subnational government can set the tax rate, perhaps within limits. As can be seen from the data presented below for this limited sample of countries, there is a considerable variation in the extent to which subnational governments rely upon purely local government taxes. In the US, there is a relatively high degree of subnational revenue autonomy. Meanwhile, in Indonesia and Russia, the second tier of government provides for about a quarter of its revenue with purely subnational government taxes, and the third tier provides for less than 25 percent of revenue from purely local government taxes.

Under a less autonomous decentralized regime, subnational governments may be allowed some true own-source revenues with some, though perhaps limited, tax rate and tax base setting authority. Often times, however, those sources are limited in scope and revenue yield. Instead, the central government may share tax revenues from more important revenue sources, such as the value added tax from time to time in Russia, through an established sharing rate or through a general intergovernmental grant. Experience has shown that property and piggyback income taxes are among the best sources of own source revenues for subnational governments. Often, user fees, including licensing, car registration and recreational fees, are also assigned as own sources of local government revenue. However, this source is often under utilized in transitional and developing countries, perhaps out of concern for horizontal equity or public choice reasons.

In those countries with substantial revenue sharing, the subnational government typically has very limited revenue autonomy. Their tax bases and tax rates often are determined by the central government, and, in some cases, the sharing rates may vary from year to year. Under such circumstances, efforts at tax reform may be opposed on at least two fronts.

Table 7.4   Intergovernmental Arrangements and Incentives for Tax Reform

Arrangement	Tension for tax reform
Shared taxes	Reforms aimed at eliminating 'bad' shared taxes met with opposition unless revenue neutral additions are made
	Rate reductions may be met with similar opposition
Piggybacked systems	Rate and base changes at the central level will affect the revenue yield at the subnational level.
Significantly autonomous subnational revenue sources	Tax reform efforts may be viewed as encroaching on subnational own source revenues

Source: compiled by the authors

Proposed changes to existing tax rates and bases will directly affect revenues of either and/or both the central and subnational governments, and any level of government that is a revenue loser under the proposed reform is likely to become an opponent of the reform. Also, changes to the structure of intergovernmental fiscal relations from proposals to substitute a more efficient revenue sharing arrangement than the status quo could also meet with significant opposition if the subnational governments view themselves as losing part of their 'traditional' revenue sources. Like people, governments often prefer the devil they know to the devil they don't, even in the case of taxes.

If, for example, the intergovernmental fiscal arrangements are stable, tax reform efforts led by the central government may arouse concerns that the reform will introduce greater revenue instability into the budgets of subnational governments or compromise revenue adequacy. If, on the other hand, the intergovernmental fiscal arrangements are not politically stable and/or failing to produce adequate revenue, then the tax reform debate will often turn to addressing these issues as well. In either, the intergovernmental governmental ramifications of central government led tax reforms cannot be ignored, at least in the case of a successful reform.

Intergovernmental Relations in the Russian Federation: Historical and Political Setting

The structure of government in the Russian Federation is multi-tiered. At the center is the President of the Russian Federation and the legislative bodies of the Federation Council and the Duma. The next tier of government, the regional or oblast level, is comprised of 89 regions of which there are 49 oblasts, 21 republics, 6 krai and 2 cities (Moscow and St Petersburg), and 11 autonomous oblasts or okrugs. Municipalities comprise the third tier; there are as many as 30,000 individual jurisdictions.

The relationship between the central government and the regions has developed over time in a series of laws and regulations (see Box 7.1). However, a number of the laws and regulations were never enforced. As a result, during the early period of the transition from 1991 to 1994, there was a lot of confusion regarding expenditure responsibilities and the intergovernmental revenue system was ad hoc and frequently changed. Beginning in 1994, the budgetary autonomy of subnational governments was strengthened, and the federal government stopped the ad hoc offloading of expenditure responsibilities onto regional and local governments. New taxes were introduced as was a new piggyback system for the enterprise income tax, whereby regional governments were given the authority to adjust the regional share of the tax anywhere from 0 to 22 percent. During the 1997–98 period, a new Tax Code and Budget Code were developed in which revenue and expenditure assignments were clarified, and these laws provided more structure to central-regional relations. Table 7.5 summarizes the evolution of the federal-regional tax sharing rates from 1999 to date.

At the local level, the system of local governance was transformed with the introduction of the 1993 Constitution.[4] The Russian Constitution guarantees local communities the right to govern local affairs separately from the sovereignty of the state. The implementation of the constitutional right for local self-government is assigned to be the joint responsibility of the federal and regional governments. Thus, the Constitution set the stage for the federal government to enact a number of laws which further developed the framework for local governance. The most important of these laws includes the Law on the Fundamental Principles of Local Self-Government in Russia, the Law on the Constitutional Right to Local Government Elections, and the Law on the Financial Foundations of Local Self-Government. Box 7.1 summarizes these legislative regulations.

While the technical distinction in the hierarchy of subnational governments is roughly spelled out in the Constitution and various pieces of legislation, there is a de facto hierarchy among regions themselves. At the top of this hierarchy are so called 'donor' regions, which contribute more revenue to the federal budget than they get back through revenue sharing and transfers. In other words, they are net revenue donors to the federal budget. The 'donor' distinction has varied over time, but generally includes Moscow City, St Petersburg, Nizhny Novgorod, Samara, Sverdlovsk, Volgograd, Tyumen, Khanty-Mansi, Krasnoyarsk and Sakha (Yakutia).

Box 7.1   Legislation Shaping Intergovernmental Relations in the Russian Federation

Federal Law No. 1550-1 On Local Self-Government in the RSFSR (July 6, 1991) Established local governments and dual subordination of local officials to local bodies and higher level executives.

Law On the Basic Principles of Taxation (1991) Established limited tax instruments for local governments: land and property taxes, business licenses, and over 20 minor taxes.

Federation Treaty of March 1992 Regulated relationships between the central and regional governments; established certain powers for ethnic republics

Russian Constitution of 1993 Allowed for bilateral treaties between the Federation and the regional governments, thus supporting asymmetric federalism.

Law on the Fundamental Principles of Local Self-Government in Russia (1995) Developed the concept of autonomy of local self-governments.

Law on the Financial Foundations of Local Self-Government (1997) Institutionalized the structure of intra-regional fiscal relations.

Presidential Decree No 1281 of October 1998 'On the Congress of Municipal Settlements' (October 1998) Established the Congress of Municipal Settlements and the Union of Russian Cities.

Concept of Reform of Intergovernmental Fiscal Relations in the Russian Federation, 1998 Established new system of formula driven intergovernmental grants between the central and regional levels of government.

Presidential Decree of May 2000 Divided Russia into seven groups of regions, each with a presidential envoy to monitor regional legislation and ensure that regional administrations were abiding by federal laws.

Amendment to the Law on the Fundamental Principles of Local Self-Government (August 2000) Established accountability of local officials to upper-level governments.

Budget Code of 2001 Imposed legal limits on subnational borrowing.

Kazak Commission Recommendations (2002-03) Recommendations include the need to adequately fund each level of government according to the expenditure responsibilities they have been assigned.

The economic strength of these regions makes them important players in the tax reform debate as their willingness to carry out reforms and administer the tax system will have direct repercussions for the remaining regions in the Federation.

Needless to say, the 'subsidy' regions, which receive a net inflow of funds from Moscow, are subordinate to the 'donor' regions in the hierarchy of regional governments. This hierarchy reflects horizontal inequities that result from basic differences in fiscal capacity. Such disparities could be mitigated by the central government through shared taxes and general grants, but there is some evidence that central government transfers have been countering equalizing rather than equalizing, at least through 2001.[5]

Over the last 15 years, the strength of various regions, general economic conditions and outside forces, including IMF conditionalities and other international pressures, have significantly shaped the design of intergovernmental fiscal relations in the Russian Federation. In the early part of the post-Soviet period through 1993, regional governments received funding from three different sources: their own revenues generated from regional and local taxes; the sharing of revenues from the major taxes, including the enterprise profit tax, personal income tax, value added tax and excise taxes; and intergovernmental transfers. The system was largely one of negotiation and, as a result, sharing rates for the major taxes varied between years, among regions and among taxes.[6] During this period, the budgets of subnational governments were under dual subordination of both the federal and subnational authorities. At the local level, rayons and cities had the same general structure of funding sources as the regions, but revenue sharing and subventions were from their respective regional regional governments rather than from the federal government. Regional governments typically shared revenues with local governments under their jurisdiction in very similar ways, replicating the relations between the federal and regional governments.

The result of various experiments with fiscal decentralization in the Russian Federation coupled with the considerable disparities in the underlying fiscal capacity of various regions has created a situation where severe vertical and horizontal imbalances put pressure on the fiscal system. The vertical imbalances in terms of the heavy expenditures placed on the subnational governments without commensurate revenue authority pressures governments to either look for additional sources of revenue or shirk responsibilities. As noted by Martinez-Vazquez and Wong (2003), subnational governments have tried various ways to reduce these imbalances, including illegal means, such as refusing to remit collected taxes to Moscow that were to be shared by various levels of government. Beginning in 1993, subnational governments were also allowed to borrow, and this also has increased budgetary pressures.

CURRENT STATUS OF INTERGOVERNMENTAL FISCAL RELATIONS IN THE RUSSIAN FEDERATION

The federal government's current approach towards regional-local relations presents a mix of rigid norms and loose guidelines. The result is a system that has decentralized significant expenditures but centralized much of the revenue (Martinez-Vazquez and Wong, 2003). This has increased pressure on subnational governments and, for understandable reasons, increased their

Table 7.5 Legislated Sharing Rates of Major Taxes in the Russian Federation

	1991 Q1		1999 Q2-Q4		2000		2001	
	Fed	Reg	Fed	Reg	Fed	Reg	Fed	Reg
Value added tax[a]	75	25	85	15	85	15	100	0
Enterprise profit tax	37	63	37	63	37	63	31	69[c]
Personal income tax	14	86[e]	14	86	16	84	1	99
Single social security tax	–	–	–	–	100	–	100	0
Energy excises	100	0	100	0	100	0	100	0
Excise on liquor	50	50	50	50	50	50	50	50
Excises on tobacco[b]	0	100	0	100	0	100	0	100
Excises on wine, beer, and jewelry[b]	0	100	0	100	0	100	0	100
Tax on property of legal entities	0	100	0	100	0	100	0	100
Land tax	30[g]	70	30[g]	70	30[g]	70	30[g]	70
Tax on gas extraction	–	–	–	–	–	–	–	–
Tax on oil extraction	–	–	–	–	–	–	–	–
Tax on extr. of com. minerals	–	–	–	–	–	–	–	–
Tax on extr. of other minerals	–	–	–	–	–	–	–	–
Tax on property of individuals	0	100	0	100	0	100	0	100

Table 7.5 Legislated Sharing Rates of Major Taxes in the Russian Federation (continued)

	2002		2003		2004		2005		2006	
	Fed	Reg	Fed	Reg	Fed	Reg	Fed	Reg	Fed	Reg
Value added tax[a]	100	0	100	0	100	0	100	0	100	0
Enterprise profit tax	31	69[d]	25	75[d]	21	79[d]	27	73	27	73
Personal income tax	0	100	0	100	0	100	0	100	0	100
Single social security tax	100	0	100	0	100	0	100	0	100	0
Energy excises	100	0	100	0	100	0	–	–	–	–
Excise on liquor	50	50	50[f]	50	50	50	50	50	50	50
Excises on tobacco[b]	0	100	100	0	100	0	100	0	100	0
Excises on wine, beer, and jewelry [b]	0	100	0	100	0	100	0	100	0	100
Tax on property of legal entities	0	100	0	100	0	100	0	100	0	100
Land tax	15	85	0	100	0	100	0	100	0	100
Tax on gas extraction	80[h]	20	80[h]	20	100	0	100	0	100	0
Tax on oil extraction	80[h]	20	80[h]	20	86	14	95	5	95	5
Tax on extr. of com. minerals	0	100	0	100	0	100	0	100	0	100
Tax on extr. of other minerals	40	60	40	60	40	60	40	60	–	–
Tax on property of individuals	0	100	0	100	0	100	0	100	–	–

Source: Ministry of Finance

Notes:

[a] Value added tax on imports, precious metals and stones is assigned 100 percent at the federal   level.

[b] These taxes could be shared with the federal government.

[c] In 2001 a local enterprise profit tax rate of 5 percent was introduced; the regional share, therefore, also includes the local 5 percent.

[d] In 2002–04 an enterprise profit tax rate earmarked for local retention was 2 percent, the regional share includes the local 2 percent.

[e] The regional share is taken as equal to the average.

[f] Since 2003, the federal government has been receiving its share of excises.

[g] Tax revenues from agricultural land were shared differently.

[h] Until 2005, for regions including autonomous areas, the remittance rate was reduced to 5 percentage points in favor of the autonomous area. Since 2005 all regions receive 5 percent while autonomous areas receive nothing (ditto for other shared and assigned taxes), possibly to encourage further merging of autonomous areas with encompassing regions started in 2005.

opposition to wide-scale tax reforms that reduce their share of major taxes such as the value added tax.

The current federal legislation does not allow any level of government to introduce taxes beyond those enumerated in the Tax Code.[7] The list of permitted taxes is broken into three categories: federal, regional, and local revenue sources. As of January 2002, the list of 'federal' taxes includes the value added tax, special excises, custom duties, the enterprise profit tax, taxes and royalties on natural resources extraction, the personal income tax, gambling tax, the unified social tax, which is levied on payroll, as well as other minor federal revenue sources. In 2004 the Gambling Tax became a regional tax.

The current list of 'regional' taxes includes the Enterprise Assets Tax, Sales Tax, the Presumptive Income Tax, the Forestry Tax, the Transport Tax, which is levied according to engine power, as well as other minor regional revenue sources. Regions that have not introduced the Sales Tax (13 out of 88 regions) are allowed to levy the 'Education Tax', which is a further tax on payrolls.[8] Proceeds from all regional taxes, except for the Education and Forestry Taxes, can serve as 'regulated' sources of revenue for local governments, so that regional governments can share those revenues with their localities on a derivation or point of collection basis. Taxes shared by the regions with local governments are often at negotiated or differential rates.

The current list of 'local' revenue sources includes the Individual Property Tax, Land Tax, the Individual Entrepreneur's Patent, the License Fee for Alcohol Retailing, the Resort Tax, the Advertisement Tax and 'Earmarked Charges.[9] In 2004 the local Patent was abolished and replaced with duty stamp for registration in the state register of businesses. In regions without the Sales Tax, local governments are authorized to levy a dozen different charges, which typically have very low yield (for example, dog license tax).[10]

Classification of a tax into a particular category does not always determine the level of government that receives the proceeds from this tax. For instance, the personal income tax is a fully retained federal tax. In other examples, the succession and gift tax (until it was abolished in 2006) was classified as a federal tax, though traditionally its full revenue yield had been allocated to the subnational budgets at the point of collection (that is, fully shared on a derivation basis). At the same time, the Land Tax, which is classified as a local tax, had been shared among all three levels of government till 2004. For some taxes also designated as 'assigned', revenue sharing is fixed in legislation. For others, designated as 'regulated' revenue sharing, revenue sharing is determined by the higher-level government as part of the annual budget process.

Part of the collections of the personal income tax and special excises on good – and up until 2001, the value added tax – are shared by the federal government with regional governments based on a derivation basis or the point of collection. In turn, regional governments can reallocate a portion of these revenues to their local government. Similarly, royalties on natural resource extraction are in part assigned to regional governments, and until the year 2002 also to localities, at the point of collection. In addition, regional governments can determine a surcharge on the federal enterprise profit tax between 10.5-14.5 percentage points while local governments retain revenue from 2 percentage points without any tax-setting powers.[11]

The pattern of revenue distribution between the central and subnational governments over the last ten years is reported in Tables 7.6a and 7.6b. The relative level of revenue transferred or generated by subnational governments has varied over the decade, but until the tightening of central control post-Putin, the split was roughly a 50-50 split between the federal and regional governments. The year 2001 was a transition year when the value added tax was assigned to the federal government and boosted the federal share of revenue. The sales tax 'experiment,' whereby regional governments were allowed to impose a sales tax and had jurisdiction over the tax base, ended in 2004, which further tilted the shares in the favor of the federal government.

At the subnational level, the importance of various revenues is obvious from Tables 7.7 and 7.8, which show the distribution of revenues by source. At the federal level, most of the revenue comes from taxes on goods and services (value added tax), income tax and trade taxes; while the subnational governments receive the majority of their revenue from the shared income taxes. This assignment of revenue is more appropriate than the early sharing of the value added tax, but there are still problems with this arrangement. In particularly, a subnational enterprise income tax is problematic because it is not evenly distributed among regions, and there is a headquarters problem. Furthermore, the current arrangement provides little scope for truly subnational taxes. From the data presented in the table, however, it is obvious that changes in the tax code that affect the tax base or rate for shared taxes are likely to meet with considerable opposition or at least arouse considerable concern among subnational government officials and the public. Tax reforms that do not take into account the intergovernmental dimension have either worsened the fiscal situation of the regional and local governments or led to increased pressure for the central government to increase transfers to subnational governments. Such pleas are likely to be received more sympathetically during national elections, which may result in macroeconomic stability and bad management practices by subnational

Table 7.6a   Fiscal Distribution of Total Pre-Transfer Revenue (Percent of Consolidated Budget Revenues)

	1995	1996	1997	1998	1999	2000	2001	2002	2003	2004
Federal	49.06	46.61	44.21	44.08	48.23	51.51	54.66	57.44	57.26	58.79
Subfederal	50.94	53.39	55.79	55.92	51.77	48.49	45.34	42.56	42.74	41.21

Source: Russian Statistical Yearbook (Goskomstat, 2005)

Table 7.6b   Fiscal Distribution of Total Tax Revenue (Percent of Consolidated Budget Tax Revenues)

	1995	1996	1997	1998	1999	2000	2001	2002	2003	2004
Federal	48.12	46.24	44.20	44.86	50.59	56.50	62.28	64.89	64.10	63.83
Subfederal	51.88	53.76	55.80	55.14	49.41	43.50	37.72	35.11	35.90	36.17

Source: Russian Statistical Yearbook (Goskomstat, 2005)

Table 7.7 Components of Federal and Subnational Revenue 2003 (billions of rubles)

	Federal	Consolidated	Subnational	
			Regional	Local
Total revenue	2,586.20	1,930.42	1,410.90	871.40
Tax revenue	2,394.20	1,341.20	893.80	447.30
Income, profit, capital gains tax	537.30	813.20	523.60	289.60
Taxes on goods and services, license fees	1,135.80	152.90	120.10	32.80
Tax on total income	10.10	20.20	6.30	13.90
Property taxes	1.70	136.10	77.40	58.70
Natural resource tax	249.50	146.20	108.10	38.10
Tax on international trade	452.80	–	–	–
Other taxes	7.10	72.60	58.30	14.20
Non-tax revenue	176.70	156.70	110.70	46
Income from government property and activities	112.70	127.50	88.20	39.30
Revenues from sale of non-material assets	0.01	0.06	0	0.06
Administrative fees	1.40	5	4.60	0.50
Fines and forfeits	2	6	1.90	4.20
Income from foreign economic activity	52.90	–	–	–
Other non-tax revenue	7.70	18.10	16	1.90
Intergovernmental grants	1	285.70	269.90	367.80
Revenue of earmarked budget funds	14.30	128.70	127.40	1.30

Source: Federal Treasury, Ministry of Finance (various years), accessed September 11, 2007: http://www.roskazna.ru/reports/fbrf

Table 7.8 Composition of Federal and Subnational Revenue 2003 (percent of total revenue)

	Federal	Consolidated	Subnational	
			Regional	Local
Total revenue	100.00	100.00	100.00	100.00
Tax revenue	92.58	69.48	63.35	51.33
Income, profit, capital gains tax	20.78	42.13	37.11	33.23
Taxes on goods and services	43.92	7.92	8.51	3.76
Tax on total income	0.39	1.05	0.45	1.60
Property taxes	0.07	7.05	5.49	6.74
Natural resource tax	9.65	7.57	7.66	4.37
Tax on international trade	17.51	–	–	–
Other taxes	0.27	3.76	4.13	1.63
Non-tax revenue	6.83	8.12	7.85	5.28
Income from government property and activities	4.36	6.60	6.25	4.51
Revenues from sale of non-material assets	0.00	0.00	0.00	0.01
Administrative fees	0.05	0.26	0.33	0.06
Fines and forfeits	0.08	0.31	0.13	0.48
Income from foreign economic activity	2.05	–	–	–
Other non-tax revenue	0.30	0.94	1.13	0.22
Intergovernmental Grants	0.04	14.80	19.13	42.21
Revenue of Earmarked Budget Funds	0.55	6.67	9.03	0.15

Source: Federal Treasury, Ministry of Finance (various years), accessed September 11, 2007: http://www.roskazna.ru/reports/fbrf

governments. The experience with state finances of India is especially instructive in this regard (McCarten, 2001).

TAX ADMINISTRATION, TAX POLICY, AND INTERGOVERNMENTAL FISCAL RELATIONS

Another important dimension of the interaction between intergovernmental fiscal relations and tax reform is that of tax administration. Tax reforms will not work if taxes cannot be collected. Furthermore, as long as tax administration is under the authority of both the federal and subnational levels of government, the intergovernmental issue will continue to play a crucial role in tax reform. The initial structure of the Russian tax administration consisted of the State Tax Service (STS) Headquarters, 89 Oblast-level State Tax Inspectorates (STIs) and almost 3,000 Territorial Tax Inspectorates (TTIs) at the level of cities and rayons. The State Tax Service headquarters organizationally has been in a state of flux since its inception. Major reorganizations have been commonplace, and there has been a high rate of turnover of officials appointed to top-level management positions. In 1999, the State Tax Service was made the Ministry of Taxes and Levies and given official cabinet status. In 2004, a wholesale reorganization of the government restored tax administration as a subordinate agency under the authority of the Ministry of Finance.

The total staff of the federal tax administration fluctuated from approximately 65,000 employees in 1990 to 197,000 in 1998 and down to 156,000 in 2000 (Tolkushkin, 2001). The vertical structure of the federal tax administration appears to be extremely deconcentrated, even more deconcentrated than the federal public administration as a whole. For example, in 1995 the State Tax Service headquarters employed 710 persons while State Tax Inspectorates and Territorial Tax Inspectorates employed 161,000 persons. The post-2004 structure has 1,051 employees in the Moscow headquarters and 166,000 employees in the territorial brunches. Interestingly, while the deconcentrated employment in State Tax Inspectorates and Territorial Tax Inspectorates accounts for more than one third of the total public administration employment of the federal government, the State Tax Service headquarters staff accounts for less than 3 percent of the federal public administration core in Moscow. This highly deconcentrated structure has allowed State Tax Inspectorates to experiment with their own innovations and approaches (Firestone, 1998). The lack of coordination and logistical support from the Moscow headquarters traditionally has made federal tax agents in the field dependent on the support of local authorities. This later has contributed to blurring the delineation of powers between the levels of government and led to the de facto 'dual subordination' of tax administrators to subnational and federal authorities. If the tax code is not enforced by the tax administration, then tax reform will have no or limited impact. The dual subordination of tax administration in Russia, which perpetuates divided loyalties among administrators between the various levels of government, is likely to continue to plague the implementation of tax reform.

TAX REFORM EFFORTS WITH INTERGOVERNMENTAL FISCAL RELATIONS

Putin's administration has continued the recentralization of revenues that started in the latter years of the Yeltsin administration. A beginning was made with the reform of the Russian tax system in 1998 as part of the emergency measures taken in response to the economic crisis of August 1998. The first part of the new Tax Code, which contains the general principles of taxation in the Russian Federation, was passed by the legislature in 1999. Subsequently, however, the government's tax reform efforts effectively stalled as the more important, second part of the Tax Code, which contained legislation defining the various taxes, became bogged down in the legislative process because of a lack of political consensus on the nature of the reforms within the executive and legislative branches. Following his election to the presidency, Putin managed to get four chapters of the second part of the Tax Code approved by the State Duma, which had a profound impact on regional finances. Subnational government sales taxes, which provided a substantial level of own-source revenues for local and regional governments, have been repealed.

The cumulative impact on the vertical fiscal balance of the post-1998 tax reforms and associated changes in revenue assignments is reflected in the changing distribution of resources across the different levels of government over time. During the early years of the transition the federal share of overall tax revenues steadily declined. In 1992 approximately 60 percent of overall tax collections were assigned to the federal government; however, by 1998, the federal share declined to 44 percent. A sharp reversal of the downward trend in the federal share of consolidated revenues began in 1999. The federal share has steadily increased since the low point in 1998. The federal government's share of overall tax collections once again reached closed to 60 percent by 2004. Thus, after a period of increasing decentralization of fiscal resources during the early phase of the transition, the revenue balance in Russia has shifted substantially in favor of the federal government in recent years.[12]

Overall, the tax reforms have tended to reduce the complexity of the tax system and lower the marginal tax rates, thereby reducing incentives for tax avoidance and evasion. While generally in line with sound fiscal practices, these reforms and changes in the assignments of tax revenues have caused a substantial loss of shared revenues for regional and local governments and added very little to the revenue autonomy of these governments. In contrast, federal revenue sources, such as the natural resource extraction tax, have been substantially increased as part of the ongoing tax reforms. In this sense, the tax reforms did not facilitate, and in fact may compromise, many of the potential benefits of a decentralized fiscal system.

The intergovernmental fiscal system of the Russian Federation continues to fall short of its goal at least with respect to decentralization of expenditures and revenues, and the hope for the result of increased efficiency in the provision of locally provided public services. While the expenditure assignments have become more transparent and more in-line with best practices, revenue autonomy for subnational government continues to lag behind the reforms on the expenditure side of the budget. As long as subnational governments lack sufficient revenue autonomy, Russia's system of decentralization will not be able to achieve the full benefits of decentralization. In fact, the long-term success of tax reform in large part will depend on the reforms made to the system of intergovernmental revenue. There are a number of viable alternatives including the re-imposition of the regional sales tax or a permanent piggyback system for the income tax. Unless the federal government is committed to and successful in reversing the degree of decentralization in Russia, the failure of tax reform to address the vertical imbalances in the fiscal system will be met with renewed demands by the subnational governments for further reforms,.

Another weakness in the tax system is the dual subordination of tax administration. As previously noted, the unreformed and highly deconcentrated system of tax administration that came out of the early reform period has made it difficult to implement tax reforms that do not meet with acceptance by subnational governments. See the discussion in Chapter 6.

NOTES

1. For a detailed discussion of the analysis of tax reform and fiscal decentralization in Russia and China, see Martinez-Vazquez and Wong (2003).
2. A more detailed discussion of asymmetric federalism in the Russian Federation can be found in Wallich (1994), Treisman (1996, 1998) and Martinez-Vazquez, Timofeev and Boex (2004).

3.   Revenue from a 100 percent shared tax is paid over to the subnational government but the rate and base setting authority remains with the central government.
4.   Local governments are defined those that are: self-governed, hold municipal property, have a budget and have elected bodies of local self-government. Currently, there are about 29,500 units of local administration below the regional level. Kurlyandskaya (2001) note that only 12,261 local 'governments' are officially registered as municipal entities; 11,691 have elected representative authorities; 11,209 municipalities are endowed with municipal property; and only 4,500 have fully independent budgets.
5.   Empirical evidence is presented in Bahl, et al. (1999), Martinez-Vazquez and Boex (2001), and Bahl and Wallace (2003).
6.   In 1992 an experimental tax assignment regime was implemented but it did not last.
7.   This section draws heavily on Martinez-Vazquez, Timofeev and Boex (2004). In the course of 2000-05, gradual enactment of the Tax Code chapters replaced respective provisions of the previous *Law on the Basic Principles of Taxation*.
8.   By 2005 the regional list had shrunk to just Transport and Enterprise Assets Tax but supplemented with the formerly federal Gambling Tax.
9.   The amount to be collected for local 'earmarked charges' was set by the local government within federal limits of 3 percent of minimum wages for natural persons and 3 percent of the minimum wage multiplied by the number of employees for enterprises. However, we are aware of only a few (unsuccessful) attempts to levy this charge on natural persons, which would constitute a poll tax.
10. By 2005 the local list had shrunk to just the Individual Property Tax and Land Tax.
11. Since 2002 the regional enterprise profit tax surtax has had both an upper and lower limit: 10.5-14.5 percentage points in 2002, 12-16 percentage points in 2003, 13-17 percentage points in 2004, 13.5-17.5 percentage points in 2005–07.The local enterprise profit tax surtax of up to 5 percent was introduced to replace revenue from the abolished turnover tax revenue in 2001; however it was turned into a fixed retention in 2002 of and eventually abolished in 2005.
12   The determination of the 'right' level of revenue centralization is a policy decision that balances competing policy objectives, including macroeconomic stability and administrative efficiency, which often require centralized control over fiscal policy tools, and the desire to provide subnational governments with own-source revenues to fund the decentralized provision of public goods and increased efficiency and accountability of subnational governments.

8. The Next Decades of Reform

Russia's tax reform path has been slow and difficult. Economic and political realities have often intruded on the ability of the government and State Duma to focus on the development of a modern, market-oriented tax code. Consequently, there have been periods of progress in tax policy reform and periods without. Some major changes have been enacted, such as the introduction of a flat rate personal income tax and progress with more limited reforms. In particular, there are now more rational penalties for nonpayment of tax, and the total burden of the enterprise profit tax has been reduced. Despite the progress on some elements of tax reform, the codified approach to tax policy has not yet been fully implemented.

In addition to completing the task of developing a fully codified tax system, Russia's tax code also must adapt over time to the evolving demographic and socio-economic conditions of the country. For example, the budgetary expansion associated with the oil-led economic boom in the first decade of the twenty-first century may be masking underlying tensions that threaten the long-run stability of the tax system. The post-1998 economic boom is attributable to several factors, including the high price of oil, growth in private investment and import substitution. If these favorable economic conditions do not continue to prevail in coming years, the country's current fiscal stance may be difficult to sustain over the long term.

In addition to the risk of changing economic circumstances, there are demographic trends currently underway in Russia that may present policy challenges in the future. Among the myriad demographic trends, the decline in the size of the population and the growing share of the elderly in the total population may present the greatest challenges.[1] In short, changing circumstances over time may raise questions regarding who and what should be taxed and by how much.

By analyzing a country's demographic and socio-economic trends, one can identify fiscal policies which may be out of sync with those trends. We refer to such demographic and socio-economic trends that may impact a country's revenue and expenditure policies as the fiscal architecture of the country. Analyzing a country's fiscal architecture is helpful in identifying future problems and designing effective policy alternatives for the future. In this concluding chapter, we focus on Russia's fiscal architecture in order to explore the sustainability of the tax reforms to date and the need for further reforms in the future.

This chapter proceeds as follows. In the next section, we explore in greater detail some important demographic and socio-economic trends that are likely to present challenges to Russia's fiscal system. The third section evaluates the likely performance of the current revenue and expenditure system in light of these trends. We conclude with a discussion of some potential options for reform.

RUSSIA'S FISCAL ARCHITECTURE

Demographic and socio-economic factors such as the size of the population, age distribution, health status and the structure of an economy influence the performance of its fiscal system. Fiscal policies may become outdated as changes in a country's architecture occur over time. For example, suppose the service sector increases as a share of the economy, a tax system built around heavy manufacturing may over time become less buoyant as the relative importance of manufacturing to the economy declines. Tax reforms that are not consistent with the evolving fiscal architecture of a country can result in growing fiscal imbalances, and, if these imbalances are not addressed, they may eventually lead to macroeconomic instability.

To take another example, consider the fiscal impact of an aging population. In many countries, government and in some cases private pensions are not included in the personal income tax base. If the elderly grow as a proportion of the population, tax exempt pension income is also likely to be a growing share of total personal income, thus narrowing the personal income tax base and making that tax less buoyant. While a less buoyant personal income tax may present challenges to policymakers seeking to raise a given level of revenue, a growing elderly population is likely to demand more and different services from the government, such as income maintenance and health services. Thus, an aging population may confront the government with the twin challenges of a less buoyant tax system and increasing demand for government expenditures.

In short, if a country's tax policy is not properly aligned with changes in the country's fiscal architecture, the buoyancy of the tax system may not be adequate to meet the evolving demand for government services. While the focus of this book is on the revenue side of the budget, we would be remiss not to mention at least in passing that Russia's evolving fiscal architecture has equally important and consequential implications for the alignment of government programs with the demand for government services.

Generally speaking, the revenue yield of a country's tax system is a function of the size of the tax bases, the rates of tax and compliance with the system. Thus, the change in revenue yield of a given tax can be expressed as follows:

$$\Delta REV_i = \Delta TXBASE_i \times TXRATE_i + \Delta TXRATE_i \times TXBASE_i$$

where:

REV_i = revenue yield from tax i
$TXBASE_i$ = size of the base of tax i
$TXRATE_i$ = rate structure of tax i

Briefly, this expression shows that the change in the revenue yield of a tax varies with changes in the tax base and rate structure of the tax. The size of the tax base, in turn, depends on the number of taxable individuals (firms), distribution of income (distribution of economic activity among sectors) and level and composition of consumption (production). In the case of value added tax and excise taxes, the size of the tax bases depends on the level and composition of consumption which, in turn, is a function of the tastes and preferences of the population as well as the level and distribution of income. Based on evidence from developing countries, the composition and level of demand for goods and services in Russia is likely to evolve as the level and distribution of income and the size and age profile of the population change over time. For example, based on experience in developed economies, people demand more and different goods and services as their personal income grows over time. Changing demands for goods and services is likely to have an impact on the revenue yield of consumption taxes, such as a value added tax, excise taxes and customs duties.

The change in revenue yield is also influenced by changes in the rate of tax compliance. However, the effect of a country's fiscal architecture on tax compliance is not well understood; therefore, we do not incorporate tax compliance into our analysis.

As discussed above, changes in a country's fiscal architecture also affect the demand for government goods and services. The expenditure needs of a country are determined by the unit costs of producing government goods and services, the size of the recipient populations, take-up rates and compliance with program eligibility rules. Thus, the change in demand for total government expenditures can be expressed as follows:

$$\Delta EXP_i = \Delta CPOP_i \times PXPS_i + \Delta PXPS_i \times CPOP_i$$

where:

EXP_i = demand for government expenditure on the ith program
$CPOP_i$ = size of the client population of the ith program
$PXPS_i$ = production costs of the ith program

Briefly, this expression says that the change in government expenditures is proportional to the change in the size of the client population and the change in the unit costs of production of the ith program. This expression does not account for take-up rates and compliance with the eligibility criteria of the program, as the influence of a country's fiscal architecture on these factors is not well understood. Demographic changes can influence both components of the expenditure calculation. For example, consider a change in the age distribution of the population. As previously discussed, the demand for government services targeting the elderly, such as income maintenance and health services, grows as the elderly grow as a share of the population. However, a growing elderly population also may influence the unit costs of providing services because the resulting labor shortages may result in higher wages or input costs.

One could develop a rigorous econometric analysis of the impact of these demographic and socio-economic changes on tax revenues and expenditures by source if the necessary detailed data are available. Such an analysis would estimate the growth in revenue by tax as a function of tax rates and the demographic and socio-economic architecture that affects the tax base. This type of analysis would give us an objective and quantitative estimate of the impact of changes in the fiscal architecture on a country's fiscal system. Such an analysis also could provide valuable insights into the efficacy of proposed policy reforms.

In the case of the Russian Federation, it is difficult to obtain comprehensive and consistent time series of government revenues, economic activity, and demographic data that would permit us to build the proposed econometric model. However, we can use empirical findings from other countries to understand the likely effect of such trends on revenue yields by tax.

During the past two decades, dramatic political and economic reforms coincided in the Russian Federation with equally dramatic changes in major demographic and socio-economic characteristics of Russia. Failure of future reforms to account for these changes in Russia's fiscal architecture may compromise the success and long-term sustainability of the existing tax system. To analyze the implications of these trends for fiscal policy, we first focus the discussion on the effect of demographic changes, and then we turn to an analysis of the effect of changes in the structure of the economy on the country's fiscal system. In both cases, we focus on the way in which the evolution of these variables is likely to affect the stability and buoyancy of Russia's tax system.

Demographics: Table 8.1 provides a convenient summary of major demographic trends currently underway in Russia. The first row of Table 8.1 shows that the size of Russia's population is decreasing. As shown in row 2, the rate of decline is approximately 5.5 percent per annum. The UNDP (2006) reports a decline in the fertility rate from approximately the population replacement rate in 1970-75 to well below this rate at 1.3 in 2000-05. This decline in the fertility rate is helping to drive the decline in total population. Another contributing factor to the population decline is the decline in life expectancy at birth. As shown in row 3, during the past ten years, life expectancy at birth has fallen from 66.8 years in 1992 to 65.4 years in 2003. This trend reflects the decline in male life expectancy. Although women outlive men by twice as many years relative to other G-8 countries (World Bank, 2006), women also are less healthy than their counterparts in many developed countries.

Although there has been progress in reducing the rates of infant mortality (row 4) and poverty (row 5), the World Bank (2006) reports that the overall physical health of the population has deteriorated due, in part, to alcohol and tobacco consumption. According to the same study, Russia also has higher levels of cancer mortality, cardiovascular disease, traffic fatalities and suicides. In fact, the death rate is high relative to that of other countries, 30th out of 224 countries when ranked in descending order. Russia also ranks high in terms of the number of people living with HIV/AIDS: 13th out of 164 countries.[2]

A healthy and growing country would typically have a substantial young and working age population relative to the retired population. Figure 8.1 shows the 'population pyramid' for the Russian Federation in 2000 and the projected pyramid for 2050. These figures show quite dramatically that Russia's population base of the young and working age population is shrinking relative to the size of the retired population. Between 2000 and 2025, the age-dependency ratio of the population over 54 years old and the number aged 20 to 54 is projected to increase from 36 percent to 57 percent. In other words, the number of workers per retiree is expected to decrease from approximately 3:1 in 2000 to less than 2:1 by 2025.[3] Furthermore, the US Census Bureau forecasts that Russia's working age population (age 20 to 59) will fall from 57.5 percent of the population in 2000 to 45.7 percent in 2050, which represents an absolute decline in the number of such individuals by 41 percent over the next 50 years. In short,

Table 8.1   Demographic Trends: 1992-2004

Variable	1992	1996	2000	2003	2003
Population, million[a]	148.3	147.6	145.6	144.2	143.4
Total increase in population, per 1000 of population[b]	7.1	4.5	−4.2	−4.5	−5.5
Life expectancy at birth, years[c]	66.8	66.0	65.4	65.4	65.4
Infant mortality, per 1000 of children younger than 1 year old[d]	20.5	16.7	16.9	16.9	16.9
People with income below poverty level, share of population, percent[e]	33.5	22.0	29.1	20.4	17.8

Source:
[a] IMF
[b] Goskomstat
[c] Goskomstat
[d] United Nations Department of Economic and Social Affairs
[e] United Nations Department of Economic and Social Affairs

Russia's age demographics are putting pressure on a smaller and smaller number of workers to support a growing population of retirees.

What are the likely fiscal consequences of these demographic trends for Russia? On the expenditure side, we would expect an increased demand for health and pension-related expenditures. Because the population of the country is shrinking – particularly the working aged population – the budget arithmetic simply does not balance. The lack of a link between inflows and outflows of a simple pay-as-you-go pension system becomes clear.

To make matters more concrete consider the following expression which describes a pay-as-you-go pension system that breaks even on an annual basis:

$$N_p \times B = t \times P_w \times W$$

where:

N_p = the number of pensioners,
B = average benefit per pensioner,

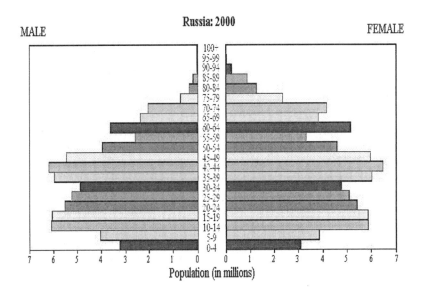

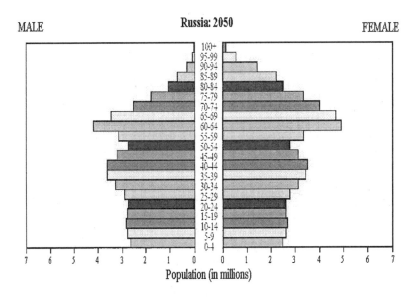

Source: US Census Bureau, International Data Base

Figure 8.1   Age Population Pyramids for Russia: 2000 and 2050

t = payroll tax rate
P_w = the number of workers, and
W = the average covered wage per worker.

This relationship can be rearranged as follows:

$$\%\Delta t = \%\Delta(N_p - P_w) + \%\Delta(B - w).$$

This expression says that the percentage change in payroll tax rate must equal the sum of the percentage change in the difference between the number of pensioners and the number of workers [$\%\Delta(N_p - P_w)$] and the percentage change in the difference between the benefit level and the wage [$\%\Delta(B/w)$]. As the number of beneficiaries grows relative to the number of workers, the age-dependency ratio (N_p/P_w) increases and ($N_p - P_w$) increases, and, if the pension system does not have adequate reserves, there is not enough revenue to service the annual pension liabilities. If wages grow faster than benefits, some of the impact of the increase in the dependency ratio may be offset. If, however, wages and benefits grow proportionately, then $\%\Delta(B - w) = 0$, and the government would eventually have to increase the payroll tax rate to maintain a given level of real benefits in the face of a growing elderly population. This is an example of the expenditure-revenue pressure that is expected to affect the Russia Federation in coming years.

In addition to affecting the benefits-contribution balance of a pay-as-you-go pension system, a growing elderly population would be expected to change the revenue yield of taxes on wages and salary, such as the personal income tax and payroll-based social fund taxes. As capital income is typically a hard to tax source, the concentration of wealth in Russia would not be expected to offset the slowing growth of wage income resulting from the aging population. Russia's personal income tax per employed worker grew from 2,289 rubles in 2000 to 8,543 rubles in 2004, more than doubling the tax burden on labor in real terms over this four year period. Such growth may be the result of increased work effort or increased compliance (Ivanova et al., 2005; Martinez-Vazquez et al. 2006). However, it is unlikely that such growth could be sustained over the long term. In addition, the expected decline in the working age population may reduce the growth of income tax receipts unless the tax burden becomes very high on those workers in the tax net.

A declining population also is likely to adversely affect the buoyancy of the value added tax. In recent years, value added tax revenues have been buoyant, growing by 68 percent in real terms from 2000 to 2004. This can be attributed in large part to growing household consumption which has experienced an average growth rate of 8.7 percent per year since 1999 (in real terms). A declining population is likely to lead to a decrease in household formation and thus substantially erode the consumption tax base. In real terms, a 5 percent reduction in population could reduce value added tax revenues by approximately the same amount, assuming consumption patterns are constant. This is a worrisome result because the value added tax is an important source of revenue in Russia's current tax structure.

However, consumption patterns are unlikely to stay constant if personal incomes continue to grow. Rather, changing consumption patterns may favor taxable goods and services thus increasing the buoyancy of the value added tax. Furthermore, a substantial share of household expenditure is not taxable under the current value added tax. Based on tabulations from the Russia Longitudinal Monitoring Survey (RLMS), we find that per capita expenditures have been averaging about 2,600 rubles, but much of this consumption is non-taxable. The USGTA (1998d) reports that food consumption is about 35 percent of total reported expenditures in Russia. Using the RLMS, we estimate that only about 27 percent of household consumption on average is taxable under the value added tax. Since such a large share of the consumption tax base is exempt from tax, this provides opportunities for base broadening to increase the yield and buoyancy of the value added tax

Economic base: During the nearly two decades of reform, there has been significant restructuring of Russia's economy. This restructuring also has implications for tax reform, past and present. Table 8.2 presents a summary of the growth in output by economic sector. The cumulative figures in the rightmost column of Table 8.2 show that construction and transportation/communication are the fastest growing sectors of the economy. The within industry classification shows that the fuel sub-industry is the only one that has recovered to the output levels achieved in 1991. In fact, the outputs of light industry, forestry, machinery and construction materials are fractions of their 1991 levels. These trends suggest that the sectoral achievements of the Soviet period may be in decline, perhaps because they were not market-based in the first place. In any event, taxes targeting these sectors may not be as productive in the future, as the economy continues to restructure.

Having said this, using the enterprise profit tax may be a more effective way for Russia to tax the industrial sector, than it would be in an economy like that of the United States which relies more heavily on the service sector. As such, the Russian Federation should consider continuing to simplify the corporate income tax thus reducing the temptation of companies to avoid or evade the corporate tax.

Table 8.2 Growth by Sector (percent)

Economic sector	1998	1999	2000	2001	2002	2003	2004	Cumulative
GDP	-5.3	6.4	10	5.1	4.7	7.3	7.1	35.3
Industry	-4.8	10.2	11.1	4.9	4	7.5	6.1	39
Agriculture	-8.1	17.1	12.7	11.4	2.9	5.7	2.9	34.6
Construction	-6.3	6	17.4	9.9	2.8	14.3	10.2	54.3
Transportation/communication	-3.4	9.6	6.1	5.7	5.8	8.7	9.5	42
Trade	-6.7	-2	12.1	3.9	8.2	10.9	10.1	36.5
Non-market services	1.3	1.9	1.4	-0.6	2.2	4	2.3	12.5

Source: IMF (2005)

With these changes in Russia's fiscal architecture in mind, we use the documented experiences of other countries to understand the effect of expected changes in Russia's fiscal architecture on the buoyancy of the current tax system. Table 8.3 provides a summary of this analysis. The information in the table provides an overview of the major demographic and socio-economic trends impinging on Russia's tax system. Due to changes in the country's fiscal architecture, many tax bases may be weakened. In fact, the income and consumption tax bases may be at risk because of the growing share of the elderly in the population and the reduced number and size of households. The recent growth in GDP, which is in part attributable to the oil sector, gives some hope for continuing growth of tax revenue. However, the volatility of the international price of oil makes this sector a weakness as well as strength over the long run. Russia's evolving fiscal architecture calls for diversification of the tax base to compensate for the negative effects of an aging population on the buoyancy of the tax system, declining size of the workforce and volatility of prices in the oil sector.

If demand for government goods and services do not fall proportionately, reduced revenue buoyancy due to changing demographics is likely to be a problem. However, there is reason to expect that, in Russia, the per capita demand for government expenditures will increase rather than remain constant. Based on the experiences of many countries, pension benefits and health care costs are likely to outstrip the potential expenditure savings associated with fewer school children. Additionally, Russia will need to continue to invest in infrastructure to sustain current economic growth rates; otherwise, infrastructure is likely to be over utilized or congested which may put a brake on continued growth. Bringing Russia's infrastructure up to developed world standards will be an expensive undertaking. Finally, Russia is likely to strive to rebuild its national defense capabilities which will also be an expensive undertaking.

Are Russia's tax reforms consistent with its changing fiscal architecture? We now turn to a summary of changes that have been made, and discuss how these changes interact with the country's evolving fiscal architecture. We include as well, a discussion of issues related to the tax climate, including the barter economy and tax administration.

THE PAST AND THE UNFINISHED AGENDA

The many changes to the tax system over the past 15 years have moved the system toward a more modern, market-oriented tax system. In this concluding section, we examine the major taxes in light of these changes and evaluate whether the changes are appropriate from the perspective of its

Table 8.3 Impact of Economic and Demographic Changes on Major Revenue Sources

Factor	Trend in Russia	Factors' Impact on Revenue Holding other Factors Constant			
		Value added tax	Excise	Enterprise profit tax	Personal Income Tax
Age distribution	Increased elderly as a share of population	Increased consumption of non-taxed goods, reduced value added tax growth	Reduced consumption of alcohol, indeterminate for tobacco, reduced revenues	Unclear, expect reduced consumption of durables may weaken tax base	Reduced elasticity to tax revenue due to reduced growth in taxable wages and other sources
Family size	Decreasing	Decreased growth in overall consumption	Indeterminate		May increase labor force participation and expand base
Health	Slowly increasing life expectancy, AIDS, environmental concerns	Reduced consumption of taxable items	Indeterminate	May reduce productivity	Reduced workforce and taxable income base
GDP	Steady growth	Steady growth	Steady growth	Steady growth	Steady growth

Table 8.3 Impact of Economic and Demographic Changes on Major Revenue Sources (continued)

		Factors' Impact on Revenue Holding other Factors Constant			
Factor	Trend in Russia	Value added tax	Excise	Enterprise profit tax	Personal Income Tax
Service sector (output composition)	Increasing	More ambiguous than for enterprise profit tax, IIT, evidence slightly for negative impact	Potential for increase due to demand for more technology	Decrease due to decrease in tax handles	Decrease due to decrease in tax handles
Oil/gas markets	Volatility in prices, increased production	General increase via employment effects	Negligible	Increase via increased profits	Increase via employment impacts

evolving fiscal architecture. We also offer some suggestions for further changes. To that end, there are some remaining reforms to part of the tax code that, while not tied as directly to the fiscal architecture story, are important options to consider as a means of enhancing the productivity and stability of the tax system.

In the most general terms, the tax code is in need of further simplification, and the tax administration needs to become more serious about developing the capacity to administer the system. The complicated types of taxes, the complicated structure of each tax and the lack of sufficient tax administration combine to create a system which is onerous and burdensome on the one hand, and for which there is little respect and compliance on the other. At the same time, the aging of the population, reduced family size, volatility of oil prices and increased international capital mobility call for changes in the tax system that continue to broaden the base of major taxes such as value added tax and diversify the revenue base.

Simplification of the system: Some of the complexity of the system associated with multiple taxes and rates has been simplified over the past several years, but small nuisance taxes remain at the regional and local levels. The enterprise profit tax is still unnecessarily complicated due to the types and number of deductions and exemptions, and the same can be said for the value added tax and even the flat rate personal income tax. The World Bank estimates that businesses must spend an average of 256 hours per year on complying with the tax system.[4] This is high relative to the OECD average (197.2 hours) but not substantially different from countries in East Asia and the Pacific (249.9 hours) and the Middle East and North Africa (241.9 hours).

There are obvious ways to simplify these taxes. This could be accomplished in a revenue-neutral way by eliminating a number of exemptions and deductions. Simplification may offer the added benefit of increasing tax morale and thus compliance with the tax system, at least insofar as the tax administration can enforce these changes. Over time, it may be possible to reduce tax rates. Care needs to be taken not just to eliminate the smaller nuisance taxes levied by local and regional governments. Such an action would further reduce the very limited revenue autonomy of subnational governments, particularly that of local governments. Simplification of the system should include a rationalization of the tax-sharing and tax-assignment arrangements among the federal, regional and local governments.

Taxation of capital income: The taxation of capital is an example of a system which has been 'fixed' too many times. The result is a system where dividends, capital gains and interest income are treated differently and are also treated differently according to the recipient of the income.

For residents, interest income earning a return less than the central bank refinancing rate on ruble deposits is taxed at 13 percent, while interest above this rate is taxed at 35 percent. After accounting for the deductibility of interest expenses under the enterprise profit tax, the effective marginal tax rate is approximately 9.9 percent. Dividends paid to physical persons are taxed at 9 percent, but these payments are not deductible at the corporate level. Thus, the effective rate on dividends paid to physical persons is approximately 33 percent. Corporate capital gains are taxed at 24 percent, and the capital gains of physical persona are taxed at 13 percent. Finally, non-resident individuals typically pay a higher tax rate on all sources of income.

Options: The changes to capital taxation have improved the situation from the pre-1998 tax code. Yet, there is a considerable differential between the effective marginal tax rate on dividends and interest income paid to physical persons. This tax differential creates opportunities for tax avoidance. Rather than issuing equity and distributing earnings as dividends which are taxed at an effective rate of 33 percent, the firm could issue debt and 'distribute' earnings to their bond holders as interest payments which face an effective rate of 9.9 percent. If one of the goals of tax policy is to avoid interfering with market decisions, then it is difficult to rationalize the tax preference for debt financing as opposed to equity finance, particularly in a country in which firms may already be thinly capitalized.[5]

An obvious reform option would be to give dividends and interest the same tax treatment. A further flattening of the tax rates on capital gains could improve incentives to save and investment and would further simplify the system. An option is to create a capital tax whereby interest, dividends and capital gains are all taxed at a flat rate of 13 percent.

Personal income tax and other taxes on labor income: The maximum tax rate on labor income due to the combined effect of the personal income tax and social taxes is 39 percent. The combined rate has come down significantly since the mid-1990s as a result of reducing the social taxes, though in a regressive manner, and the introduction of the flat rate personal income tax. Including the pension fund tax which has a maximum rate of 14 percent and the workplace accident insurance tax with a maximum rate of 8.5 percent, the overall tax burden on labor income is 61.6 percent which is still quite high by international standards.

Options: The list of exemptions and deductions under the personal income tax includes deductions for education expenses, property purchase expenses, gains from the sale of property and the cost of employer provided medical insurance. A number of these could be eliminated. This reform would simplify the personal income tax and create fiscal space to decrease the tax rates on labor income in a revenue neutral manner.

The Tax Code also provides for personal deductions for special category taxpayers, such as victims of Chernobyl, war veterans and so on. Eliminating the special category deductions and the standard deduction and replacing them with a more generous and uniform standard deduction may be an attractive option. In addition to promoting greater horizontal equity, this change would greatly simplify compliance with the personal income tax because it is generally paid by withholding at source.

Corporate and other business taxes: The taxes paid statutorily by businesses end up affecting either the return to capital, labor and/or output prices. Generally speaking, firms in Russia face an enterprise profit tax of 24 percent, a value added tax of 18 percent and an assets tax of 2.2 percent, among other business taxes. Overall, the statutory tax schedule for businesses is now reasonably consistent with international best practice.

Options: The enterprise profit tax has been cleaned up substantially in recent years. The depreciation of capital expenses has been simplified. There are now ten asset categories, and firms can use either the straight line or declining balance methods. Most business expenses are allowed as deductions for tax calculations, and those that are not allowed are explicitly enumerated in the tax code. In other words, business expenses are deductible, unless explicitly stated otherwise in the tax code. Still, there are over 48 non-allowable deductions listed in Article 270 of Chapter 25 of the tax code. Many of these are very specific an example of which is the limitation on the deductibility of expenses of firms working in natural resource development, where the work proved 'unsuccessful' (Article 270, number 35). Retaining an exemption list with this level of detail within the tax code could make administration of the enterprise profit tax more cumbersome.

Loss carry forwards have been extended to ten years, which is an improvement over earlier versions of the tax code. However, there is no provision for loss carry backs.

Value added tax: The value added tax has seen a number of improvements over the past several years. The number of exemptions has been reduced, a long-awaited move to accrual accounting has been implemented and differential treatment of the construction industry has effectively been eliminated. The two-tiered system now in place for necessities and other goods is not optimal from the perspective of minimizing compliance and administrative costs, but it is a practical and widely accepted approach to dealing with the otherwise regressive nature of a uniform consumption tax.

Options: The list of value added tax exemptions is long but not necessarily so in comparison with other countries. Of course, the list of exemptions should be evaluated in terms of their effect on revenue yield, efficiency, horizontal and vertical equity and administration and compliance burden. An entrenched culture of tax evasion and the weaknesses in the capacity of the tax administration to enforce complicated taxes may advise against a long exemption list. The code exempts many medical services and applies the lower rate to prescription drugs and other medications. This is significant in Russia because the population is aging and therefore likely to spend more on healthcare over time. Exempting medical services may adversely affect the buoyancy of the value added tax, but this may be mitigated by the fact that prescription drugs are taxed, though at a lower rate.   Finally, government should consider a statutory indexing of the threshold for value added tax filing.

Small businesses: A number of changes to the tax system over the years have affected small businesses. Currently, the simplified tax system (Chapter 26.2) governs organizations and individual entrepreneurs. The system is meant to simplify the tax regime for small businesses by wrapping the income taxes, social taxes and assets tax into a single tax and exempting such businesses from the value added tax. Small business is defined by sales (11 million rubles or less in 2005), employment (100 or fewer employees) and assets (100 million rubles or less). Certain types of businesses, including banks, gambling enterprises and investment funds, among others, are not allowed to file under the simplified tax system.

The unified presumptive tax system (Chapter 26.3) applies to a relatively small set of service-oriented businesses. The code allows regional governments to determine some of the parameters of the unified presumptive tax including those businesses that are eligible, within the overall list contained in Chapter 26.3. Like the simplified tax system, the presumptive system replaces income taxes, the asset tax and the unified social tax. In addition, these taxpayers are not required to pay value added tax. The imputation is made based on a fairly complex formula that includes parameters associated with profitability, type of physical building, location, season, work hours and so on. Regional governments are responsible for setting the coefficients for the size of the business and actual location. Besides these two specific taxes related to small businesses, those entities with sales of 1 million rubles or less per quarter are exempt from value added tax.

Options: Simplified tax schemes are important components of tax policy. They can help reduce the compliance burdens for small businesses. They also bring taxpayers into the tax net by making the system easier for taxpayers. If not monitored, however, they can create opportunities for tax evasion. Larger firms can make themselves appear eligible for the simplified system if the net tax liabilities from doing so are positive and large enough. In Russia, the net tax benefit of the simplified system is positive and large because the combined rates of income tax, social taxes and asset taxes are very high. The imputed system sets no threshold for sales or employment, so some large businesses may qualify for the imputed system. The imputed tax should be made creditable against ordinary tax liability and either made a tax on small business or apply to all taxpayers.

CONCLUSIONS

Russia's economy and fiscal structure is among the great success stories in recent experience. Real GDP growth is strong and consequently government revenues are strong, particularly standard taxes like the personal income tax and enterprise profit tax are yielding increasing amounts of revenue.

The Tax Code of the Russian Federation has come a long way through its post-Soviet life. The system has been rationalized, and this has yielded what at this point in time seems to be a relatively buoyant revenue system. There are some specific difficulties with the current system, including complications with the list of exemptions and deductions for individuals, the three-tiered value added tax (0, 10 and 18 percent tax rates) and carry-back rules for the enterprise profit tax. The larger challenge appears to be transforming the tax administration into a modern and efficient collection agent for the government.

As previously noted, Russia has a number of difficult demographic and socio-economic problems. The size of the country's population is decreasing, and the health status of the population is relatively low. The economy has moved, like that of many countries, toward services and construction, which are both relatively hard to tax sectors. As a result, we expect downward pressure on the buoyancy of the income tax and the value added tax. While Russia, in theory, taxes consumption broadly, past practices suggest that it is not capturing the full extent of its consumption base. Further elimination of exemptions and increased focus on tax administration could help guarantee value added tax collections. The income tax has come a long way in Russia. The flat rate tax is a positive development both from the perspective of tax administration and revenue yield. However, Russia's fiscal architecture casts some doubt on the continued buoyancy of the income tax. Furthermore, Russia needs to diversify the sources of government revenue, but this is just another way of saying that the country needs to diversify its economy because it is too reliant on the raw material producing sectors.

There also are concerns related to Russia's surplus oil and natural gas revenues as the price of oil has increased in recent years. The central government has witnessed a large increase in revenue and reserves associated with climbing world price of oil. The Stabilization Fund has been used as the repository for these windfall revenue gains. As the World Bank (2006) points out, this fund may no longer be needed solely for providing a cushion against future declines in world oil prices. In early 2006, the fund stood at 1.5 trillion rubles (World Bank, 2006) which is sufficient to support the entire budget of the Russian Federation for three or more years, even if oil prices fall by one-half or more. The fund may be helpful in maintaining fiscal balance as the country's fiscal architecture begins to have a larger and larger impact on the economy and government revenues and expenditures. This provides Russia with an opportunity that few countries enjoy: the ability to address the country's pension issues arising from the growing elderly population.

NOTES

1. The US Census forecasts a decline in Russia's population from a high of 148,495,015 in 1995 to 143,420,309 by 2005 (US Census, 2006: International Data Base: http://census.gov/ipc/www/idbacc.html).
2. Data from http://en.wikipedia.org/wiki/List_of_countries_by_death_rate.
3. Calculations based on US Census Bureau International Population Statistics: http://www.census.gov/ipc/www/idbnew.html
4. The World Bank, Doing Business from: http://www.doingbusiness.org/ExploreTopics/PayingTaxes/
5. According to the 'new' view of the effect of taxation of dividends, however, individual taxes on dividends from investments financed with retained earnings are irrelevant.

References

Alexeev, Michael (1998), 'Review of the methodologies for estimating the tax gap and the size of the underground economy', unpublished manuscript.

Alm, James and Jorge Martinez-Vazquez (2003), 'Institutions, Paradigms, and Tax Evasion in Developing and Transition Countries', in James Alm and Jorge Martinez-Vazquez (eds), *Public Finance in Developing and Transitional Countries*, Cheltenham, UK and Northampton, MA, USA: Edward Elgar, pp. 146-78.

Alm, James, Jorge Martinez-Vazquez and Friedrich Schneider (2006), '"Sizing" the Problem of the Hard-to-Tax', in James Alm, Jorge Martinez-Vazquez and Sally Wallace (eds), *Taxing the Hard-to-Tax: Lessons from Theory and Practice*, Amsterdam: Elsevier, pp. 11-76.

Alm, James, Jorge Martinez-Vazquez and Benno Torgler (2006), 'Russian attitudes toward paying taxes – before, during, and after the transition', *International Journal of Social Economics*, **33**(11-12): 832-57.

Alm, James, Jorge Martinez-Vazquez and Sally Wallace (2006), 'Do Tax Amnesties work? The revenue effects of tax amnesties in the Russian Federation', International Studies Program Working Paper, Atlanta, GA: Andrew Young School of Policy Studies, Georgia State University.

Antel, Scott (2002), 'News analysis: Recent tax reforms helps Russian economy', *Tax Notes International*, August 26, p. 996

Antel, Scott and Svetlana Lozovskaya (2005), 'Russia 2005: Tax year in review', *Tax Notes International*, January 9, pp. 95-6.

Antel, Scott, Ruslan Vasutin and Sergei Etdzaev (2006), 'Russia 2006: Tax year in review', *Tax Notes International*, December 25, pp. 1100-101.

Aslund, Anders (1995), *How Russia Became a Market Economy*, Washington, DC: The Brookings Institute.

Aslund, Anders (2000), 'Go long on Russia', *International Economy*, **14**(4): 38-9.

Bahl, Roy (1971), 'A regression approach to tax effort and tax ratio analysis', *IMF Staff Papers*, No. 18: 570-610.

Bahl, Roy (1994), 'Revenues and Revenue Assignment: Intergovernmental fiscal relations in the Russian Federation', in Christine Wallich (ed.), *Russia and the Challenge of Fiscal Federalism*, Washington, DC: The World Bank, pp. 129-80.

Bahl, Roy (1999), *Fiscal Policy in China: Taxation and Intergovernmental Fiscal Relations*, San Francisco: The 1990 Institute.

Bahl, Roy and Sally Wallace (2003), 'Fiscal Decentralization', in James Alm and Jorge Martinez-Vazquez (eds), *Public Finance in Developing and Transitional Countries*, Cheltenham, UK and Northampton, MA, USA: Edward Elgar, pp. 5-34.

Bahl, Roy, Galina Kurlyandskaya, John Mikesell, Sally Wallace, Natalia Golovanova, Dmitry Shiskin, Andrey Timofeev, Alexander Derugin, Yelena Nikolayenko, Inna Verbina and Natasha Minkova (1999), 'Intergovernmental Fiscal Relations in Leningrad Region', International Studies Program Working Paper 99-2, Atlanta, GA: Andrew Young School of Policy Studies, Georgia State University.

Bahl, Roy, Jorge Martinez-Vazquez and Sally Wallace (1996), *The Guatemalan Tax Reform*, Colorado: Westview Press.

Berkowitz, Daniel and Wei Li (2000), 'Tax rights in transition economies: a tragedy of the commons?', *Journal of Public Economics*, 76(3): 369-97.

Bird, Richard (1999), *Rethinking Subnational Taxes: A New Look At Tax Assignment*, Washington, DC: International Monetary Fund.

Bird, Richard (2004), 'Administrative dimensions of tax reform', *Asia-Pacific Tax Bulletin*, March, pp. 134-150.

Bird, Richard M. and Pierre-Pascal Gendron (2001), 'VATs in federal countries: International experience and emerging possibilities', *Bulletin for International Fiscal Documentation*, 55(7): 293-310.

Blanchard, Olivier and Andrei Schleifer (2000), 'Federalism with and without political centralization: China and Russia', MIT unpublished manuscript.

Bosquet, Benoit (2002), 'The Role of Natural Resources in Fundamental Tax Reform in the Russian Federation', Policy Research Working Paper 280, Washington, D.C.: The World Bank.

Bureau of Economic Analysis of the Russian Federation and the Higher School of Economics (1998), *On Personal Income Tax Avoidance in 1995-1997*, Moscow: Bureau of Economic Analysis of the Russian Federation and the Higher School of Economics.

Celarier, Michelle (1997), 'Privatization: A case study in corruption', *Journal of International Affairs*, 50(2), 531-43.

Chelliah, Raja (1971), 'Trends in taxation in developing countries', *IMF Staff Papers*, No. 18: 254-321.

Cohen, Stephen F. (2001), *Failed Crusade America and the Tragedy of Post-Communist Russia*, New York: W.W. Norton & Company.

Easter, Gerarld M. (2003), 'Building political compliance in transition economies: Russia', Paper presented in the State Capacity, Trust and Tax Evasion Conference, St. Gallen, Switzerland.

EBRD (1997), *Transition Report: Economic Transition in Eastern Europe and the Former Soviet Union*, London, UK: European Bank for Reconstruction and Development (EBRD).

Ebrill, Liam P. and Oleh Havrylyshyn (1999), 'Tax Reform in the Baltics, Russia, and Other Countries of the Former Soviet Union', IMF Occasional Paper No. 182, Washington, DC: International Monetary Fund.

Ebrill, Liam P., Michael Keen, Jean-Paul Bodin and Victoria Summers (2001), *The Modern VAT*, Washington, D.C.: International Monetary Fund.

Ernst and Young (2005), *Doing Business in Russia,* Moscow, Russia: Ernst and Young.

Federal Treasury, Ministry of Finance (various years), available from http://www.roskazna.ru/reports/fbrf.

Firestone, Alan (1998), 'Modernization of the Tax Administration of the Russian Federation', International Studies Program Working Paper Series, Atlanta, GA: Andrew Young School of Policy Studies, Georgia State University.

Fowkes, Ben (1997), *The disintegration of the Soviet Union: A Study in the Rise and Triumph of Nationalism*, New York: St Martin's Press.

Frank, Charles (2000), 'The best and worst of times for Russia's economy', *Moscow Times*, Moscow.

Freeland, Chrystia (2000), *Sale of the Century, Russia's Wild Ride from Communism to Capitalism*, London: Little Brown and Company.

Gaddy, Clifford and Barry Ickes (1998), 'Russia's virtual economy', *Foreign Affairs,* 77(5): 53-67.

Garibaldi, Pietro, Nada Mora, Ratna Sahay and Jeromin Zettelmeyer (1999), 'What Moves Capital to Transition Economies?' IMF Working Paper 02/64, Washington, DC: International Monetary Fund.

Gillis, Malcolm (1989), *Tax Reform in Developing Countries*, Durham: Duke University Press.

Glinkina, Svetlana (1999), 'Russia's Underground Economy during the Transition', in Edgar Feige and Katarina Ott (eds), *Underground Economies in Transition: Unrecorded Activity, Tax Evasion, Corruption and Organized Crime,* Aldershot, UK, Brookfield, VT and Sydney: Ashgate, pp. 101-6.

Goode, Richard (1984), *Government Finance in Developing Countries*, Washington, DC: Brookings Institution.

Gorodnichenko, Yuriy, Jorge Martinez-Vazquez and Klara S. Peter (2007), 'Myth and Reality of Flat Tax Reform: Micro estimates of tax evasion and productivity response in Russia', ISP WP 0720, Atlanta, GA: Andrew Young School of Policy Studies, Georgia State University.

Goskomstat (2005), *Statistical Yearbook of Russia 2005*, Moscow, Russia: Federal State Statistics Service.

Gregory, Frank and Gerald Brooke (2000), 'Policing economic transition and increasing revenue: A case study of the federal tax police service of the Russian Federation 1992-1998', *Europe-Asia Studies,* **52**(3): 433-55.

Hellman, Joel (1997), 'Constitutions and Economic Reforms in the Post-Communist Transitions', in Jeffrey Sachs and Katharina Pistor (eds), *The Rule of Law and Economic Reform in Russia*, Boulder, CO: Westview Press, pp. 55-78.

Hellman, Joel, Geraint Jones, Daniel Kaufmann and Mark Schankerman (2000), 'Measuring Governance, Corruption, and State Capture: How firms and bureaucrats shape the business environment in transition economies', World Bank Policy Research Working Paper 2312, Washington, DC: The World Bank.

Highfield, Richard and Katherine Baer (2000), 'Tax Administration for Russia', Paper presented in the Post-Election Strategy Conference, Moscow, April 5-7.

IMF (2000), 'Russian Federation: Selected issues', Country Report 00/150, Washington, DC: International Monetary Fund.

IMF (2004), 'Russian Federation: Selected issues', Country Report 04/316, Washington, DC: International Monetary Fund.

IMF (2005), 'Russian Federation: Selected issues', Country Report No. 05/379, Washington, DC: International Monetary Fund.

IMF (2006), *Government Finance Statistics*, CD 2006, Washington, DC: International Monetary Fund.

Ivaneev, Alexander (2000), 'Ideology and key mechanisms of tax reform', *Banking Business*, No. 9, Moscow.

Ivanova, Nadezhda and Charles Wyplosz (1999), 'Arrears: The tide that is drowning Russia', *Russian Economic Trends*, **8**(1): 24-35.

Ivanova, Anna, Michael Keen and Alexander Klemm (2005), 'The Russian "Flat Tax" reform', *Economic Policy*, **20**(43): 397-435.

Johnson, Simon, Daniel Kaufmann, John McMillan and Christopher Woodruff (2000), 'Why do firms hide? Bribes and unofficial activity after communism', *Journal of Public Economics*, **76**(3): 495-520.

Karpov, Piotr (1997), 'On causes of low tax collection rate: General causes for "non-payment crisis" and possibilities for restoration of Russian enterprises' solvency', Moscow: Interdepartmental Balance Commission.

Kasper, Wolfgang and Manfeld E. Streit (1998), *Institutional Economics: Social Order and Public Policy*, Cheltenham, UK and Northampton, MA, USA: Edward Elgar.

Klebnikov, Paul (2000), *Godfather of the Kremlin: The Decline of Russia in the Age of Gangster Capitalism*, New York: Harcourt Inc.

Korolenko, Dimitry (1998), 'Russian tax collection practices', *International Tax Journal*, 24(4): 48-61.

Kwon, Goohoon (2003), 'Post-crisis fiscal revenue developments in Russia: From an oil perspective', *Public Finance and Management*, 3(4): 505-30.

Kurlyandskaya, Galina (2001), *Budgetary Pluralism of Russian Authorities*, Budapest: Open Society Institute.

Lapina, A. A. (1995), 'Taxation of natural persons', International Center of Finance and Economic Development conference proceedings, October.

Lavrov, Aleksei, John M. Litwack and Douglas Sutherland (2000), 'Fiscal Federalism in the Russian Federation: Problems and reform options', Paper presented in the Russian Economic Reform, Moscow, April 5-7.

Levin, Mark and Georgy Satarov (2000), 'Corruption and institutions in Russia', *European Journal of Political Economy*, 16(1): 113-32.

Libman, Aleksei and Lars P. Feld (2007), 'Strategic Tax Collections and Fiscal Decentralization', CESifo Working Paper No. 2031, June.

Lotz, Jorgen and Elliot Morss (1967), 'Measuring Tax Effort in Developing Countries,' *IMF Staff Papers*, 14

Loungani, Prakash and Paolo Mauro (2001), 'Capital flight from Russia', *World Economy*, 24(5): 689-706.

Mahi, Raksaka (2002), 'Managing Local Revenue in Indonesia', International Studies Program working paper, Atlanta, GA: Andrew Young School of Policy Studies, Georgia State University.

Martinez-Vazquez, Jorge (2007), 'Asymmetric Federalism in Russia: Cure or Poison', in Richard Bird and Robert Ebel (eds), *Fiscal Fragmentation in Decentralized Countries: Subsidiarity, Solidarity and Asymmetry*, Cheltenham, UK and Northampton, MA, USA: Edward Elgar, pp. 227-66.

Martinez-Vazquez, Jorge and Jameson Boex (2001), 'Russia's transition to a new federalism', Washington, DC: The World Bank.

Martinez-Vazquez, Jorge and Robert M. McNab (1998), 'Tax Systems in Transition Economies', in W. Bartley Hildreth and John Richardson (eds), *Handbook on Taxation*, New York: Marcel Dekker Publishing, pp. 911-63.

Martinez-Vazquez, Jorge and Robert M. McNab (2000), 'The tax reform experiment in transitional countries', *National Tax Journal*, **53**(2): 273-98.

Martinez-Vazquez, Jorge and Andrey Timofeev (2006), 'Regional-Local Dimension of Russia's Fiscal Equalization', International Studies Program Working Paper 06-16, Atlanta, GA: Andrew Young School of Policy Studies, Georgia State University.

Martinez-Vazquez, Jorge and Sally Wallace (1999), 'The ups and downs of comprehensive tax reform in Russia', *Tax Notes International*, 13, Special Reports, December, pp. 2261-73.

Martinez-Vazquez, Jorge and Christine Wong (2003), 'Two Large Experiments in Fiscal Decentralization Compared: China and Russia', International Studies Program Working Paper 03-13, Atlanta, GA: Andrew Young School of Policy Studies, Georgia State University.

Martinez-Vazquez, Jorge, Mark Rider, Riatu Qibthiyyah and Sally Wallace (2006), 'Who Bears the Burden of Taxes on Labor Income in Russia?', International Studies Program Working Paper 06-21, Atlanta, GA: Andrew Young School of Policy Studies, Georgia State University.

Martinez-Vazquez, Jorge, Andrey Timofeev and Jameson Boex (2004), 'Russia's continuing transition toward a new federalism: Subnational finance in the Russian Federation', Atlanta, GA: Andrew Young School of Policy Studies, Georgia State University.

McAuley, Alastair (1997), 'The determinants of Russian federal-regional fiscal relations: equity or political influence', *Europe-Asia Studies*, **49**(3): 431-44.

McCarten, William (2001), 'The Challenge of Fiscal Discipline in the Indian States', in Jonathan Rodden, Gunnar Eskeland and Jennie Litvack (eds), *Decentralization and Hard Budget Constraints*, Cambridge: MIT Press, pp. 249-86.

McDonald, Joel (2001), 'Sales tax in Russia ruled unconstitutional', *Tax Notes International*, March 5, pp. 1115-116.

McLure, Charles (1992), 'A simpler consumption-based alternative to the income tax for socialist economies in transition', *The World Bank Research Observer*, **7**(2): 221-37.

McLure, Charles and George Zodrow (1997), 'Thirty Years of Tax Reform in Colombia', in Wayne Thirsk (ed.), *Tax Reform in Developing Countries*, Washington, DC: The World Bank, pp. 57-125.

McLure, Charles and George Zodrow (1996), 'A hybrid consumption-based direct tax proposed for Bolivia', *International Tax and Public Finance*, **3**(1): 97-112.

Ministry of Finance of the Russian Federation (2005), *Tax Code of the Russian Federation*, Moscow: Ministry of Finance of the Russian Federation.

Moscow Times (2000), 'Tax, finance officials blast tax reforms', November 23.

Musgrave, Richard (1959), *The Theory of Public Finance*, New York: McGraw-Hill.

Musgrave, Richard A. and Peggy Musgrave (1976), *Public Finance in Theory and Practice,* New York: McGraw- Hill.

Nerre, Birger (2001), 'The Role of Tax Culture in the Russian Transformation Process', in Michael H. Stierle and Thomas Birringer (eds), *Economics of Transition: Theory, Experiences and EU Enlargement*, Berlin: VWF, pp. 111-28.

New York Times (1999), 'Tax evasion scheme in Russia', May 26.

Oates, Wallace E. (1972), *Fiscal Federalism*, New York: Harcourt Brace Jovanovich.

Ostrow, Joel (2000), *Comparing Post-Soviet Legislatures: A Theory of Institutional Design and Political Conflict*, Columbus: Ohio State University Press.

Owen, Thomas C. (1997), 'Autocracy and the Rule of Law in Russian Economic History', in Jeffrey Sachs and Katharina Pistor (eds), *The Rule of Law and Economic Reform in Russia*, Boulder, CO: Westview Press.

Poterba, James (1989), 'Lifetime incidence and the distributional burden of excise taxes', *American Economic Review*, **79**(2): 325-30.

Rao, M. Govinda (forthcoming), 'Fiscal Decentralization in India: Trends and Reform Issues', in Roy W. Bahl and Sinichi Ichimura (eds), *Decentralization Policies in Asian Development*, Singapore: World Scientific Press.

Romanovskii, Mikhail and Natalia Ivanova (1999), 'Tax System of Russia', Working Paper, St. Petersburg: St. Petersburg State University.

Rosen, Harvey (2003), *Public Finance*, Boston: McGraw-Hill.

Russian Federation Government (2001), *Workplan of the Russian Government in the Area of Social Policy and Modernization of the Economy for 2000-2010*, Moscow: Russian Federation Government.

Rutkowski, Michael (1999), 'Russia's Social Protection Malaise: Key reform priorities as a response to the present crisis', Discussion Paper No. 9909, Washington, DC: The World Bank.

Sachs, Jeffrey and Katharina Pistor (1997), *The Rule of Law and Economic Reform in Russia*, Boulder, CO.: Westview Press.

Salacuse, Jeswald W. (1998), 'Undertaking a Direct Foreign Investment', in Streng and Salacuse (eds), *International Business Planning*, New York: Mathew Bender.

Schmidt, Diana (2006), 'Fighting against corruption, and struggling for status', *Russian Analytical Digest*, No. 11, December 5, pp. 2-17.

Schneider, Friedrich and Dominik H. Enste (2000), 'Shadow economies: Size, causes, and consequences', *Journal of Economic Literature* **38**(1): 77-114.

Schneider, Friedrich and Dominik H. Enste (2002), *The Shadow Economy: An International Survey*, Cambridge, New York and Melbourne: Cambridge University Press.

Shatalov, Sergey (1996), 'Tax code as a guarantee for stability of the system of taxation', Paper presented in the International Center of Finance and Economic Development Conference, October.

Shleifer, Adrei and Daniel Treisman (2000), *Without a Map: Political Tactics and Economic Reform in Russia*, Cambridge: MIT Press.

Silvani, Carlos and Katherine Baer (1997), 'Designing a tax administration reform strategy: experiences and guidelines', *Tax Notes International*, August 4.

Spilimbergo, Antonio (2005), 'Measuring the Performance of Fiscal Policy in Russia', IMF Working Paper 05/241, Washington, DC: International Monetary Fund.

Statistics Canada (2008), available from http://40.statcan.ca/101/cst01/govto 4a.htm.

Stiglitz, Joseph (2000), 'What I learned from the world economic crisis', *The New Republic*, April 14.

Summers, Victoria and Emil Sunley (1995), 'An Analysis of Value-added Taxes in Russia and Other Countries of the Former Soviet Union', International Monetary Fund Working Paper No. 95/1, January, Washington, DC: The International Monetary Fund.

Tait, Alan, Wildfrid Gratz and Barry Eichengreen (1979), 'International comparisons of taxation for selected developing countries 1972-76', *IMF Staff Papers*, **26**(1): 123-56.

Tanzi, Vito (2000), 'On fiscal federalism: Issues to worry about', IMF conference on Fiscal Decentralization, Washington, DC, November 20-21.

Tanzi, Vito and Howell Zee (2001), *Tax Policy for Developing Countries*, Washington, DC: International Monetary Fund.

Thirsk, Wayne (1997), *Tax Reform in Developing Countries*, Washington, DC: The World Bank.

Thirsk, Wayne (2000), 'Fiscal decentralization in Ukraine', in J.M. Szyrmer and K.M. Sultan (eds), *Ukraine through Transition: Challenges and Strategies*, Kiev: Alterpress, pp. 116-124.

Tolkushkin, A.V. (2001), *History of Taxation in Russia*, Moscow: Yurist (in Russian).

Treisman, Daniel (1996), 'The politics of intergovernmental transfers in post-Soviet Russia', *British Journal of Political Science,* **26**(3): 299-335.

Treisman, Daniel (1998), 'Fiscal redistribution in a fragile federation: Moscow and the regions in 1994', *British Journal of Political Science,* **28**(1): 185-200.

Treisman, Daniel (2000), 'The causes of corruption: A cross-national study', *Journal of Public Economics,* **76**(3): 399-457.

United Nations Development Project (2006), 'Human Development Reports', retrieved September 2006 from website, http://hdr.undp.org/statistics/data/countries.cfm.

United States Government Technical Assistance Team (USGTA) (1998a), 'The Tax Burden on Labor Income', Atlanta, GA: Andrew Young School of Policy Studies, Georgia State University.

United States Government Technical Assistance Team (USGTA) (1998b), 'The Choice Between the VAT and the Retail Sales Tax in the Russian Federation', Atlanta, GA: Andrew Young School of Policy Studies, Georgia State University.

United States Government Technical Assistance Team (USGTA) (1998c), 'Memo: Individual Income Tax Gap Estimates', Atlanta, GA: Andrew Young School of Policy Studies, Georgia State University.

United States Government Technical Assistance Team (USGTA) (1998d), 'Estimating Potential VAT Receipts Using International Data', Atlanta, GA: Andrew Young School of Policy Studies, Georgia State University.

United States Government Technical Assistance Team (USGTA) (1998e), 'Enterprise Profit Tax Collection Gap', Atlanta, GA: Andrew Young School of Policy Studies, Georgia State University.

United States Government Technical Assistance Team (USGTA) (1999a), 'The Problem of Arrears in the Russian Federation', Atlanta, GA: Andrew Young School of Policy Studies, Georgia State University.

United States Government Technical Assistance Team (USGTA) (1999b), 'The Distribution of Tax Burden in the Russian Federation', Atlanta, GA: Andrew Young School of Policy Studies, Georgia State University.

United States Government Technical Assistance Team (USGTA) (1999c), 'Taxation of Capital Income under the Current Law and Draft Tax Code', Atlanta, GA: Andrew Young School of Policy Studies, Georgia State University.

United States Government Technical Assistance Team (USGTA) (1999d), 'Depreciation Rules', Atlanta, GA: Andrew Young School of Policy Studies, Georgia State University.

United States Government Technical Assistance Team (USGTA) (1999e), 'Evidence from the Russian Longitudinal Monitoring Survey on Alcohol Consumption in Russia', Atlanta, GA: Andrew Young School of Policy Studies, Georgia State University.

US Census Bureau (2004), 'State and local government finances', retrieved August 2004 from website http://www.census.gov/govs/www/estimate02 .html.

US Census Bureau (2006), International Data Base: http://www.census.gov/ cgi-bin/ipc/idbagg, accessed August 2006.

Wallich, Christine (1994), 'Intergovernmental Fiscal Relations: Setting the Stage', in Christine Wallich (ed.), *Russia and the Challenge of Fiscal Federalism*, Washington, DC: The World Bank, pp. 60-61.

Woller, Garry M. (1999), 'Taxation in East Asian countries: Japan, Korea, Taiwan, and China', in B. Hildreth and J.A. Richardson (eds), *Handbook on Taxation*, New York: Marcel Dekker, pp. 835-76.

Woodruff, David M. (1999), *Money Unmade: Barter and the Fate of Russian Capitalism*, Ithaca, NY: Cornell University Press.

World Bank (1992) *Russian Economic Reforms: Crossing the Threshold of Structural Changes*, Washington DC: The World Bank.

World Bank (2002), 'Project Appraisal for a Second Tax Administration Project in the Russian Federation', Report No: 23565-RU, Washington, DC: The World Bank.

World Bank (2003), 'Project Appraisal for a Customs Development Project in the Russian Federation', Report No: 24690-RU, Washington, DC: The World Bank.

World Bank (2006), *World Development Indicators 2006*, Washington, DC: The World Bank.

World Bank (2007), 'Enterprise Surveys 2005-2006', retrieved September 29 http://www.enterprisesurveys.org/.

Yakovlev, Andrei (2001), '"Black cash" tax evasion in Russia: its forms, incentives and consequences at firm level', *Europe-Asia Studies*, **53**(1): 33-55.

Yakovlev, Andrei and Olga Vorontsova (1997), 'Black cash turnover and behavior of wholesale trade enterprises', *Russian Economic Barometer*, **6**(4): 14-26.

Zolotareva, Anna and A. Shishkov (2000), *General Problems of Tax Administration in Russia*, Moscow: Institute for The Economy in Transition.

Zolt, Eric (1999), 'Prospects for fundamental tax reform: Comparisons between the United States and Japan', *Tax Notes International*, May 10.

NOTE

The USGTA worked under a grant from USAID from 1997 through 2000 and the team includes faculty and staff of the Andrew Young School of Policy Studies, Coopers and Lybrand, Barents, LLC, and the US Treasury Department. The publication archives are available at the Andrew Young School of Policy Studies, Georgia State University, Atlanta GA and publication of the joint USGTA work is therefore listed at that address. Original publications were available in the USGTA office in Moscow, Russia.

Index